TRANSPARENCY IN POLITICS AND THE MEDIA

TRANSPARENCY IN POLITICS AND THE MEDIA

ACCOUNTABILITY AND OPEN GOVERNMENT

Edited by NIGEL BOWLES,
JAMES T. HAMILTON,
and DAVID A. L. LEVY

REUTERS
INSTITUTE for the
STUDY of
JOURNALISM

Published by I.B.Tauris & Co. Ltd in association with
the Reuters Institute for the Study of Journalism, University of Oxford

The Reuters Institute would like to acknowledge the assistance of Richard Sambrook and Robert G. Picard as readers on behalf of the Institute.

Published in 2014 by I.B.Tauris & Co. Ltd
6 Salem Road, London W2 4BU
175 Fifth Avenue, New York NY 10010
www.ibtauris.com

Distributed in the United States and Canada Exclusively by Palgrave Macmillan
175 Fifth Avenue, New York NY 10010

ISBN: 978 1 78076 675 1 (HB); 978 1 78076 676 8 (PB)

A full CIP record for this book is available from the British Library
A full CIP record is available from the Library of Congress

Library of Congress Catalog Card Number: available

Typeset by 4word Ltd, Bristol

Printed and bound in Great Britain by T.J. International, Padstow, Cornwall

Contents

Tables and Figures

Tables

Figures

Contributors

Philip Bennett is Eugene C. Patterson Professor of the Practice of Journalism and Public Policy, Duke University.

Patrick Birkinshaw is Professor of Public Law and Director of the Institute of European Public Law, University of Hull.

Paul Bradshaw is a reader in Online Journalism at Birmingham City University and a Visiting Professor at City University's School of Journalism in London.

Nigel Bowles is Director of the Rothermere American Institute, University of Oxford.

Sarah Cohen is a reporter at the *New York Times*.

Leonard Downie Jr. is Weil Family Professor of Journalism, Walter Cronkite School of Journalism and Mass Communication, Arizona State University, and Vice President at large and former executive editor of the *Washington Post*.

Joel Gurin is Senior Advisor at the Governance Lab at New York University.

James T. Hamilton is Charles S. Sydnor Professor of Public Policy at Duke University's Sanford School of Public Policy and Director of the DeWitt Wallace Center for Media and Democracy.

Robert Hazell is Professor of British Politics and Government and Director of the Constitution Unit, University College London.

Jennifer LaFleur is Director of Computer-Assisted Reporting, ProPublica.

David A. L. Levy is Director of the Reuters Institute for the Study of Journalism, University of Oxford.

Charles Lewis is Professor and Executive Editor, Investigative Reporting Workshop, at the American University School of Communication.

John Lloyd is Director of Journalism, Reuters Institute for the Study of Journalism, University of Oxford, and a contributing editor to the *Financial Times* and a columnist for Reuters.com.

Helen Margetts is Director of the Oxford Internet Institute and Professor of Society and the Internet, University of Oxford.

Beth Simone Noveck is Founder and Director of the Governance Lab and The Jacob K. Javits Visiting Professor at the New York University Robert F. Wagner Graduate School of Public Service, and a visiting professor at the MIT Media Lab. She is on leave as Professor of Law at New York Law School.

Peter Riddell is Director of the Institute for Government and a former political journalist for the *Financial Times* and *The Times*.

Michael Schudson is a professor at the Columbia University Graduate School of Journalism.

Benjamin Worthy is a lecturer in the Department of Politics, Birkbeck, University of London.

Introduction

Nigel Bowles, James T. Hamilton, and David A. L. Levy

Around the world, governments are experimenting with initiatives in transparency and open government. These involve announcements of new government websites, more access to government datasets, and broader attempts to involve the public in government decision-making. The role of the media in open government, however, is often left unremarked and unexamined. This book explores the particular challenges and opportunities that journalists face in holding governments accountable in an era of professed transparency.

On his first day in office, President Obama issued a Memorandum on Transparency and Open Government that emphasised that government should be transparent, participatory, and collaborative. Prime Minister Cameron has similarly emphasised the value of opening up government data to wider access. Open government commitments have also become part of international policy discussions, with the adoption and implementation of national freedom of information laws in countries such as India, Mexico, and South Africa attracting widespread attention. In the US and UK many of these initiatives focus on data helpful to people in their role as consumers (rather than voters), or aim to draw on knowledge from citizens or experts to aid in the development of policies and regulations. To examine how transparency and open government initiatives have affected the accountability function of the press in the US and the UK, scholars and practitioners from both countries met at Oxford University's Rothermere American Institute in October 2012. This book emerges from the ideas generated at this interdisciplinary conference, convened by Duke University's DeWitt Wallace Center for Media and Democracy, the Reuters Institute for the Study of Journalism, and the Rothermere American Institute.

Rather than giving a chapter-by-chapter summary of key points, this introduction has three aims: to provide a context for how information works in theories of government transparency and accountability; to highlight themes that ran across discussions of how government and the media approach openness in their institutional operation; and to project how policies and changes in technology might affect the paths that journalists and government officials will follow as they consider questions of transparency and accountability.

Information and accountability, in theory

Delegated decision-making lies at the core of representative democracies. In the US and UK electoral systems voters delegate choices to elected officials, who ultimately face the sanction of defeat if their decisions stray too far from the preferences of voters. Economists call this type of arrangement a principal–agent relationship, where the principal (here a voter) delegates decision-making power to an agent (who could be a Member of Congress, or Member of Parliament). Principal–agent relationships in politics offer multiple advantages. The division of labour allows government officials to become experts in particular policy areas, and leaves voters free to pursue other interests without significant attention to the details of government decisions. The prospects of constituent dissatisfaction and electoral defeat in theory police the actions of agents and make them attentive to voter interests.

Principal–agent relationships, both in politics and markets, carry the potential for the agent to make different decisions from those that the principal might choose (see Kiewiet and McCubbins, 1991, the basis for the following discussion of delegation incentives). This potential arises because of hidden actions and hidden information. Since the principal cannot always be there to observe the choices of an agent, the agent can enjoy some power to make choices with which the principal might disagree. Principals cannot always see what choices an agent is making, and cannot often see the full set of ideas and data that an agent faced when making a selection.

In a relationship such as the hiring of bureaucrats and regulators, there are multiple ways to align the decisions of agents with principals: screening agents before they are hired to predict what they would do if given discretion; developing contracts and incentives to reward agents who follow the terms of delegation; providing for the generation and processing of information that makes the actions of agents more apparent; and delegating tasks to multiple agents whilst requiring them to compete for the work's completion. Assessing how well the delegation of decision-making works, between shareholders and company managers or voters and elected officials, always involves looking at a set of trade-offs. What is gained by the delegation of choices to others, what are the possibilities that they will use the advantages of hidden action and hidden information to pursue their own agenda, and how can different institutional arrangements lead agents to make the choices that principals desire?

Examining how this works in political relationships carries two additional burdens. In the market one can assume that principals have similar preferences – for example, stockholders wish managers to maximise profits. Within an electoral district, a representative may have constituents with very different goals and values, which makes it difficult to measure whether a vote or regulatory decision is consistent with voter interests. Within the US system, a regulator may have multiple principals (e.g. a Democratic president, a Republican-controlled House of Representatives, and a Democratic-controlled Senate). Interpreting whether a regulator has chosen actions consistent with the agenda of her principals is challenging in a world of multiple principals. Delegation in representative democracies also carries an additional twist: voters in effect delegate power that can lead to their oppression. In policy areas relating to national defence or criminal justice, agents who go astray can ultimately deprive principals of liberties and their freedom, with little recourse for objection.

Since information is costly and attention spans limited, knowledge in the series of delegated decision-making relationships that make up government and market institutions is imperfect. Leaders may not know well the circumstances or ideas of their constituents, who in turn may lack data on the actions or choice sets of their representatives. Consumers may not know well the quality of products and services they buy, or the social impact of the companies which produce these goods.

Enter the media. News outlets offer information that can make agents work more closely to match the interests of their principals. The set of stories and outlets that survive in the marketplace will depend on the types of information individuals demand and the incentives of producers. In his *Economic Theory of Democracy*, Anthony Downs (1957) noted that people have four distinct information demands. As consumers, they search out data that help them make purchases. As workers, they want news that helps them do their jobs. Some information is simply enjoyable to consume, thereby satisfying a demand for entertainment. As voters, people might benefit from learning more about candidates and issues as elections draw close. The degree to which producers will seek to meet these demands depends on a mix of incentives. Producers will create information to generate payments, advertising, votes, the satisfaction of changing people's views, or the pleasure of sharing ideas. These correspond to different models of news provision: subscription, advertising, partisan, nonprofit, and expression (Hamilton, 2004, 2011).

This mix of demands and incentives means that news about public affairs is likely to be underprovided in the commercial marketplace. Even if a voter cares deeply about politics and new information would help alter his selection of candidates, the likelihood that a single individual's showing up at the polls and casting his ballot will alter the election outcome is so small that the costs of becoming better informed outweigh the benefits of searching out additional information. Downs termed this calculation rational ignorance since it meant that, from an individual's perspective, investing in gaining more knowledge about government and politics might not pay, even though society as a whole might benefit if voters were more informed. Some people will seek out political news, because they believe they have a duty to be informed, have an intrinsic interest in learning, or like to follow politics as a sport or human interest drama. But the low return to an individual to reading about politics as a strategic investment of time means that news outlets face reduced demands for serious stories about public affairs.

The investigative reporting often involved in accountability journalism faces particular hurdles in the marketplace. The group 'Investigative Reporters and Editors' defines investigative reporting as 'the reporting, through one's own initiative and work product, of matters of importance to readers, viewers or listeners. In many cases, the subjects of the reporting wish the matters under scrutiny to remain undisclosed' (Houston and IRE, 2009: v). In economic terms, the time and resources a reporter spends on an investigation means that stories that hold institutions accountable can have high fixed costs, not least because the nature of investigative journalism often requires a far greater investment of resources than do other, more routine forms of reporting. If the stories generate changes in policies that translate into better outcomes in society, the news outlet that produced these positive spillovers on society might be unable to monetise these benefits. If an investigation were to reduce corruption or improve the environment, for example, a paper might not see much additional subscription or advertising revenue despite residents benefiting from the stories' outcomes. The natural desire of agents, whether elected officials or corporate managers, to be free from scrutiny means that people running institutions will make it hard to follow their actions. One of the biggest recent investigations in British journalism in recent years, the *Daily Telegraph*'s exposure in 2009 of information regarding the expenses of UK Members of Parliament that Parliament had sought to conceal, brought much public attention and comment, a change in the rules and several criminal prosecutions, but did nothing to arrest the long-term decline in the *Telegraph*'s circulation. The transaction costs of finding out what agents are doing can thus be high.

Policies that make governments more transparent and open can potentially make it easier for voters, interest groups, and journalists to track the origin and implementation of policies. For investigative reporters, were more of the documents and data available to officials also available to the public, officials would be more easily held accountable. The costs of discovering stories might fall, the likelihood of positive spillovers from exposés increase, and the transaction costs of gathering and assembling information decline. Transparency is thus a highly valued instrumental good, since it is an input into a process of monitoring that increases the odds that voters or consumers get what they want from institutional actors. Transparency is also an intrinsic good for some voters, who believe that they have a fundamental right to know about the actions of public officials.

Discussions of the instrumental value of transparency often assume the desirability of institutions that lead representatives to make choices that are in the best interests of citizens (Przeworski et al., 1999). Assessing the functioning of transparency involves many questions at the heart of democratic theory: how to define representation, whether leaders should respond to short-run assessments of voters or long-run values not currently shared or appreciated by voters, and the importance of placing some policies (e.g. the rights of minorities) beyond quick decisions by majority rule. While open government policies that make monitoring by reporters easier might appear to be an unqualified good, there are some areas of policy-making (such as court decisions or monetary policy) where those who craft the division of labour in government try to make it easier to insulate decision-makers from popular opinion. The opposite may also happen. Ferejohn (1999) explains that agents will sometimes take steps voluntarily to make their decisions more transparent, in order to increase the willingness of principals to delegate more power to them. This in part explains why prior to the age of freedom of information laws and transparency policies, governments adopted institutional designs to make their actions more visible to voters without labelling such policies as transparency. Overall, most theories of open government rest on assumptions that transparency begets responsiveness by those with delegated decision-making power, and that this responsiveness increases the value of policies formulated and implemented.

The desirability of transparency as an instrumental good involves trading off the real costs of making information and actions more accessible and observable versus the gains that come from decisions that more closely mirror the desires of voters and consumers. The benefits of transparency as an intrinsic good will involve similar trade-offs, including the balancing of other intrinsic goods such as rights to privacy of the people (e.g. government employees) whose actions are tracked in the data. In assessing the net benefits, some observers stress the 'dark side of transparency'. They cite a number of potential drawbacks when government debates and data are made more open: the skilful use by interest groups of government information to bend policy toward their ends; the chilling effect on internal debate within the executive branch because of potential revelation of internal policy disputes; and the focus by audience-driven media outlets on using FOI to ferret out politicians' foibles and scandals. Former prime minister Tony Blair shared this critical view of FOI policies in his memoir (2010), noting they were used as a 'weapon' by journalists and asserting that they undermined 'sensible government'.

The political economy of transparency means that the actual development and implementation of open government policies will be made by decision-makers concerned with a very specific trade-off, namely how transparency might affect their career prospects. As both politics and communications strategies designed to set the news agenda become increasingly professionalised, tensions between transparency and media management risk becoming acute. The benefits of transparency are widely dispersed across voters, while the costs are often highly concentrated on bureaucrats and elected officials whose actions are being monitored. The formulation of transparency policies that truly bind officials may depend on hoping that political actors will act against their short-term political interests. Transparency policies that sound desirable in election programmes, or as legislation is proposed, but have little or no effect might constitute a more desirable outcome for re-election-oriented officials. Accordingly, open government can be more symbolic than real, since imperfect information might well hide the lack of enthusiasm or action in implementation from constituents.

The degree to which information might be produced and used in an open government initiative will depend on a set of political economy questions, including the following.

What specific information demands are met by the data?

Individuals will search out data in their roles as consumers, workers, or entertainment seekers, since if they do not consume the information they will derive no benefit. People will often sit back and remain rationally ignorant about political information since, from an individual's perspective, time invested in remaining apprised of policy brings little reward because the probability that an individual will determine the outcome of an election or policy dispute is tiny. It is precisely because the study and scrutiny that holds government accountable is a public good that so many potential voters are apt to free ride and let others pay attention to policy debates.

Who will use the data, given the problems of collective action and rational ignorance?

Interest groups and journalists are intermediaries that may bear the costs of collecting and analysing open government information. Which government data are extracted and used will thus depend on the set of interest groups, including NGOs, and media outlets which are sustained in a market. The rapid financial decline of local newspapers in the US and UK means that the likelihood that accountability coverage will be generated of local government actions has declined over the last decade.

How can you reduce transaction costs of use?

Some of the information released by government is unstructured data, such as pdfs of documents or live streaming of meetings, which are cheap to produce but require ordering and interpretation. While government agencies (and companies) have invested significant resources in mining data for their own analyses, they have been less willing to share or subsidise the creation of software tools that would allow voters and their intermediaries, including journalists and NGOs, to mine government data.

What is the underlying regulatory context? Implementation strategy?

Regulatory programmes can involve a mix of command and control mechanisms, market incentives, and information provision requirements. If data are released in a command and control system, the feedback generated may be less immediate than data released in a market system, where prices may react more quickly to new information. The implementation of policy may be planned as a police patrol, where regulators check a sample of firms or areas for problems, or a fire alarm, where regulators rely on residents, consumers, or voters to complain (McCubbins and Schwartz, 1984). Insofar as political participation varies by income, reliance upon information to spur changes through political pressure at the neighbourhood level is likely to result in areas where income and education levels are lower being less likely to experience the benefits of information provision.

Is there a budget?

Making information freely available comes at a cost, in terms of making data accessible, readable, and clean. The time and resource demands generated by freedom of information laws and other transparency measures can be unfunded mandates, or can be explicitly budgeted for. The likelihood that open government policies will flourish and survive beyond initial implementation depends in part upon the dedication of specific funding.

Transparency and accountability, in practice and in the future

Transparency theories consider how information affects the operation of delegated decision-making in government and market institutions. Because of the longer lineage of freedom of information laws in the USA and the backdrop of the First Amendment, many in the UK see the USA as advancing more rapidly in the scale and scope of transparency policies. Though political and media structures are very different between the UK and the US, the authors in this volume show some common problems that arise in the actual implementation of policies of openness and transparency in government and the media in both countries. This may be because of the similarity of incentives government officials and reporters face when they consider whether they want to reveal more fully their actions and methods, and whether consumers and voters seek out particular information about products, policies, and politicians.

The chapters in this volume follow a roadmap with four clear destinations. Chapters 1 to 4 outline the history of freedom of information laws and policies in the US and UK, discuss evidence about how these policies have been implemented, and reflect on the values inherent in government transparency requirements. Chapters 5 to 8 shift the focus to journalism and transparency, including discussions of how media outlets themselves could operate more openly and discussions of the difficulties that reporters still face in gathering data about the operation of administrations and agencies that profess to be open and transparent. Data are at the forefront of Chapters 9 to 11, which explore what open data and big data will mean for journalists trying to hold governments accountable and what smart disclosure requirements placed on private sector actors may reveal about the actions of market participants. How the digging that goes into the generation of new information will be paid for is the topic of the final two chapters (12 and 13), which examine the degree that nonprofit media and other NGOs can generate the scrutiny of public, private, and nonprofit sector institutions that is a necessary component of holding these institutions accountable.

Common themes

Transparency

Announced government policies of transparency and openness in the US and UK have made more information available to the public, but the data provided are more frequently those that government officials wish to release rather than those that might hold officials accountable.

Open government may involve government agencies inviting input from stakeholders to enlarge the set of ideas and facts considered in public decision-making, thereby involving public participation in deliberations.

A high priority for the release of government data will often be 'big data' sets generated by regulation of private activities or the operation of government services, information which entrepreneurs can use to build private sector businesses. In the US this process is often termed 'DC to VC', to capture the sense the federal government information can be released and used by new businesses (funded by venture capital funds) in regulated fields such as healthcare and finance. The potential for jobs and profits to be generated by the release of the data means that government officials concerned about generating economic growth will often spur the release of this type of data.

Regulators will be willing to facilitate the collection and release of data that hold companies accountable, such as 'smart disclosure' programmes which require reporting by firms about their product and service quality. Journalists are often not the envisioned users of open data, and policies set and formats offered do not always take into account the specific needs of reporters. Media organisations with reputations for high quality in public affairs coverage are often leaders in the use of data journalism to take advantage of information released by governments. The provision of databases and underlying documents used in stories, through innovative features such as DocumentCloud, means that reporters can be more transparent about the data underlying their conclusions. NGOs and media nonprofits have also been leaders in translating newly available data into accessible formats and into accountability stories.

Accountability

In marketplaces where advertising support for traditional media is often declining, it is difficult to fund the expensive, time-intensive reporting projects that help hold government officials accountable.

Media companies have not often chosen to use transparency to make the actions of their own editors and reporters more accountable to consumers. While the web holds great promise in allowing reporters to show more of their work, in terms of data gathered in the production process, and decisions made about what goes into a final story, few to date have been willing to experiment with giving readers the underlying data that would facilitate the making of alternative assessments. Quality competition in media markets on the web might eventually lead some outlets to be more transparent and accountable, as a means of building their brand reputation for substantive coverage.

The chapter authors acknowledge that the contexts for transparency policies differ between the two countries. US authors were likely to discuss the First Amendment, severe drops in newspaper staffs caused by declines in advertising, the rising role of nonprofit media and NGOs to fill gaps in accountability coverage, and the hard line taken by President Obama's administration on leaks relating to national security. UK authors are more likely to reference the Official Secrets Act, discuss cracks in the support for the BBC, and acknowledge the uncertainties surrounding press regulation in the wake of the phone-hacking scandals and Leveson Inquiry.

These contextual differences notwithstanding, the authors conclude that there are common policy changes in the US and UK which would facilitate the translation of transparency into greater government accountability.

Policies

Freedom of information laws and transparency policies should make it easier for reporters to get data that are the artefacts of governing – for example, officials' appointment calendars, expenditure contracts, personnel records. Too often the information provided under transparency policies takes the form of a second set of books – that is to say, information created expressly for release to the public.

Since journalists need to search for patterns and tell individual stories, government data provided should be in machine-readable, standardised formats. Tables of information locked in pdfs or emails printed out on paper and sent to reporters do not constitute effective transparency.

In an era of big data and time of heightened domestic security concerns, governments have invested in algorithms that permit the monitoring of actions of individuals as residents and consumers. This software allows the government to turn unstructured information, such as hours of video or audio recordings or mountains of reports and documents, into structured data for analysis. If officials wished to increase government accountability, however, they could support research into the development of software tools that would allow reporters, NGOs, and citizens to process the flood of government data made available.

Government should be willing to release information about government decisions, not simply government information about consumer or producer actions. This would lower the costs of journalists to constructing accountability coverage focused on public officials.

Tax policies should be changed to make it easier for media organisations to form as nonprofits, so that donors who support these public affairs news outlets would enjoy tax benefits akin to those derived from supporting other educational or charitable organisations.

The ancient phrase *Quis custodiet ipsos custodies*, 'Who will guard the guards themselves?,' captures the dilemma at the heart of transparency and open government. Institutions inevitably involve delegated decision-making, and once the power to make choices passes from principals to their agents there arises the chance that the agents will act in hidden and surprising ways. Officials with delegated powers do push for transparency policies, but the authors here show that these policies often reveal the actions of others. Open government programmes might invite public participation, require other government agencies to reveal their actions, or mandate reporting by private sector actors. Less frequent are those occasions when policy-makers make their own actions more readily observable and accountable.

The sharp drop in the costs of monitoring, brought about by advances in technologies of data creation, transmission, and storage, have increased the expectation of what information could be made easily available. In media markets, this change might be expected to lead to greater competition in transparency about the reporting process among media outlets. In the political arena, it might increase voters' expectations of what they should be able to know about government actions, especially actions involving provision of services and expenditure of funds. Under such changed circumstances, individual citizens both in the US and UK are likely in their roles as consumers, producers, and voters to be better informed. Yet the conflict between officials' desires to have their choices examined and the increasing ease of tracking their actions means that, in the realm of transparency and open government policies, the gap between what is possible and what is probable will likely remain.

References

Blair, T. (2010) *A Journey: My Political Life* (Knopf).

Downs, A. (1957) *An Economic Theory of Democracy* (Harper Books).

Ferejohn, J. (1999) 'Accountability and Authority: Towards a Model of Political Accountability', in A. Przeworski, B. Manin and S. C. Stokes (eds.), *Democracy, Accountability, and Representation* (Cambridge University Press).

Hamilton, J. T. (2004) *All the News that's Fit to Sell: How the Market Transforms Information into News* (Princeton University Press).

Hamilton, J. T. (2011) 'What's the Incentive to Save Journalism', in R. W. McChesney and V. Packard (eds), *Will the Last Reporter Please Turn out the Lights: The Collapse of Journalism and What Can be Done to Fix it* (New Press).

Houston, B., and Investigative Reporters and Editors Inc. (2009) *The Investigative Reporter's Handbook: A Guide to Documents, Databases, and Techniques* (St Martin's).

Kiewiet, D. R., and McCubbins, M. D. (1991) *The Logic of Delegation: Congressional Parties and the Appropriations Process* (University of Chicago Press).

McCubbins, M., and Schwartz, T. (1984) 'Congressional Oversight Overlooked: Police Patrols versus Fire Alarms', *American Journal of Political Science*, 28: 165–79.

Przeworski, A., Stokes, S. C., and Manin, B. (eds) (1999) *Democracy, Accountability, and Representation* (Cambridge University Press).

1

Origins of the Freedom of Information Act in the United States

Michael Schudson

The US Congress approved the Freedom of Information Act (FOIA) on 20 June 1966, a reluctant President Lyndon Johnson signed it into law 4 July 1966, and it took effect one year later. It declares that every federal agency subject to the Act (this exempts Congress and the courts) shall post for public view in the Federal Register and elsewhere information regarding its operation, procedures, opinions and orders, staff manuals, and indexes to these materials. Important as this provision is, the originality of the Act lies elsewhere, in a section that obliges executive agencies also to make records available 'promptly' to 'any person' who requests information the person 'reasonably describes' and requests in accord with published rules and fees. Moreover, if the records are denied, the requester may file a complaint with a US district court.

FOIA was a negotiated settlement between competing values – what information belongs to the public because the people are sovereign in a democracy, and what information must be withheld from the public in the service of legitimate governmental objectives that require confidentiality. The balancing of desired openness with justifiable confidentiality is struck in the law's list of nine exemptions. When an executive agency successfully invokes any one of them, it is relieved from the obligation to disclose the information requested, although this decision may ultimately rest in the hands of a federal judge. FOIA permits the government to withhold information that falls within any of these exemptions: (1) information designated by an executive order to remain secret for the sake of national defence or foreign policy, (2) information related exclusively to internal personnel practices, (3) information specifically exempt from disclosure by statute, (4) trade secrets, (5) information that would be available only to an agency in litigation with the agency in question (information that judicial opinions later refer to as 'predecisional deliberation', as in the records of meetings in which agency officials consider alternative courses of action: see Goldenson, 2001–2), (6) information, like personnel and medical files, whose disclosure would invade personal privacy, (7) information compiled for law enforcement purposes that might impair law enforcement or the rights or privacy of an individual involved in criminal law enforcement proceedings, (8) information concerning agency regulation of financial institutions, and (9) geological and geophysical information.

If an agency does not release some or all of the information that a requester has demanded, the requester may go to court to seek a ruling that would require the agency to comply. This, of course, can be time-consuming and expensive. Prominent news organisations, among other parties, have been willing to do it, however. In recent years, free law clinics have been established to help news organisations file FOIA requests and appeal FOIA denials to the courts. (Yale Law School's Media Freedom and Information Access Practicum was established in 2009 with the sponsorship of Professor Jack Balkin's Information Society Project. The Online Media Legal Network, associated with Harvard Law School's Berkman Center for Internet and Society, was founded in 2010.)

Although FOIA is a significant law and one that has been a model for scores of other countries, one will look in vain in almost all US history books to find the name of John E. Moss, a workaholic Democrat from Sacramento, California, who served in the US House of Representatives from 1953 to his retirement in 1978, and who is acknowledged to be the father of FOIA (the one biography of Moss is the admiring Lemov, 2011, by a lawyer and former employee of his; more thorough work is provided in the older dissertations listed in the References to this chapter). Moss was not a colourful figure, not much of a self-promoter, and for that matter no legislative craftsman (see *New York Times*, 1956). But he was a bulldog about the cause that consumed the first half of his Congressional career, the effort to limit the power of the executive branch of government to withhold public information from the Congress and the people.

During his first term, according to his own later account, Moss became interested in freedom of information. The Democrats in 1953 were the minority party in the House. Moss, as a freshman assigned to the lowly Post Office and Civil Service Committee, was concerned that Republicans were charging the outgoing Truman administration with being lax about dismissing federal employees for security reasons.

> *This was disturbing to me because I had every confidence that the Truman administration had been diligent in administering the laws and had attempted to hire loyal Americans. I insisted in committee that we get the facts from the Civil Service Commission. Well, the Commission refused to supply the information requested by the committee. This was my first experience with an agency refusing to respond to the legitimate demands of the legislative body. (Berdes, 1969: 61)*[1]

When the Democrats gained control of the House in 1955, Moss was appointed chair of a Subcommittee on Government Information of the Government Operations Committee. Early in the subcommittee's efforts to investigate government information policies, staff consulted with James Russell Wiggins of the *Washington Post*, then head of the Freedom of Information Committee of the American Society of Newspaper Editors, other leaders in journalism, and a dozen reporters who could testify to specific instances when government agencies withheld information or suppressed news (Blanchard, 1966: 62). Moss's efforts from that point on for more than a decade were buoyed by media support, and he was not shy about asking for it. 'I hope more of you will bring your complaints to the Subcommittee,' he told news executives in 1957. 'By demanding your right of access to Federal information – and by bringing the case to the attention of the Subcommittee if your right is disregarded – you can help reverse the present Federal attitude of secrecy' (Moss, 1957a).

That there were journalists to consult with in 1955 was itself novel. The American Society of Newspaper Editors (ASNE), founded in 1923, had taken no interest in government secrecy until World War II, and then only as a problem in other countries, holding to the premise that Americans could and should instruct the rest of the world in press freedom. Only as the Cold War developed did journalists became concerned about press freedom at home.

The ASNE created its first committee on the subject – the Committee on World Freedom of Information – in 1948. In the same year, Sigma Delta Chi, the national journalism honour society, created a Committee on Advancement of Freedom of Information – again, with a global, not a national focus. The ASNE dropped 'World' from the committee's name in 1950 and Sigma Delta Chi's committee moved towards a domestic focus in

1951 (Kennedy, 1978: 20–30: information largely from ASNE and Sigma Delta Chi contemporaneous publications). ASNE recruited the retired media lawyer Harold Cross to examine the legal environment for freedom of information in the United States with respect to local, state, and national government. His work led to a book, *The People's Right to Know* (1953), that became the much-cited Bible of the freedom of information movement. Cross himself intended the work to be a 'manual of arms' for media lawyers and journalists (1953: xvi). He boldly began the book: 'Public business is the public's business. The people have the right to know. Freedom of information is their just heritage. Without that the citizens of a democracy have but changed their kings' (1953: xiii).

A freedom of information movement was taking shape, and as much or more at state and local levels as at the national level – which is to say, it was by no means focused on secrecy in the interests of national security. The freedom of information movement gained momentum in the 1950s at the state level. By 1959, fifteen states enforced both open meetings and public records disclosure, fifteen others open meetings only, and a handful of others public records disclosure only. Journalism professional groups – Sigma Delta Chi, the AP Managing Editors, the American Society of Newspaper Editors, the National Editorial Association, and state press associations – promoted these laws (Scher, 1960: 41–52).

Moss could be very entertaining – and headline-grabbing – in firing away at government secrecy. In a speech to the Magazine Publishers Association in 1958 – Moss spoke frequently to journalism associations and conferences – he recounted how the Air Force had tested a missile, hoping to get the nose cone back safely through the atmosphere, but the experiment failed. Major General Bernard Schriever told the press the next day that there had been nothing living in the nose cone. Several days later the *New York Times* reported that a mouse had been in the nose cone and the Air Force admitted this. Moss added that he disagreed with the Washington correspondents who said the Air Force had denied the existence of the mouse passenger until next of kin could be notified. Moss (1958b) told the magazine publishers that he asked General Schriever if the existence of the mouse was classified under Executive Order 10501 and, if so, why was the information eventually released? If not, why was the information originally withheld?

Moss doggedly attacked executive secrecy even after Democrat John F. Kennedy came to the White House in 1961. In June 1962, he insisted that a much larger share of complaints his subcommittee pursued in the first year of the Kennedy administration than in the final half-year of Eisenhower's presidency were initiated by the subcommittee itself (Kennedy, 1978: 102, citing an address by Moss to the New Mexico Press Association, 29 June 1962). In fact, in an address to the California Press Association on 30 November 1962, just a month after the dramatic, frightening, and effective 'brinksmanship' of the Cuban missile crisis, Moss criticised the Kennedy administration not just for continuing the secrecy policies of the Eisenhower administration but for expanding them – especially, for centralising policy in the White House and for making information release in defence and security matters more and more a matter of political advantage, less and less justified by defence and national security. In this speech, Moss used the framework of the Cold War to needle the Kennedy administration. 'I'm not worried,' he said, 'because the society reporters for Washington newspapers were not permitted backstage when the President and the First Lady talked to members of the Bolshoi Ballet, even though they were scooped by a Tass representative who was backstage as an official of the Russian government' (1962: 15).

This was a rhetorical move that Moss perfected – to show instances where the Soviets were more open in their information policies than the US. In a 1957 speech to the Associated Press Managing Editors, for instance, he had observed that the Russians published much of their research concerning the use of nuclear energy for domestic purposes: 'This has been going on in open Russian technological publications for more than a year; but practically all information in the same areas are still classified in the United States' (Moss, 1957b).

Although FOIA is a monument to the ideal of government transparency, it emerged in a climate of opinion far different from the mood and momentum of openness and disclosure that would emerge in the years after FOIA became law. True, 1974 amendments to the law made it far more effective, and these were passed in the wake of Watergate, buoyed by the very different atmosphere of the early 1970s (see Sundquist, 1981: 315–18). The 1974 amendments provided for the 'segregation' of information so that agencies could not classify whole documents or categories of documents as exempt; they provided for *in camera* review by the courts of materials the executive agencies judged to be protected by the national security exemption, they made more concrete what fell under the investigatory law enforcement exemption, they standardised the fee schedules the requester must pay, they provided fee waivers for requests that were for the benefit of the general public, and they established deadlines for agencies to respond to requests. (On the importance of these 1974 post-Watergate amendments, see Cate et al., 1994, and Wald, 1984 – who as judge in the US Court of Appeals for the District of Columbia heard many FOIA cases.) But why did FOIA become law in 1966? Why did the efforts to achieve its passage begin in 1955?

Clearly, the Cold War offered a rhetorical framework that served supporters of freedom of information. Moss spoke repeatedly of the 'paper curtain' of executive secrecy in Washington, an obvious reference to Winston Churchill's 1946 popularisation of the phrase 'iron curtain' to refer to the Soviet domination of its Eastern European satellite countries. Moss may have picked up 'paper curtain' from journalists themselves, although the term was in use in a closely related context as early as 1952, referring to the barriers the government had erected to foreign scientists seeking visas for visits to the United States (Shils, 1952; see also Weisskopf, 1954). At the first set of hearings in his subcommittee, Moss invited a group of leaders in journalism to present their views. This included Victor 'Red' Newton, then chair of the Freedom of Information committee of Sigma Delta Chi. His committee, he observed, had produced a report that warned of a 'paper curtain'. He testified,

> *This report ... exposed clearly an alarming picture of a 'paper curtain' draped securely over the release of news in the executive branch of Federal Government; of direct censorship in many departments, agencies, and bureaus; of arrogance on the part of many of our public servants; of much propaganda for political gain and privilege; of utter public confusion as to the facts in the big stories of the day; and, in some cases, of favoritism, intimidation, and revenge in the release of news of government to the people. (House Committee, 1956: 14).*

Other journalists picked up the 'paper curtain' phrase and Moss used it regularly. In the summer of 1955, Moss was asked to make a public report on the work of the subcommittee. His aide, J. Lacey Reynolds, a former journalist, drafted remarks for him, entitled 'Is there a "Paper Curtain" in Washington?' (Blanchard, 1966: 73; speech published in Congressional Record, 84th Cong., 2d Sess., 25 Aug. 1965, A6213–14). In a 1956 speech to the American Society of Newspaper Editors, Moss proudly reported, 'We feel we have punched a few holes in the "paper curtain" of secrecy which has been lowered between the people and their Government.' In 1958 he gave credit to journalists themselves in a speech at the Syracuse University

Journalism School: 'The great majority of Washington correspondents – backed by their editors and by nearly every news organization – have been fighting hard to punch a few more holes in the paper curtain surrounding Washington bureaucracy' (Moss, 1958a).

Concern about government information control accumulated some force in Washington without any support from the executive branch. Every single government executive agency that testified in the hearings on the FOIA bill in 1966 testified against it. As for the general public, there is no sign that the issue ever attracted any powerful support or opposition. But the legislators favouring curbs on the government's power to withhold information from the public had one very significant ally: the news media, particularly the newspapers, and notably some of their organised groups – of journalists, of editorial writers, and of publishers. They all saw their own interests at stake and, with some hesitation on the part of some in the media about playing an active role in encouraging a specific piece of legislation, they went ahead precisely to do this. Journalists testified in its support. They fed Rep. Moss information he could use in promoting his cause. They praised Moss and his efforts in editorial after editorial. They gave good coverage to his hearings.

There is no 'right to know' in the Constitution. The First Amendment protects a free press from government interference, but it offers no affirmative requirement that the government help the press in its task of covering government.[2] A regard for 'popular information' is protected by the Constitution only in Article I, section 5, where Congress is required to maintain journals and make them public 'from time to time ... excepting such Parts as may in their Judgment require Secrecy'. And what did 'from time to time' mean to the founders? We do not know for sure, but we can make a reasonable guess because the Virginia ratification convention proposed an amendment (none of its proposals were adopted) that specified that the House and Senate journals 'shall be published at least once in every year'. (Uhm, 2008: 402, argues that a 'right to know' can be traced back to the founding era but acknowledges that leading scholars do not agree: BeVier, 1980; O'Brien, 1981; Stewart, 1975.) Patrick Henry, one of the most ardently libertarian of the founders, objected to the ambiguity of 'from time to time', but he made no headway with his colleagues (cited in O'Brien, 1981: 39). Even the most radical of the framers on liberty of speech and press – Henry and George Mason – acknowledged that secrecy would sometimes be necessary, particularly in military matters and the conduct of diplomacy (O'Brien, 1981: 39).

Did the founders believe that republican government required informed citizens? The most that may be claimed, as legal scholar David O'Brien has cogently argued, is that the founders judged that the public had a right to know 'as an abstract political right' derived indirectly from the First Amendment – but that the First Amendment is not a freedom-of-information act as such (1981: 29 and 141). It does not say that citizens should be able to make demands for information upon those serving in the government; it says only that Congress 'shall make no law abridging freedom of speech, or of the press'. It offers a negative liberty, not a right to information.

The Freedom of Information Act, for all of its originality, was not born from nothing. The Federal Register Act of 1935 was an important first step in making public the rule-making actions of executive agencies. The Federal Register has been an official gazette of US executive activity, modelled on an 1893 'Rules Publication Act' in Britain (Feinberg, 2001: 359–70). The Administrative Procedure Act (APA) (1946) – to which FOIA was technically an amendment – required public disclosure of government records 'to persons properly and directly concerned' except when 'secrecy in the public interest' is required, when the information relates 'solely to the internal management of an agency', or when 'otherwise required by statute', except, even then, 'information held confidential for good cause found' (U.S.C. 1002). Openings like 'the public interest' and 'good cause' were big enough to drive through as many federal trucks as any administration might want (on legislative precedents to FOIA, see Feinberg, 1986). Supporters of the APA urged that it would be a 'bill of rights' for individuals facing the rapidly growing administrative state that the founding fathers had never anticipated, but Joanna Grisinger, the historian who has written most extensively about the APA's origins and its evolution, concedes that 'The APA ultimately worked little change in administrative practice' (2012: 10, 11).

Moss understood this. In practice, officials felt free to do what they wished about informing – or not informing – the public. As Moss said in a 1959 speech to the Aviation Writers Association, federal officials make information available to the press:

> – unless the information is restricted on grounds of security;
> – unless the information is specifically restricted by law; such as personal income tax returns and trade secrets;
> – unless the official decides that the information is merely 'preliminary';

– unless the official decides the information is part of an 'internal' document;

– unless the official believes the information would cause 'controversy';

– unless the official believes release of the information is not 'timely';

– unless the official believes that the information might be 'misunderstood' or 'misinterpreted' by the people of the United States;

– unless the official believes the information might cause a 'publicity build-up';

– or unless he feels merely that release of the information would not be 'in the public interest.' (Moss, 1959)

FOIA changed this. It was a landmark of historic proportion, but it was also badly flawed. In an early (1967) analysis, Kenneth Culp Davis, a widely respected expert in administrative law, was particularly scathing:

That the Congress of the United States, after more than ten years of hearings, questionnaires, studies, reports, drafts, and pulling and hauling, should wind up with such a shabby product seems discouraging. The drafting deficiencies cannot be explained away as the product of extreme complexity, intractable subject matter, or unruly struggles between irreconcilable political philosophies. The failures in this instance are in the nature of inattention and indifference. (1967: 803, 804, 807)

FOIA's shortcomings came to the attention of Senator Edward Kennedy's Administrative Practice and Procedure Subcommittee of the Senate Judiciary Committee some years later and a FOIA reform bill was under consideration in both Houses early in 1973. Passed in the autumn of 1974 – unanimously in the Senate and 349-2 in the House, it was promptly vetoed by President Gerald Ford. He objected to its authorising the courts to examine classified documents, the vulnerability of law enforcement records to disclosure, penalties for agencies that failed to comply with the law, and the introduction of time limits for agencies to respond to FOIA requests. Congress overrode the veto (371–31 in the House and 65–27 in the Senate), with Sen. Kennedy declaring the override 'a visible and concrete repudiation by Congress of both the traditional bureaucratic secrecy of the federal establishment and the special antimedia, antipublic, anti-Congress secrecy of the Nixon administration' (cited in Foerstel, 1999: 48; see also Congressional Quarterly, 1977: 805–6; O'Reilly, 2000: 43–9). In these remarks, Kennedy paired the new Ford administration with its predecessor Nixon administration whose Watergate ignominy was the dark shadow that hung fatefully over the Ford White House.

The efforts of John Moss to make Congress a more effective watchdog on the burgeoning executive, pursued with the willing collaboration of leaders of the nation's press and with avid support from some Republicans (notably Illinois Representative Donald Rumsfeld) as well as Democrats, produced something novel for the United States and – since the 1766 freedom-of-information law in Sweden had not had global influence – something of a small miracle for the world as other nations borrowed from the American example and enacted freedom-of-information laws of their own (on Sweden see Holstad, 1979, and Pedren, 1987). Flawed as the American FOIA was, it proved the modern renewal of what Thomas Blanton, director of the National Security Archive, has dubbed 'The Openness Revolution'. Blanton (2002) sees FOIA's passage and the 1974 amendments that strengthened it as the point of origin for the worldwide spread of a revolution that in the key decade between the fall of the Soviet Union and 9/11 would reach around the globe. The Cold War national security state with its apparatus of secrecy generated a hunger for its opposite – and a legislative mechanism that could begin to achieve it.

The drive to make government more open over the past half century has been part of a broad cultural movement to make society more open, to make human relations more equal, and to make visibility itself an axis on which progress turns.

Many forces and factors have contributed to open and undisguised communication, and this in general is a virtue in and for democracy. But it is a virtue with limits. There really are things that governments should keep secret. There really is information about constructing nuclear, biological, or chemical weapons that circulates within parts of the government and that should not be made available to the general public. There really is such a thing as 'diplomacy' that requires leaders to say in public something different from what they say behind closed doors. Making publicly available the personnel records of individual government employees would violate personal privacy; disclosing certain information related to ongoing law enforcement investigations (say, of organised crime or terrorism) could jeopardise legitimate law enforcement objectives.

Advocates of transparency have been far too casual in presenting it as an ultimate value rather than what Alasdair MacIntyre has labelled a 'second-order virtue', a virtue more of process than of ultimate good (1967: 24). Of concern are limitations on disclosure that on their face are an indignity to democracy or gross violations of personal autonomy. Many such practices, routine through most of American history, changed in the period from 1960 to 1980. Various efforts in these years, touched by and in turn contributing to a profound cultural change, made disclosure and its positive valuation more central in American society than ever before. Transparency is not coincident with republican government or representative democracy. Representative democracies have taken a great deal of non-transparency for granted for generations. Some features of democracy have not only accepted non-transparency but even placed it on a sacred pedestal, most notably the secret ballot. One might also add – since it is sacred at least among journalists – the confidentiality of reporters' relationships with their sources. The secret ballot protects citizens' autonomy and privacy; the confidentiality of reporter–source relationships upholds the effective operation of a free press. Both pay tribute to a single value above transparency – a norm of non-coercion, that individuals may be empowered to act according to conscience without fear of reprisal.

Far from being a traditional element in representative government, freedom of information laws are part of what political theorist John Keane (2009) has labelled 'monitory democracy', what he has also called a 'post-parliamentary' form of democracy that has developed largely since 1945, especially from the 1960s and after. In the American context, I think the label 'trans-legislative democracy' would be apt. These names are not meant to signal that elections and elected legislatures have become unimportant but that they have been massively supplemented by a wide variety of practices in both government and civil society that enable citizens to monitor the work of government and even to impress their views upon it not only on election day but year-round. 'Any person' may file a FOIA request at any time, may join an organised interest group, may alert the news media to suspected malfeasance or corruption, and may pursue political objectives through litigation.

Meanwhile, governments have devised a set of new instruments for government to monitor itself – in the United States, the Inspector General Act of 1978 established a substantial and largely new federal bureaucracy for self-monitoring designed to curb mismanagement, corruption, and law-breaking in executive agencies. The work of the inspectors general has recovered hundreds of millions of dollars, led to thousands of successful prosecutions, and spawned hundreds of prominent news stories about error, mismanagement, and malfeasance in government. In recent years, more readily available online government data and smarter, more user-friendly design of agency websites have also made citizen access and oversight more possible. While one cannot doubt that the Enlightenment inspiration of the American founders lies behind such developments, it lies rather far behind them. The Freedom of Information Act was a relatively early harbinger of what Keane (2011: 212–23) describes as

> the rapid growth of many different kinds of extra-parliamentary, power-scrutinising mechanisms. These monitory bodies take root within the domestic fields of government and civil society, as well as in cross-border settings once controlled by empires, states and business organisations. In consequence, the whole architecture of self-government is changing. The central grip of elections, political parties and parliaments on citizens' lives is weakening.

Keane's discussion seems to me the best and most fitting characterisation of democratic developments since 1945, but others have pointed in the same direction. I review some of them in Schudson (forthcoming).

This is certainly not to say that we have yet figured out just how to make the various institutions of trans-legislative democracy work. Consider this example of the journalistic uses of FOIA. In May 2008, *New York Times* reporter Nina Bernstein wrote a front-page story about the imprisonment of immigrants who violated conditions of their visitor status, sometimes languished in detention, and in some horrifying cases died while in custody. Bernstein had got wind of the story several years before, at which time her sources told her there were some 20 deaths involved. She filed a FOIA request. Her request was met with a long silence – that is, until November 2007 when a package was delivered to her desk with the information she had requested and the shocking evidence that there were 66 deaths, not 20.

Bernstein's FOIA request became a topic of the *Times*'s 'public editor' column by Clark Hoyt. Hoyt observed that *Times* reporters make aggressive use of FOIA and that in recent weeks the *Times* had published two leading stories based on FOIA-obtained government information, Bernstein's and a story by David Barstow that revealed how the Pentagon influenced TV military analysts to get a more favourable spin in the television news. Barstow had filed his FOIA request at the end of April 2006. It was denied. He appealed. The appeal was turned down in August 2006. Barstow kept trying – and in the end received 687 pages of documents from the Defense

Department. A bit more information trickled in thereafter but it was far less than Barstow had requested and the explanations for the denial were not credible. The *Times* took the Pentagon to court – and won. Still the Pentagon moved slowly. Finally the *Times* ran the story with what it had on 20 April 2008. Several days later Barstow received an additional 2,800 pages.

According to Hoyt (2008), Barstow judged FOIA 'a cruel joke', and every indication is that Hoyt agreed. The phrase 'cruel joke' hangs in the air at the end of Hoyt's column. Nevertheless, early in 2009, Barstow's stories on the Pentagon and TV military analysts won the Pulitzer Prize for investigative reporting, confirming the importance of the work and amplifying its influence.

Two stories, deeply critical of federal policy, both of them embarrassing to Washington, were made possible, in part, by FOIA even as they were substantially delayed while the journalists struggled with the FOIA apparatus and recalcitrant agencies. And the frustrations were enough to make journalists themselves only half-hearted advocates of FOIA-as-it-exists (rather than FOIA as they might like it to be). Would 100 such stories a year justify all the expense and trouble of FOIA? Ten such stories? One?

In 2006, in recognition of the 40th anniversary of FOIA, the National Security Archive published a list of 40 notable news stories that relied on information obtained through FOIA. In most cases, a news organisation initiated the FOIA request – the Associated Press, the *Baltimore Sun*, the *Chicago Sun-Times*, the *Chicago Tribune*, the *Des Moines Register*, Knight Ridder, the *Los Angeles Times*, the *Minneapolis Star Tribune*, *Newsday*, the *New York Times*, the *Richmond Times Dispatch*, the *San Francisco Chronicle*, *USA Today*, and the *Washington Post*. In other cases, the FOIA request came from nonprofit civic, advocacy, and research organisations – the American Civil Liberties Union, Electronic Privacy Information Center, Judicial Watch, Migration Policy Institute, People for Ethical Treatment of Animals, Public Employees for Environmental Responsibility, Texans for Public Justice, Transactional Records Access Clearinghouse, Union of Concerned Scientists, and in several cases the National Security Archive at George Washington University itself (National Security Archive, 2006).

The law can be improved, perhaps overhauled, and the government's faithfulness to its spirit can be strengthened. FOIA is often awkward, difficult, and frustrating – but it is no joke.[3] It affixes a right to petition for information to 'any person' and thereby makes it clear that no question of 'standing' is relevant in court review of FOIA requests – everyone had standing. It places the burden of proof on executive agencies to defend the withholding of information, not on the FOIA requester to offer reasons for disclosure. Even in its early years, FOIA requesters fared well in the courts more often than not (Clark, 1974–5: 745–8).

Why does it exist at all? It emerged as an effort of members of Congress to defend the prerogatives of the legislative branch against a rapidly expanding administrative state that displayed an arrogance of power. The Congressional effort acquired some energy thanks to the way John Moss and others employed the rhetoric of the Cold War itself to advertise their intentions in a persuasive way. While Congressional advocates did not have and did not generally seek popular support, they worked hard to rally journalists and journalism organisations to their side, with considerable success. Later, in 1973 and 1974, as supporters of freedom of information sought to strengthen FOIA, they rode the wave of a Vietnam, Pentagon papers, and a popular Watergate-inflected distrust of government and government secrecy. But that was well into a future that John Moss in 1955 or even in 1966 could not have readily imagined.

The American Freedom of Information Act was not the first law to provide for government disclosure of information – that honour goes to Sweden – but the American law brought this practice into modern times, planted it in the most powerful democracy in the world, and helped to inspire scores of other countries to enact comparable laws of their own and to make disclosure the new, legitimate ideal in government relations with the general public. There are more than 90 countries with freedom of information laws today, 70 of them enacted since 1990 (Michener, 2011). With all of FOIA's faults, it is worth remembering how this unlikely and indispensable law came to be.

Notes

1   This interview took place 13 Apr. 1965. Although not published by Marquette until 1969, it is cited in Blanchard, 1966: 53–4. Paul E. Kostyu reports that Moss requested from the Civil Service Commission a breakdown of the 2,200 loyalty-security firings in the Truman administration – he asked especially about postal employee dismissals. Philip Young, chair of the Civil Service Commission, responded that the Commission had 'neither the responsibility nor the

authority' to release this information (see *Washington Evening Star*, 26 Jan. 1954, cited by Kostyu, 1991). See also Kostyu, 1990. Consistent with the Berdes interview in 1965 is George Kennedy's 1 June 1977 interview where Moss said he was denied information he requested from the Civil Service Commission during his first term. 'My experience in Washington quickly proved that you had a hell of a time getting any information.' See Kennedy, 1978: 64.

2   David M. O'Brien declares 'the First Amendment is not a Freedom of Information Act' (141). This seems indisputable although Justices William J. Brennan and Thurgood Marshall argued (in dissenting opinions) otherwise. See O'Brien, 1981: 141–6, 165–7.

3   There are many accounts of both successful and unsuccessful FOIA requests and the many cases that fall in between. See, for instance, Martin, 2008, Marks, 1979 – Marks received 16,000 pages of CIA documents in response to his FOIA requests and in his acknowledgments thanks the Congressional sponsors of FOIA. Historian David Garrow told National Public Radio that he waited seventeen years for some of the documents he requested. (See Martin, 2008: 92, 228.) When I contacted Garrow about this (personal communication by email, 2013) he did not remember the specific time span but wrote that seventeen years sounded about right. Nonetheless, in his biography of Martin Luther King, Jr., Garrow reports that he received 'tens of thousands of pages' through FOIA requests, and thanks by name seven individuals at the FBI and the Department of Justice's Civil Rights Division and Community Relations Service who helped him. See Garrow, 1986: 627–8. Requests to the CIA and FBI have often produced the most egregious delays and denials. Philip H. Melanson titles his chapter on FOIA, 'The User-Unfriendly Law.' The chapter opens with his assertion that the law is weighted toward the government, not the requester, and that, even so, its procedures 'are often ignored or manipulated by agencies'. This is followed immediately by a quotation from a booklet of the Reporters Committee for Freedom of the Press: 'The possibilities of the act are endless. All that is required is that you use it.' Melanson comments: 'Both positions are correct.' See Melanson, 2001: 31. Lawyer and political scientist Peter Irons, thanks in part to Department of Justice disclosures in response to his FOIA requests, found that government lawyers suppressed evidence in presenting the government's defence of the forced internment of Japanese-Americans during World War II. This revelation ultimately led the Supreme Court to reopen the cases of Gordon Hirabayashi and Fred Korematsu who had tried unsuccessfully to challenge the constitutionality of the executive order establishing the internment camps. Irons's FOIA-based research led to the vacating of the cases against Hirabayashi and Korematsu and ultimately to

financial compensation for the surviving Japanese-American citizens who were interned or their descendants. See Irons, 1983.

References

Berdes, G. R. (1969) *Friendly Adversaries: The Press and Government* (Center for the Study of the American Press, College of Journalism, Marquette University).

BeVier, L. R. (1980) 'An Informed Public, an Informing Press: The Search for a Constitutional Principle', *California Law Review,* 68: 482.

Blanchard, R. O. (1966) 'The Moss Committee and a Federal Public Records Law,' Ph.D. dissertation, Syracuse University, 1966.

Blanton, T. S. (2002) 'The Openness Revolution: The Rise of a Global Movement for Freedom of Information', *Development Dialogue,* 1: 7–21.

Cate, F. H., Fields, D. A. and McBain, J. K. (1994) 'The Right to Privacy and the Public's Right to Know: The "Central Purpose" of the Freedom of Information Act', *Administrative Law Review,* 46: 41–74.

Clark, E. (1974–5) 'Holding Government Accountable: The Amended Freedom of Information Act', *Yale Law Journal* 84: 741–69.

Congressional Quarterly (1977) *Congress and the Nation,* vol. 4, 1973–76 (Congressional Quarterly): 805–6.

Cross, H. L. (1953) *The People's Right to Know: Legal Access to Public Records and Proceedings* (Columbia University Press).

Davis, K. C. (1967) 'The Information Act: A Preliminary Analysis', *University of Chicago Law Review,* 34: 761–816.

Feinberg, L. E. (1986) 'Managing the Freedom of Information Act and Federal Information Policy', *Public Administration Review,* 46: 615–21.

Feinberg, L. E. (2001) 'Mr. Justice Brandeis and the Creation of the Federal Register', *Public Administration Review,* 61 (May/June): 359–70.

Foerstal, H. N. (1999) *Freedom of Information and the Right to Know: The Origins and Applications of the Freedom of Information Act* (Greenwood Press).

Garrow, D. J. (1986) *Bearing the Cross: Martin Luther King, Jr., and the Southern Christian Leadership Conference* (Random House).

Goldenson, D. G. (2001–2) 'FOIA Exemption FIVE: Will it Protect Government Scientists from Unfair Intrusion?', *Boston College Environmental Affairs Law Review,* 29: 311–42.

Grisinger, J. L. (2012) *The Unwieldy American State: Administrative Politics Since the New Deal* (Cambridge University Press).

Holstad, S. (1979) 'Sweden', in D. C. Rowat (ed.), *Administrative Secrecy in Developed Countries* (Columbia University Press): 29–50.

House Committee on Government Operations (1956) Availability of Information from Federal Departments and Agencies: Hearings Before a Subcommittee of the Committee on Government Operations, 7 Nov. 1955, 84th Cong., 1st Sess. (Government Printing Office, 1956).

Hoyt, C. (2008) 'Information that doesn't Come Freely', *New York Times*, 11 May.

Irons, P. (1983) *Justice at War* (Oxford University Press).

Keane, J. (2009) *Life and Death of Democracy* (Simon & Schuster).

Keane, J. (2011) 'Monitory Democracy?', in S. Alonso, J. Keane, and W. Merkel (eds), *The Future of Representative Democracy* (Cambridge University Press): 212–35.

Kennedy, G. (1978) 'Advocates of Openness: The Freedom of Information Movement,' Ph.D. dissertation, University of Missouri.

Kostyu, P. E. (1990) 'The Moss Connection: The Freedom of Information Movement, Influence and John E. Moss, Jr.,' Ph.D. dissertation, Bowling Green State University.

Kostyu, P. E. (1991) 'Partners in the Freedom of Information Movement: The Press and John E. Moss Jr.', paper presented at AEJMC National Convention, Boston, MA.

Lemov, M. (2011) *People's Warrior* (Fairleigh Dickinson University Press).

MacIntyre, A. (1967) *Secularization and Moral Change* (Oxford University Press).

Marks, J. (1979) *The Search for the 'Manchurian Candidate': The CIA and Mind Control* (Times Books).

Martin, S. E. (2008) *Freedom of Information: The News the Media Use* (Peter Lang).

Melanson, P. H. (2001) *Secrecy Wars: National Security, Privacy, and the Public's Right to Know* (Brassey's).

Michener, G. (2011) 'FOI Laws around the World', *Journal of Democracy*, 22/2: 145–59.

Moss, J. E. (1956) Speech before American Society of Newspaper Editors 1956 convention, 20 Apr. John E. Moss Papers, Box 334 Folder 16.

Moss, J. E. (1957a) Address to the Upper Midwest News Executives Conference, Minneapolis, MN, 3 May. John E. Moss Papers, Box 427 Folder 3.

Moss J. E. (1957b) Speech to Associated Press Managing Editors Association Convention, New Orleans, 20 Nov. John E. Moss Papers, Box 427 Folder 9.

Moss, J. E. (1958a) Convocation Speech, Syracuse University School of Journalism, 21 Feb. John E. Moss Papers, Box 427 Folder 15.

Moss, J. E. (1958b) Speech of 5 May. Moss Papers, Box 427.

Moss, J. E. (1959) Remarks for 'Freedom of Information Symposium', Aviation Writers Association annual meeting, Washington, DC, 12 May. John E. Moss Papers, Box 428 Folder 16.

Moss, J. E. (1962) 'Excerpts from an Address by Congressman John E. Moss, Chairman, Special Subcommittee on Government Information, at the California Press Association Conference, San Francisco, November 30, 1962', p. 15. John E. Moss Papers, Box 429 Folder 19.

National Security Archive (2006) 'FOIA in the News – 2004–2006': www.gwu.edu/~nsarchiv/nsa/foia/stories.htm.

New York Times (1956) 'A Quiet Investigator', 16 Nov., p. 16.

O'Brien, D. M. (1981) *The Public's Right to Know: The Supreme Court and the First Amendment* (Praeger).

O'Reilly, J. T. (2000) *Federal Information Disclosure*, 3rd edn (West Group).

Pedren, G. P. (1987) 'Access to Government-Held Information in Sweden', in N. S. Marsh (ed.), *Public Access to Government-Held Information* (Stevens & Sons): 35–54.

Scher, J. (1960) 'Access to Information: Recent Legal Problems', *Journalism Quarterly*, 37: 41–52.

Schudson, M. (forthcoming) 'Linking Media Sociology to Political Development in Trans-Legislative Democracies', in S. Waisbord (ed.), *New Developments in Media Sociology* (Polity Press).

Shils, E. A. (1952) 'America's Paper Curtain', *Bulletin of the Atomic Scientists*, 8/7 (Oct.): 210–17.

Stewart, Justice Potter (1975) 'Or Of the Press', *Hastings Law Journal*, 26: 636.

Sundquist, J. L. (1981) *The Decline and Resurgence of Congress* (Brookings Institution).

Uhm, K. (2008) 'The Founders and the Revolutionary Underpinning of the Concept of the Right to Know', *Journalism and Mass Communication Quarterly*, 85/2: 393–416.

Wald, P. M. (1984) 'The Freedom of Information Act: A Short Case Study in the Perils and Paybacks of Legislating Democratic Values', *Emory Law Journal*, 33: 649–83.

Weisskopf, V. F. (1954) 'Visas for Foreign Scientists', *Bulletin of the Atomic Scientists*, 10/3 (Mar.): 68.

2

Impact of Transparency on Accountability

Peter Riddell

British government is much more open than it was 10, 20, and certainly 30 years ago. But what impact has this increased transparency had on accountability? In this chapter, I examine three main themes: the various changes in the UK since the late 1980s to make government more open; the use of them made by the media in seeking accountability by public officials; and the impact on public attitudes towards political institutions and the elusive trust question.

It was one of the clichés of media and political debate that Britain was historically one of the most secretive countries in the world; although, in practice, that meant by comparison with the USA, some Scandinavian countries, and Australia, Canada, and New Zealand, which were much earlier to introduce freedom of information legislation. That reflected both statutory controls in the UK, such as a very restrictive Official Secrets Act of 1911 which banned disclosure of virtually anything happening or said within government, and, as important, a culture of 'them and us' secrecy. That, in turn, was the legacy of Britain's strong executive style of government and the absence of a formal codified constitution guaranteeing rights. The civil service were able to argue for a long time – if often unconvincingly – that information should first be disclosed to Parliament by ministers, virtually all of whom were members of the House of Commons or the House of Lords. This doctrine of ministerial accountability was interpreted in terms convenient to the executive, and had the effect of restricting access to information which was determined by ministers and civil servants.

The cultural change in the past two decades is harder to measure and still patchy. There has been a longstanding and respected Campaign for Freedom of Information, a nonprofit and non-partisan organisation set up in 1984 by Maurice Frankel to improve public access to official information. Mr Frankel has led the campaign for almost three decades. Pressures for change came not only in response to the British official tradition and practice of secrecy but also as a result of the experience of Westminster systems which all introduced freedom of information legislation: Australia, Canada, and New Zealand (all in 1982 or 1983) and Ireland (1997), as well as the example of the United States (where an Act was passed in 1966). While the evidence from overseas inspired campaigners in the UK, the British initiatives were largely home grown, rather than adopting tried and tested models developed elsewhere.

There have been three formal phases of government-inspired change: the open government initiative of the early 1990s; the Freedom of Information Act of 2000, which fully came into operation in 2005; and the transparency agenda of the coalition government since 2010. But as important as these has been the arrival of the internet which has broken down barriers, opening up access to government information, not only to the media but also to the public broadly. So there has been a combination of proactive and reactive openness. Following the implementation of the Freedom of Information Act in 2005, there has been an increase in the amount of information proactively released, especially since 2010, as part of the coalition government's wider transparency agenda.

First, the open government initiative. A gradual increase in government transparency began in the late 1980s, as a result of various initiatives by individual MPs, notably the now Liberal Democrat peer Archy Kirkwood, to increase individuals' right of access to various records about themselves. This included access to medical and other personal records. The main government step was the repeal in 1989 of the key provisions of the pre-World War I Official Secrets Act, replacing them with a narrower measure protecting information about security, defence, international relations, and law enforcement. But the new Act did not include any public interest defence and was still regarded as too restrictive by campaigning groups. At the 1992 general election, Labour and the Liberal Democrats, both then in opposition, promised Freedom of Information legislation. The re-elected Conservative government decided against such an Act, but, under the leadership of William, now Lord, Waldegrave, pursued an 'open government' policy. This was mainly through a Code of Practice which came into force in 1994 and gave access to information, but not documents. If there was limited initial impact on access to contemporary information, historians welcomed the review and release of many previously withheld official files. Nonetheless, this marked a change of tone, and approach, in central government.

Second, after a lengthy and tortuous campaign, the Freedom of Information Act finally became law in November 2000 and came into full effect in January 2005. This followed the election of the Blair government in May 1997. The original proposals, put forward in July 1998 by Dr David Clark, were watered down after he was dropped as a minister and replaced by the more cautious Jack Straw. His draft bill was widely criticised for being too weak since it included a voluntary public interest, which the Information Commissioner could not rule on. Public authorities would be able to insist on knowing why someone wanted information. The draft bill was subject to extensive scrutiny by both Houses of the British Parliament. The Public Administration Committee of the Commons commented in its (1999) report that, judged by international standards, the draft bill was restrictive in its absence of a purpose clause; the absence of a statutory duty to advise and assist people requesting information; in exempting information to be disclosed on a voluntary basis, not when the public interest requires it; and in the 'unusually restrictive class exemptions for policy advice, information from investigations and commercial information'. Many of these flaws were remedied during the debates on the bill. The government was criticised for not fully understanding the difference between open government and freedom of information.

> Open government means the Government publishing information largely for its own purposes: information that the Government think we need to know or might like to know. Freedom of information requires the Government to disclose information which we decide for ourselves we want to know. (Public Administration Committee, 1999)

The Act gave the public, for the first time, a statutory right (subject to several limitations) to find out if a public authority holds specific information and, if so, to be provided with access to it. The Act applied to more than 100,000 public authorities, ranging from large government departments to local authorities, schools, hospitals, and individual GPs and dentists. The Act was subsequently extended in 2012 to academies (independent but taxpayer-funded schools), to the Association of Chief Police Officers, and to the university admissions body, amongst other organisations. At the time of writing, there are consultations about extending this list to harbour authorities, legal regulators, and housing associations. The large number of bodies affected makes it hard to make an accurate assessment of the level of requests under the legislation. But, according to an analysis by the Ministry of Justice, over 220,000 non-routine information requests were made to central government bodies between 2005 and 2010, and nearly 700,000 to local authorities over the same period. There has been a variable response depending in part on exemptions, such as relating to national security, international relations, and court and prison records, which apply more in some departments than others.

Third, there is the transparency agenda. This can be seen as a development of the two earlier initiatives and was launched in 2010 by Francis Maude, the Conservative minister responsible for administration, as a key part of the coalition government's efficiency and reform agenda. The main focus has been on freeing up data about public services in order to enable the public to hold politicians and public bodies to account, thereby delivering better value for money in public spending. Details have been made available online of all new items of government spending over £25,000 for goods and services; all new items of local government spending over £500; all new central government contracts and tender documents over £10,000 featuring performance indicators, break clauses, and penalty measures; and all new local government contracts and tender documents over £500. Lists have been published of civil servants earning over £150,000 a year and of special advisers earning above £58,200. Monthly crime statistics are being published online by the police on a street-by-street level, with hospitals releasing weekly online data on MRSA and C-difficile infection rates. There are, of course, pressures to go further, with increasingly sensitive issues over the amount of information available as a result of the growing use of private contractors to provide public services. An Open Data Institute has been set up to promote innovation in using the data published by the government.

There is, however, a danger of exaggerating the significance of these administrative and statutory changes compared with technological ones. The internet has made government information much more accessible than before, not just to the media but also to the public. Roll back 20 to 30 years, and if you wanted to find out what the government had done, you would have to buy an official document or Hansard, the official record of parliamentary debates – or hope that they were fully covered in a newspaper or in the broadcast media. This limited not only the range of information available but also the access to it. That has all changed. All government and parliamentary documents are now available online free of charge – together with more supporting material. In this respect, there is a link between the administrative/technological changes and the legislative ones. The figures for visits to various official websites are impressive, suggesting that far more people are reading government and parliamentary statements than in the past. This has far more than offset the decline in 'paper of record', comprehensive factual coverage in newspapers of what is said in Parliament and of official documents. The most recent report by the House of Commons Commission (2012) recorded a rise in website requests from 49 million in 2007–8 to more than 67 million in 2011–12. Similarly, on average, every UK resident visits a central government website ten times a year: in practice, of course, this implies that many people visit sites a great deal more frequently. There is also evidence that the public thinks that public authorities are becoming more open, with a balance of about a half to a third agreeing this has happened, according to regular polls for the Ministry of Justice.

The media have used this greater openness to varying extents. The Freedom of Information Campaign argued in its submission to the House of Commons Justice Committee inquiry in 2012 into the working of the Act (ev. 65) that the media failed to make use of the 1994 Code of Practice on Open Government, which was one of the reasons why the code had little impact. By contrast, there is general agreement that the Freedom of Information Act has been used on a large scale by newspapers, broadcasters, and others. There is still, however, a patchiness in the use, depending in part on the work a journalist is doing, and also generationally, since younger journalists have grown up with the Freedom of Information Act. The Society of Editors told the same inquiry (vol. 1, p. 9) that: 'The Act has become an essential journalistic tool which has helped create a climate of genuine openness and transparency in British public life.' However, there are caveats. Martin Rosenbaum, a specialist at the BBC on the issue, told the inquiry (vol. 1, pp. 9–10) that the changes were

> partial and inconsistent ... Characterising the sort of information that the Act now enables us to obtain on a very crude level, you will now find that it is much easier to gets facts and figures – how much was spent on this, statistics about the performance of public services and so on. The sorts of things that were harder to get previously now tend to be very easy to get, but what it has not produced and the civil service is very resistant to that, is internal discussion documents, policy discussion, minutes of meetings and so on.

The BBC's online website has a section devoted to freedom of information, which lists a number of stories which have been unearthed through the use of the Act, from allegations of abuse in care homes; sponsorship of the Metropolitan Police; and the detention of children in police cells.

Some fears have been expressed that journalists can be tied to computers in assessing published data (open government) and in making applications under the FOI Act (freedom of information), rather than getting out and seeking stories in the traditional way. So, the internet can be both a blessing, in broadening sources of information, and a curse, in providing perverse incentives to journalists to limit the range of their activities, especially in an age of cost-cutting.

At the local government level in Britain, the experience has been uneven, partly depending on the specific authority concerned. There have been contradictory trends. The pressures towards greater openness have been offset by changes in the structure of local government in England, notably the introduction of the 'cabinet' system, which may have reduced the flow of information. This change introduced an executive model of leadership, either through a directly elected mayor, or some councillors being given executive responsibilities. This replaced a more collective, and open, system where decisions were taken in committees. On balance, however, local newspaper groups think there is greater openness not only in local authorities but also, crucially, in local health trusts running hospitals and in universities.

The Justice Committee concluded (2012: vol. 1, p. 11) that 'the strength of the new culture of openness is variable and depends on both the type of organisation, and the approach to freedom of information of the individual public authority'. Moreover, 'proactive publication cannot substitute for a right to access data because it is impossible for public bodies to anticipate the information that will be required'. There has also been friction as some public authorities have appeared to regard the media's use of the Act as illegitimate compared to requests by individuals, so that some journalists have used private email accounts in order to make requests. This had led to complaints that the media are making excessive use of the Act, diverting already stretched resources. So, as discussed below, alongside a culture of greater openness, ministers and officials, especially in central government, have looked for various ways of making policy discussions 'FOI proof' – that is resistant to applications under the FOI Act. For them, the Act is seen as a challenge. There has also been grumbling about the cost of the Act from the government and whether cost limits need to be introduced.

A very small number of requests contribute to a relatively large proportion of the costs: 8% to central government cost more than £500 to answer, making up a third of total staff costs.

Overall, however, there is little dispute among either the media or public bodies that the net effect of the Act and associated measures has been to make government more accountable. The media have played a key role here, not only via the traditional outlets of the press and broadcasters but also increasingly via the internet. The world of blogging and Twitter has forced public officials to respond, or else the story runs away from them.

Government and other public authorities have been made more accountable less as a result of the administrative and legal changes discussed above than the existence of the internet and the slightly earlier development of 24-hour news in the broadcast media. Both have shifted the balance from an essentially hierarchical structure in which government can determine who knows what and when, to a more open one in which ministers and advisers find it hard to set the terms of the media debate. Even such a skilful media operator as Tony Blair attacked the media as a 'feral beast' in a lecture shortly before he left 10 Downing Street in June 2007 and criticised the Freedom of Information Act for limiting the scope for ministers to discuss policy options. He described the passage of the Act as one of the mistakes of his administration. He wrote about it vividly in his memoirs (Blair, 2010: 516): 'Freedom of Information. Three harmless words. I look at those words as I write them, and feel like shaking my head till it drops off my shoulders. You idiot. You naïve, foolish, irresponsible nincompoop. There is really no description of stupidity, no matter how vivid, that is adequate. I quake at the imbecility of it'.

Blair described the Act as 'utterly undermining of sensible government'. It undermined the government's ability to discuss issues 'with a reasonable level of confidentiality'. The Act had 'strayed far beyond what it was sensible to disclose'. This is in stark contrast to his view (Blair, 1996) before becoming prime minister that such an Act would be 'absolutely fundamental to how we see politics developing in this country'. In his later view, the Act had become part of the battle between the government and the media and shifted the balance towards the media who used the Act as 'a weapon'. The same line has been taken by Alastair Campbell, his long-serving communications director. A common view of those in power, particularly in 10 Downing Street, was that they had been put on the defensive and that increased transparency had made governing harder.

Consequently, there has been tension between the media, often supported at later stages by the Information Commissioner appointed to oversee the implementation of the legislation, and the government over the extent of disclosure. This turns on what has become known as the 'chilling effect' – that is, anticipatory action to keep discussions off paper where they might have to be disclosed under the Act. That has been reinforced by uncertainty about the exact extent of the exemptions in view of the Commissioner's rulings on disclosure. In addition, revelations about the internal workings of government – in particular, the disclosure of emails between senior officials and advisers by Lord Hutton's inquiry into the death of Dr David Kelly – have acted as further deterrent to recording advice. (The Hutton Inquiry was into the suicide of Dr Kelly, a government scientist who had spoken to journalists about the evidence over weapons of mass destruction at the time of the Iraq War in 2003.) The argument is that fear of subsequent disclosure under the Act will reduce the frankness and quality of advice to ministers (itself threatened by more adversarial relations between politicians and civil servants). Outside bodies may become more cautious in their communications with government. Aided by developments in information technology, ministers and their advisers have increasingly held discussions in a medium not covered by the Act, notably by the use of mobile phones. This undermines not only transparency but also formal, collective decision-making. The British convention of government is that there should be frank and candid discussions between ministerial colleagues, but this can only work if they remain confidential and are not subject to FOI or similar disclosure. While a desire to be outside the Act is not the sole, or main, reason for the increase of mobile phones, the outcome is a weakening of collective, as opposed to bilateral, political judgement, as well as accountability. So a law intended to increase transparency and accountability may turn out, in practice, to reduce both. Lord O'Donnell, the former Cabinet secretary, has repeatedly stressed these dangers, warning that the result may be worse government, as less is formally recorded and therefore available for later scrutiny, either by official inquiries or by historians.

The Justice Committee concluded (2012: vol.1, p. 57) that:

> the ability for officials to provide frank advice to ministers, the opportunity for ministers and officials to discuss policy honestly and comprehensively, the requirement for full and accurate records to be kept and the convention of collective Cabinet responsibility, at the heart of our

system of Government, might be threatened if an FOI regime allowed premature or inappropriate disclosure of information.

The Information Commission and the Tribunal have recognised the need for a 'safe space' for policy discussions, as well as for protecting certain categories of information, such as intelligence and national security, trade secrets, and legal professional privilege. But there have remained grey areas and disagreements, leading both to the exercise of the ministerial veto, mainly against the disclosure of Cabinet minutes and records, and to outside, especially media, resentment about government secretiveness. A central problem has been a lack of certainty about where the lines will be drawn, since both the Commissioner and the Tribunal have to weigh up a balance of factors in individual cases. While research by the Constitution Unit of University College London has pointed to a negligible or marginal impact of the Act in constraining discussions by policy-makers, that is not the view of many leading ministers and civil servants who fear that the ability to provide frank advice has been impaired.

The crucial question is the impact on public life more broadly and, in particular, on confidence and trust in public authorities. There is the paradox that the availability of far more information than was available previously has reduced, rather than increased, public confidence in government and political leaders. There is no dispute that having greater access to information held by public authorities has increased knowledge of what they do, but that has not meant approval. Often the reverse. The Freedom of Information Act has been used most frequently by the media and others to highlight problems and mistakes in decision-making. Research by the Constitution Unit found that 58% of analysed newspaper articles arising from FOI requests tended to be negative in tone.

Overall, the evidence from the annual survey of British Social Attitudes is that levels of political trust in British governments of any party have recovered a little since the nadir in 2009 in the wake of the parliamentary expenses scandal and are much the same now as in 2006. This scandal was when, after lengthy proceedings under the FOI Act, the parliamentary authorities were forced to reveal the details of the expenses claimed by MPs. In fact, the disclosure occurred a few months earlier when a CD including all the details was obtained by the *Daily Telegraph* and the claims were published, day after day, with banner headlines. Some turned out to be illegal claims and a number of MPs were subsequently sent to prison. In other cases, the claims, while within the existing lax rules, caused media and public outrage because they appeared to be both extravagant and have no justification in terms of an MP's duties – notably those related to housing costs. So while, as the 2012 *British Social Attitudes* report noted, 'the MPs' expenses scandal has not contributed to any significant, further, long-term erosion of trust', this is scant comfort. The number trusting British governments 'just about always/most of the time' rose from 16 to 22% between 2009 and 2011, but this compares with 26% just before the 1997 election (and 33% immediately afterwards), and 40% back in 1986. As the report added, 'even so, it is evident that Labour did not achieve its aspiration to reverse the decline in trust that had become marked during John Major's 1992–97 administration, if anything levels of trust fell away even more during its time in office' (National Centre for Social Research, 2012).

Similarly, the annual research carried out for the Hansard Society's Audit of Political Engagement shows that fewer than a quarter of the public think the system of governing works well, a decline of seven percentage points in a year, and twelve points less than in the first in the series of audits in 2004. The results of both the BSA and Hansard surveys, of course, cover the period of the various initiatives to increase transparency and the passage and implementation of the Freedom of Information Act. These findings are influenced by political attitudes towards the government of the day – views of the Iraq War or the highly unpopular sharp rise in tuition fees for students in higher education – as much as, or more than, views about government openness and accountability which few voters ever consider as such. The Hansard Audit notes that levels of satisfaction with the system of governing almost exactly reflect levels of satisfaction with the incumbent government. It is hard to disentangle current voter dissatisfaction with the policies of a particular government from low levels of trust and dissatisfaction with the system of government. Given this finding, it is necessary to be cautious about assessing the impact of the initiatives described earlier in this chapter about public trust in government – though it is certainly plausible that greater openness and transparency have not helped by highlighting scandals and flaws, like the revelations about the abuse of MPs' expenses in 2009. It is only fair to point out that, despite the fluctuations of recent years, trust in politicians and the government system has not been high since the 1950s.

In a separate analysis in 2012, the Hansard Audit has also looked at the media and politics. This shows quite clear differences of view between readers of 'broadsheets' (an anachronistic term) and 'red tops' which have tended to be most critical about politicians and the political class. Some 42% of broadsheet readers think that the system of governing works extremely or mainly well. This is double the proportion of those who read local papers or no papers at all, but three times the 14% of 'red top' readers who think the system works reasonably well. The Hansard Society authors conclude: 'The media – particularly the print press and specifically tabloids – do not appear to greatly benefit our democracy from the perspective of nourishing political engagement.' In particular,

> *in the opinion of most members of the public, the press are simply not effective at conveying information and knowledge to their readers, nor at performing their crucial watchdog role of holding politicians and government to account. Indeed, it is not always clear exactly how some sections of the press perceive their watchdog role: denigrating politicians and undermining the political system and citizens' faith in it, is not the same as holding the political class accountable. (Hansard Society, 2012)*

This raises, finally, the trust question and the issues highlighted by Onora O'Neill, the eminent philosopher, now Baroness O'Neill of Bengarve, over the past decade and more. Back in her Reith lectures in 2002, she warned that some of the regimes of accountability and transparency developed since the 1980s may have damaged rather than reinforced trustworthiness. She noted the paradox that we, as citizens, still depend on the very people whom we claim not to trust. She argued that the new mechanisms of accountability and targets have undermined the professionals on whom the public sector depends, and have created a culture of suspicion and low morale which may increase public distrust. She has talked of transparency as a fetish: 'Transparency is an antidote to secrecy but it is not a mode of communication, too often it is honoured by dissemination, disclosure, putting things on websites.' In her view, it may be public but it is not a form of communication. Her analysis has also examined conceptions of media freedom and the ethics of communication. In her evidence to the Leveson Inquiry into the practices and conduct of the media in June 2012, she argued that it was 'hard, sometimes impossible, for readers, listeners and viewers to assess what they read, hear or see ... It is all too often hard for members of the public to judge the credibility or importance of media claims: are they true or false, report or rumour, evidenced or invented, balanced or tendentious, important or trivial?'

The evidence of this chapter is that a combination of administrative/ statutory and technological changes have made the government and public authorities more transparent and this has improved their accountability. But there are considerable ambiguities over what this means for public attitudes towards both government and the media. We, the media, citizens, are now better informed about how we are governed, but it does not mean that we like what we see.

References

Blair, T. (1996) Speech at the Campaign for Freedom of Information awards, 25 Mar.: www.cfoi.org.uk/blairawards.html.

Blair, T. (2010) *A Journey* (Hutchinson).

Hansard Society (2012) *Audit of Political Engagement*, 25 Apr. (Hansard Society): www.hansardsociety.org.uk/blogs/press_releases/archive/2012/04/25/audit-of-political-engagement-9-part-one.aspx.

House of Commons Commission (2011–12) *Annual Report* (The Stationery Office): www.parliament.uk/documents/commons-commission/commission-annual-report-2011-12.pdf.

Justice Committee, House of Commons (2012) *Post-Legislative Scrutiny of the Freedom of Information Act (2000)*, vols 1 and 2, House of Commons papers 96-1 and 96-11 (The Stationery Office).

National Centre for Social Research (2012) *British Social Attitudes Survey* (National Centre for Social Research): www.bsa-29.natcen.ac.uk.

O'Neill, O. (2002) *Reith Lectures* (BBC): www.bbc.co.uk/programmes/b00729d9/broadcasts/2002/04 (accessed Mar. 2013).

O'Neill, O. (2012) 'Witness Statement for Leveson Inquiry', 14 June: www.levesoninquiry.org.uk/wp-content/uploads/2012/07/Witness-Statement-of-Professor-Baroness-ONeil.pdf.

Public Administration Committee, House of Commons (July 1999) *Freedom of Information Draft Bill*, vol. 1, House of Commons paper 570-1 (HMSO).

3

The Impact of the Freedom of Information Act in the UK

Benjamin Worthy and Robert Hazell

Transparency broadly means making 'decisions, rules and other infor-mation visible from outside' (Hood 2010: 989). The rise of transparency as a central reform and goal of policy-makers has been powered by a mixture of technological change, ideological shifts, and political crisis (Hood, 2010).

One of the key ways of promoting transparency is via Freedom of Information (FOI) legislation. Between 80 and 90 countries around the world have now passed some form of FOI legislation, with many more considering or developing it (Vleugels, 2011). At the centre of every law is the right to request access to government information, subject to certain restrictions, and often an external appeal system in the shape of a commissioner, tribunal, or the courts system. Many Acts also promote wider proactive disclosure of information by government through publication schemes (records of documents held) and online disclosure. In the UK the government has a final veto on release.

Supporters and advocates hope that FOI will bring many universal benefits including increased transparency and accountability. These could have further beneficial spin-off effects, increasing public understanding and increasing public trust in government (see Darch and Underwood, 2010; Hazell et al., 2010). Some also see it as an important tool for individuals to meaningfully exercise many civil, political, and social rights and entitlements (Darch and Underwood, 2010; Roberts 2010). However, some scholars are sceptical of the power of FOI: the objectives are 'overstated as well as vague' and the more revolutionary or transformative claims over trust or participation concern deeply embedded long-term problems that FOI alone may not 'cure' (Darch and Underwood, 2010, 46; Roberts, 2010).

Since 2007, the Constitution Unit based at University College London has studied the impact of the Freedom of Information Act on British central government (Hazell et al., 2010), English local government (Worthy et al., 2011), and Parliament (Hazell et al., 2012). In all three cases we have looked at whether FOI has met six main objectives set for it by its supporters, as highlighted in reports and speeches:

1. increased openness and transparency;
2. increased accountability;
3. improved decision-making in government;
4. better public understanding of government decision-making;
5. increased participation; and
6. increased public trust in government.

We have also examined whether FOI has had an impact on the day-to-day operations of these bodies, either positively or negatively. This chapter is an extended version of evidence submitted to the House of Commons Justice Committee in 2012.

Research methods

The research used five main methods. Interviews were conducted with 56 officials in eight British central government departments, 90 officials and others across 16 local authorities, and 30 MPs, peers, and officials at Westminster, as well as journalists, requesters, and campaigners. An online survey of FOI requesters was created which collected the views of 200 requesters in total, half from local government and half from central government. This was a low number and was backed up by interviews and, in the case of local government, analysis of FOI 300 requests.

The media are a key user of FOI. As less than 1 in 1,000 people uses FOI the media are also a key source of information for the wider public. We analysed a selection of articles in the national, regional, and local press that used FOI, as well as interviewing a selection of journalists. We also analysed case law emerging out of the appeal system, the ICO and Tribunal, to estimate its impact on how the law works.

The different methods helped measure the different objectives, but each had limitations. For example, the online survey of requesters, while giving an insight, did not achieve a large number of responses. The media analysis similarly is only a 'proxy' for how people receive information through FOI. How exactly the public interprets information is a complex and much debated issue (James, 2011).

The methods are supported by other official UK studies of FOI, including scrutiny by the Ministry of Justice (MOJ, 2011), the House of Commons Justice Select Committee (Justice Committee, 2012), and a response from the government (MOJ, 2012b).

Requests and requesters

The key driver of any regime is requests. In Britain there was an initial 'big bang' which tailed off slightly for central government and is now increasing again. Local government is the recipient of the vast majority of requests and requests to local government have increased more than three-fold in five years. Parliament has also experienced rising request numbers (see Table 3.1).

A key problem underlining all FOI analysis is the lack of knowledge about requesters and their motivations. Table 3.2 is based on estimates of requester types to central and local government from FOI officers (see Hazell et al., 2010; Worthy et al., 2011).

Table 3.1 Number of information requests to central and local government in the UK, 2005–2011

Year	Local government	Central government
2005	60,000	25,000
2006	72,000	30,000
2007	80,000	33,000
2008	118,000	35,000
2009	165,000	40,000
2010	197,000	43,000
2011	n/a	47,000

Source: MOJ 2012a and Constitution Unit 2010

Table 3.2 Estimated percentage of information requesters by type

Requester	Local government (%)	Central government (%)
Public	37	39
Journalist	33	8
Business	22	8
Academic	1–2	13

Contrary to the expressed view of Tony Blair, FOI requesters are not predominantly journalists. The largest group across central and local government appears to be members of the public, a trend reflected elsewhere in the world. Among the public users are a small group of those politically engaged with FOI and a larger group using the Act to pursue issues of 'micro-politics' or of private importance (see Hazell et al., 2010; Worthy et al., 2011). In terms of motivations, there was a clear rise and fall of public interest with the news agenda and requests followed issues highlighted by the media, from government surveillance to the gritting of roads.

One of the critiques of FOI is that it is only used by those already engaged. Rather than widening public participation it merely gives a new tool to the minority of 'usual suspects' already engaged (Worthy, 2010). Others, such as former Scottish Information Commissioner, argue such 'suspects' are better seen as a vanguard of innovators (Dunion, 2011).

However, 'private' interest requests or issues of 'micro-politics' far outweighed 'political' use. Many requests by members of the public were focused, 'quite niche' or on 'specialised' issues such as a planning dispute or parking fine at local level or access to benefits at central government level.

An analysis of a small sample of 300 FOI requests found 55% were specific, with a focus on a single issue/event/location, and 20% very specific to a particular incident or place (see Worthy et al., 2011: 37). The important point is that FOI is mostly used for niche issues of personal importance rather than broadly 'political' issues. FOI is more of a personal or 'micro-political' tool – for example, about holes in roads and refuse. This means there can be a so-called 'iceberg' effect with a few high-profile 'attention grabbing' requests while the vast majority of more quotidian uses go unseen (see White, 2007). The variable impact of FOI is also down to the variability of requester motivations.

This is also seen in other FOI regimes. Under the separate Scottish FOI regime the Scottish Information Commissioner spoke of how use of the Act is about personal issues and 'the real worth of freedom of information [is] to be found in the pages of the local rather than the national newspaper'. In Ireland 'many non-personal [FOI] requests can disguise [their] true nature' as personal and focused (Dunion, 2011: 458; McDonagh, 2010: 82). The problem is that there may then be a dissonance between what politicians hope FOI will be used for and how it is used.

Another significant group is journalists. Although small in number, they have a large influence (see Cain et al., 2003; Hayes, 2009). They act as innovators and their requests often become press stories. Despite claims from government that journalists are heavy users, only a few have the time and patience to use FOI, which proves somewhat slow in relation to journalistic deadlines.

Business appeared to have used FOI for central government rarely but a great deal at local level (Worthy et al., 2011: 5). A final group of users were a very small group of MPs and a few members of the House of Lords, who regularly deploy FOI as part of their 'armoury' of weapons to hold government to account (Worthy, 2012).

What impact has FOI had?

Central government

FOI has made British central government more transparent both in terms of the information it provides and the 'culture' within departments. This is despite the fact that publication schemes were seen as rather antiquated and poorly used, having been superseded by the webpage and internet search engine. It has also led to increased accountability, particularly when FOI is used alongside other 'traditional' mechanisms of accountability, such as the media, NGOs and, albeit a few, MPs (see Hazell et al., 2010: Worthy, 2010). The Justice Committee also concluded FOI had led to greater openness across public bodies, particularly central government which was formerly 'highly secretive' (Justice Committee, 2012: 11).

It has not had an impact on any of the other objectives. This is not because FOI has failed. Complex issues such as public participation and public trust are influenced by many other factors. In this sense FOI, as with many policies, was 'oversold' by politicians (Justice Committee, 2012; Worthy, 2010).

If it hasn't realised all its supporters' hopes, it has not realised the fears of others. It has not had any significant impact on the decision-making process or some of the key constitutional conventions such as collective responsibility. Nor does it appear to have led to a chilling effect (see Hazell et al., 2010: Worthy, 2010).

English local government

FOI has made local government more transparent, though to a lesser extent than at central level because local authorities have been opening up since the 1960s. Recent innovations in online publication are beginning to have some impact, particularly third-party innovations (Worthy et al., 2011).

Accountability has also been improved, with FOI often used with other mechanisms (such as the local media or NGOs) to build a wider picture of an issue. FOI has only influenced decision-making and public understanding at low levels. It has not affected participation and has had no generalisable impact on trust.

As with central government, local authorities' key functions have not been changed by FOI. It has had no impact on how authorities deliver services or work with others, though there is tension around private companies working for local authorities and national and local media requests (see Worthy et al., 2011).

UK parliament

FOI has helped to make the UK Parliament more transparent and more accountable, though the revealing of MPs' expenses, partly through FOI, in 2009 overshadowed all other effects (Kelso, 2009; Worthy, 2013). It does not appear to have improved public understanding of Parliament, or public participation; nor has it increased public trust, simply because of the overwhelming coverage of expenses which led to resignations and embarrassment (see Hazell et al., 2012; Worthy and Bourke, 2011).

Although it has led to the creation of the Independent Parliamentary Standards Authority (IPSA) and a new expenses system, it is not clear how much it has changed parliamentary culture more generally. FOI has also led to smaller changes over, for example, how MPs pay restaurant bills and the tax status of peers (see Hazell et al., 2012; Worthy and Bourke, 2011).

We also looked at whether MPs have used FOI as an accountability mechanism. While only a small number of MPs, mostly the opposition, use FOI, it has proved to be a powerful tool. It has helped to uncover information about a range of topics, from visitors to Chequers to extraordinary rendition and the Libor banking scandal (Worthy, 2012).

Does FOI have a chilling effect?

One possible unintended consequence of FOI may be a 'chilling effect', where decisions go unrecorded or are sanitised due to fear of future requests. Finding hard evidence for such an effect is very difficult as it requires proving a negative and asking interviewees to admit unprofessional conduct. Studies are divided as to whether FOI has this effect (see Badgley et al., 2003; Hood, 2007).

The former head of the Swedish National Audit Office, Inga Britt Ahlenius, identified the 'empty archives' phenomenon in Sweden, whereby 'important issues are discussed orally [or] by telephone' (in Östberg and Eriksson, 2009: 118–19). Tony Blair claimed FOI had led to more caution over recording decisions, and the former Cabinet Secretary and Justice Minister claimed to have had experience of it (Justice Committee, 2012: 74–5).

Our central government study found little clear evidence. FOI was lost amid wider issues around resources, fear of leaks, and changing decision-making styles (Worthy, 2010: 571). Many officials were concerned more by the consequences of not having a record than having one. Others believed leaks or recording styles proved more significant. Many felt the 'politics' of a decision is 'always off paper'.

There was one very clear example, in one local authority; following a damaging FOI request, members no longer commented on drafts in writing. Interviewees elsewhere said care was taken in controversial decisions or negotiations. Most were keen to point out that this was not a general tendency and said it had also led to more professionalism in some cases.

It is difficult to draw a firm conclusion due to lack of evidence and the problem of disentangling causal factors. The Justice Committee 'was not able to conclude, with any certainty, that a chilling effect has resulted from the FOI Act' (2012: 75). An Irish local government survey found 30% of local officials claimed a chilling effect and just fewer than 50% denied it (McDonagh, 2010: 11). There appears to be no systematic evidence for alteration of records. However, FOI can and has caused a 'negative' chilling effect in specific instances, particularly with difficult or controversial topics and in problematic political situations.

The overall impact of FOI

FOI has met its core objectives at central and local government level and in Parliament. Public authorities are more transparent in terms of the information they release and how they work. FOI has also encouraged proactive disclosure of a range of information, from salaries to road maintenance. The Justice Committee scrutiny (2012) concluded that 'The Act has contributed to a culture of greater openness across public authorities ... We welcome the efforts made by many public officials not only to implement the Act but to work with the spirit of FOI to achieve greater openness.' The government agreed in its response that the 'Act has contributed to a culture of greater openness across public authorities' (Ministry of Justice, 2012a: 4).

FOI has also made public bodies more accountable. FOI works well with other mechanisms (such as the media, MPs, or NGOs) as a tool to put together information for campaigns. Although high-profile cases, such as MPs' expenses, attract publicity, FOI actually works as part of wider campaigns as a 'jigsaw' tool to put together information rather than to obtain scandalous 'smoking guns' (Worthy et al., 2011).

FOI has not improved the quality of decision-making. FOI has not increased public understanding of decision-making at central government and has little impact on public participation except via 'proxies' either centrally or locally. A chilling effect can be seen in a few politically sensitive cases but is not happening systematically.

At local level FOI has increased public understanding of decision-making at a low level, though it is mostly used to get information rather than learn about the decision-making process. Locally it may have helped the public obtain very specific and low-level information about day-to-day things such as licences or car parking (Worthy et al., 2011).

Superficially FOI does not appear to have increased trust in central government but the data are sparse and point in different directions. However, the effect is very variable for local government. At local level, use of FOI is diverse and trust in local government is more heavily influenced by performance and 'community visibility' than openness. Trust is a complex issue and the Justice Committee concluded that FOI had 'no generalisable impact' on it (2012: 17–18). Even the seemingly clear case of trust decline created by the MPs' expenses scandal shows nuance, as the disclosure came as confirmation not a revelation to many (Hansard Society, 2012). The government agreed that such an objective may not have been entirely 'realistic' but was a little more optimistic that it had shifted slightly upwards (Ministry of Justice, 2012b: 6).

'Iron laws' of FOI

Some key points about FOI are:

- *The media have a key influence on the impact of FOI.* Not only are the media a key user of FOI (and defender when reforms threaten it) but, given so few people make a request, they are a key conduit for shaping wider perception of FOI.
- *There is no going back.* The FOI Act cannot be repealed, however much the government may dislike it. Interviews and leaked ministerial correspondence showed how much some ministers resent FOI, but it is now part of the framework of government.
- *Government holds all the cards.* Despite its evident discomfort at the continuing pinpricks of FOI, the government remains in a very strong position. It holds the information. It can resist disclosure for years if it wants to play the system and fight appeals.
- *Both sides will game the system.* As in any field of legal regulation, there is scope to game the system. Officials and ministers will play things long if they want to delay disclosure, and they face few penalties for doing so. This was a constant refrain of requesters, especially journalists.
- *FOI never settles down.* In terms of bureaucratic routine and a body of case law, FOI does begin to settle down after the early years. But at a wider political level it never does and conflict is ongoing.
- *A few FOI requests cause most of the trouble.* The Pareto principle operates in FOI, as in other fields of policy. In the UK and elsewhere (e.g. New Zealand), a few high-profile cases cause disproportionate effort, media attention, public controversy, and political pain. Most requests are for 'non-political' information.

What makes FOI work or not?

Leadership is crucial to FOI

Senior support improves internal cooperation and mitigates internal resistance. By contrast, nervousness leads to defensiveness and a lack of internal cooperation.

Administrative culture is also important

A whole range of factors mean that individual departments and bodies vary in their attitude. Internal cultures, experience of FOI, and particular context (a local political environment, controversy over a policy) can lead to different impacts (see Piotrowski, 2010).

Resources

Resources are vital and are likely to be the Achilles' heel of FOI. How much FOI 'costs' is a difficult issue, with competing methodologies offering competing answers, with bias in measuring cost as the benefits are more difficult to assess (Colquhoun, 2010; MOJ, 2011).

The media

The media are a further crucial influence both in their use and reporting of stories. Pre-existing relations shape this dynamic. Some public bodies experienced heavy and aggressive use of FOI, others none. It seems that only a small proportion of journalists use the Act but they defend it, innovate with it, and raise awareness.

Political factors

Political balance can be crucial, though ideology has little bearing. A secure administration can cope with a damaging FOI request in a way that a party with a small majority cannot. Some local areas or particular departments have high levels of activism or long-running controversial issues which often involve the use of FOI.

The final crucial factor is the requester

FOI is built upon one very unpredictable variable: public use. Use varies hugely from the political to the 'micro-political' or personal.

The future

So what does the future hold for FOI? The two key forces that may shape developments are, on the one hand, growing technological innovation and, on the other, dwindling resources.

Open Data

FOI is increasingly merging with online developments (Grimmelikhuijsen and Welch, 2012). The Obama administration's reforms or David Cameron's agenda of Open Data and online transparency reforms share many of the same objectives as FOI (Halonen, 2012; Huijboom and Van Den Broek, 2011). These reforms include the development of new platforms for data, publication of frontline service and spending data as well as innovations such as online crime maps (Cabinet Office, 2012).

The new Open Data push is likely to drive increased transparency and provide support and impetus for FOI officers and transparency advocates within organisations. To date the impact of Open Data has been variable. The Public Accounts Committee (PAC), reviewing the progress to date, pointed to a lack of user interest at all levels, partly because the information was 'raw' (2012).

One flagship innovation in the UK has been to publish all local authority spending over £500 online. Early research into the publication indicates very different experiences, from no effect and no interest to high-profile use. Kent County Council had only 3,000 visits to the webpage in sixteen months, which included internal hits (Justice Committee, 2012: 15). Others had use of the data by the local media and trade unions (Worthy et al., 2011: 16). There appears to be little use by the public yet, according to a (2012) Local Government Association survey of local authorities. There is no sign of the 'army' of citizen auditors holding authorities to account that the government had hoped for, and this is unlikely to appear given the reluctance of the public to look through raw data (LGA, 2012). Some are concerned, both in the UK and elsewhere, that publishing spending data encourages emphasis on 'costs' rather than impact (Fung and Weil, 2010: 106–7).

However, while not directly used by the public the local spending data have launched several interesting third-party innovations, some of which have been created 'upwards' from the community and others between public bodies (LGA, 2012). Within local government there is a sense that the publication may have had other beneficial effects on accountability and efficiency (LGA, 2012). Open Data advocates and officials feel online publication, FOI, and new innovations will serve to mutually reinforce each other (Cabinet Office, 2012; PAC, 2012). This can already be seen with sites run by mySociety (such as What Do They Know) that publishes FOI's publically or Openly Local that provides a platform to analyse and compare local spending data at the push of a button.

Resources

Across the world government austerity drives are having the side-effect of undermining FOI systems, due to staff loss and resource cutbacks, reinforced, in some countries, by a feeling that FOI is neither 'essential' nor well used (see Roberts, 2012). A lack of resources may lead to a slowing down or, in the worst case scenario, a 'stagnation' of FOI operations, as seen in Canada in the early 2000s (Roberts, 2012). The danger is that request numbers will increase and innovations proliferate but resources will be taken away. FOI is not yet seen as a 'frontline' service and is likely to suffer financially in favour of 'vital' services, especially in bodies where support for FOI is 'lukewarm' (see below). FOI is already facing growing numbers of officers feeling they are at, if not over, capacity. In the UK the government recently expressed concern that FOI was not providing 'value for money' and spoke of reviewing the way in which the 'costs' of each request was calculated (Justice Committee, 2012: 4). The contracting out of service delivery may also create gaps in FOI coverage.

Transparency lessons for government and media

Government

Leadership is crucial to making FOI work. For transparency to be successful senior politicians both within organisations and nationally need to push for and support it. Senior support allows experimentation and ensures compliance. By contrast, lack of support (and even resistance) leads to defensiveness and internal resistance. The failure of leaders to take FOI seriously can have repercussions, as seen in the MPs' expenses case where the speaker's defensiveness helped lead to his resignation (Hazell et al., 2012). Those local authorities with a supportive leadership, who saw FOI as part of their wider engagement, appeared to fare better than those who saw it as an additional burden.

However, the problem is that leaders quickly go off FOI. The government warned that 'the formative years of open government will be difficult, tricky and uncomfortable at times' (Cabinet Office, 2012: 6). Tony Blair, who passed the FOI Act, later controversially summed up this view in his memoirs:

> *The truth is that the FOI Act isn't used, for the most part, by 'the people'. It's used by journalists. For political leaders, it's like saying to someone who is hitting you over the head with a stick, 'Hey, try this instead', and handing them a mallet. (Blair, 2010: 516–17)*

Blair's assertions are not borne out by the facts about who uses FOI. However, negative perceptions create resistance. His comments were supported by others. The former head of the civil service claimed FOI undermined good government. David Cameron, a supporter of transparency, also spoke of how it can 'occasionally fur up the arteries of government' (BBC, 2012a). The danger is that such negativity may encourage poor behaviour and lead to a small 'anti-FOI' group at the very top of government (BBC, 2012b).

In several local authorities there is a similar rumble of discontent at the time and resources FOI uses and the damage 'frivolous' requests cause. One County Council leader spoke of how they 'boiled over with rage' at 'spurious requests' over the cost of tea bags and elsewhere there was concern at 'politically difficult' requests (Worthy et al., 2011: 27). The problem is how FOI is encountered: senior officials only ever see a few requests, often the most sensitive or most potentially damaging and often from journalists. They thus get a very narrow, and negative, view of what requests are received. This, combined with a politician's natural dislike of 'surprises', leads to perception that FOI is a 'problem' and is 'abused' by the media. These views of FOI can then percolate through the institution.

The dislike of FOI can also translate into action detrimental to FOI. The government has a veto to prevent the release of information, even if the appeals system rules in favour of release. In the UK the veto has now been used five times to prevent the release of information, including for Cabinet discussions over the war in Iraq and correspondence between Prince Charles and the government (House of Commons Library, 2012). While use has been relatively restrained by international standards, each use is seen as signalling lack of faith in the system and the government has mentioned changing the circumstances in which it can be used (House of Commons Library 2012: 5; Justice Committee, 2012: 17–20).

More than use of the veto, a government can also reform the Act. In 2006 an attempt was made by the Blair government to introduce fees for FOI, as happened in Ireland in 2005. This was closely followed by an attempt by a group of MPs to remove Parliament from the FOI Act (Hazell et al., 2012). Although both ultimately failed, it is possible that future governments, sceptical of FOI, may try again, whether directly through changes or indirectly through 'resource starvation'.

The media

Tony Blair claimed that FOI 'results in a battle between the government and media' and 'tilted the scales on various contentious issues towards the media' (2012). In a hostile environment like the UK it is unsurprising that FOI is seen as another weapon in the battle between parts of the media and government. Officials and politicians complained of 'abuse' of the Act, while journalists spoke of evasion and resistance from government.

It appears that only a small group of journalists use FOI regularly as it can be time consuming: the process of obtaining the MPs' expenses took from January 2004 until June 2009 (Kelso, 2009). Some use it forensically on key issues while others use it to ask all authorities or departments the same question. It is these 'round robins' that often cause frustration. Journalists often use it alongside other tools – the MPs' expenses was partly an FOI but also a leak (Winnett and Rayner, 2009: 347).

At national and local level there is use of FOI by journalists that frequently highlights 'negative' behaviour, such as poor policy, scandal, or wasted money. Some of this may be 'spurious' (though this is a subjective judgement). At central and local level the national press used FOI to focus on the wasting of public money, unethical behaviour, or poor performance:

this stretched from controversial issues such as surveillance legislation to salaries, costs of away days or payments to celebrities for switching on Christmas lights (Worthy et al., 2011: 23–4).

On the other hand, FOI has played a key role in exposing corruption in the MPs' expenses scandal as well as in the Scottish Parliament and Northern Ireland Assembly (Hazell et al., 2010: 225–6, 209–12). Requests by journalists at the BBC also helped force access to high-level Cabinet Office papers as part of the recent Hillsborough Inquiry (BBC, 2011).

However, how or if the local press uses FOI varies greatly: some local authorities have had heavy use but others virtually none (see Worthy et al., 2011). This can depend on pre-existing relationships. Those with poor relations experienced strong campaigns against particular policies or even individuals. Others with better relations (or a weak local press) have had none. Here politics can come into play: an authority in a strong position can weather controversy better than, for example, a governing party with a small majority.

Fung et al. (2007) highlighted two key forces that shape how or if a transparency system works. On the one hand, external political coalitions must 'apply pressure' and, as seen above, the media is key player in this. On the other hand, FOI needs 'champions within government'. Without these two features, applying momentum and force, transparency policies 'remain in [a] political dead end … underutilized, implemented weakly and subject to gradual erosion' (ibid.: 112).

References

Badgley, K., Dixon, M., and Dozois, P. (2003) 'In Search of the Chill: Access to Information and Record-keeping in the Government of Canada', *Archavia*, 55: http://journals.sfu.ca/archivar/index.php/archivaria/issue/view/414.

BBC (2011) 'Hillsborough Files: Cabinet Office Settles with BBC', 30 Nov. www.bbc.co.uk/news/uk-politics-15938394.

BBC (2012a) 'Cameron's Dividing Line on Access to Information', 7 Mar.: www.bbc.co.uk/news/uk-politics-17286328.

BBC (2012b) 'Freedom of Information: Whitehall Warned over "Bad Behaviour"', 14 Mar.: www.bbc.co.uk/news/uk-politics-17365222.

Blair, T. (2010) *A Journey* (Arrow).

Blair, T. (2012) 'Letter by Rt. Hon.Tony Blair MP To the Rt. Hon Alan Beith MP': www.publications.parliament.uk/pa/cm201213/cmselect/cmjust/96/tb01.htm.

Cabinet Office (2012) *Open Data: Unleashing the Potential*, White Paper, Cm 8353 (The Stationery Office).

Cain, B., Fabbrini, S., and Egan, P. (2003) 'Towards More Open Democracies: The Expansion of FOI Laws', in B. E. Cain, R. J. Dalton, and S. E. Scarrow (eds), *Democracy Transformed? Expanding Political Opportunities in Advanced Industrial Democracies* (Oxford University Press): 115–39.

Colquhoun, A. (2010) *The Cost of Freedom of Information* (Constitution Unit).

Constitution Unit (2011) 'FOI and Local Government: Surveys by the Constitution Unit Covering the Five Years from 2005 to 2010': www.ucl.ac.uk/constitution-unit/research/foi/foi-and-local-government/FOI-Surveys-5-year-Summary-01Dec2010.pdf.

Darch, C., and Underwood, P. (2010) *Freedom of Information in the Developing World: Demand, Compliance and Democratic Behaviours* (Chandos).

Dunion, K. (2011) *Freedom of Information in Scotland in Practice* (Dundee University Press).

Fung, A., and Weil, D. (2010) 'Open Government and Open Society', in D. Lathrap and L. Ruma (eds), *Open Government: Collaboration, Transparency, and Participation* (O'Reilly): 105–14.

Fung, A., Graham, M., and Weil, D. (2007) *Full Disclosure: The Perils and Promise of Transparency* (Cambridge University Press).

Grimmelikhuijsen, S., and Welch, E. (2012) 'Developing and Testing a Theoretical Framework for Computer-Mediated Transparency of Local Governments', *Public Administration Review*, 72/4: 562–71.

Halonen, A. (2012) 'Being Open about Data: Analysis of the UK Open Data Policies and Applicability of Data': http://finnish-institute.org.uk/images/stories/pdf2012/being%20open%20about%20data.pdf.

Hansard Society (2012) *Audit of Political Engagement*, 25 Apr. (Hansard Society): www.hansardsociety.org.uk/blogs/press_releases/archive/2012/04/25/audit-of-political-engagement-9-part-one.aspx.

Hayes, J. (2009) 'A Shock to the System: Journalism, Government and the Freedom of Information Act 2000': https://reutersinstitute.politics.ox.ac.uk/fileadmin/documents/Publications/Hayes_A_Shock_to_the_System.pdf.

Hazell, R., and Worthy, B. (2010) 'Assessing the Performance of FOI in Different Countries', *Government Information Quarterly*, 27/4: 352–9.

Hazell, R., Bourke, G., and Worthy, B. (2012) 'Open House? Freedom of Information its Impact on the UK Parliament', *Public Administration*, 90/4: 901–21.

Hazell, R., Worthy, B., and Glover, M. (2010) *The Impact of Freedom of Information on British Central Government: Does FOI Work?* (Palgrave Macmillan).

Hood, C. (2007) 'What Happens When Transparency Meets Blame Avoidance?', *Public Management Review*, 9(2): 191–210.

Hood, C. (2010) 'Accountability and Transparency: Siamese Twins, Matching Parts, Awkward Couple?', *West European Politics*, 33: 989–1009.

House of Commons Library (2012) *FoI and Ministerial Vetoes Standard Note* (SN/PC/05007) (The Stationery Office).

Huijboom, N., and Van Den Broek, T. (2011) 'Open Data: An International Comparison of Strategies', *European Journal of ePractice*, 12: www.epractice.eu/files/European%20Journal%20epractice%20Volume%2012_1.pdf.

James, O. (2011) 'Performance Measures and Democracy: Information Effects on Citizens in Field and Laboratory Experiments', *Journal of Public Administration Research and Theory*, 21/3: 399–418.

Justice Committee (House of Commons) (2012) *Post-Legislative Scrutiny of the Freedom of Information Act 2000*, vols 1 and 2, HC 96-i (The Stationery Office).

Kelso, A. (2009) 'Parliament on its Knees: MPs' Expenses and the Crisis of Transparency at Westminster', *Political Quarterly*, 80/3: 329–38.

Local Government Association (LGA) (2012) *Local Government Transparency Survey 2012* (LGA): www.local.gov.uk/c/document_library/get_file?uuid=bfad418d-1be8-43c8-bb9a-40faf3d41b82&groupId=10171.

McDonagh, M. (2010) 'Access to Local Government Information in Ireland: Attitudes of Decision Makers', *Open Government Journal*, 6/1: www.opengovjournal.org/article/view/5617.

Ministry of Justice (2011) *Memorandum to the Justice Select Committee Post-Legislative Assessment of the Freedom of Information Act 2000* (Ministry of Justice).

Ministry of Justice (2012a) *Freedom of Information Act 2000: Statistics on Implementation in Central Government 2011 Annual and Q4: October–December 2011* (Ministry of Justice): www.justice.gov.uk/downloads/statistics/mojstats/foi-statistics/foi-stats-bulletin-q4-2011.pdf.

Ministry of Justice (2012b) *Government Response to the Justice Committee's Report: Post-Legislative Scrutiny of the Freedom of Information Act 2000* (Cm 8505): www.justice.gov.uk/downloads/publications/policy/moj/gov-resp-justice-comm-foi-act.pdf.

Östberg, K., and Eriksson, F. (2009) 'The Problematic Freedom of Information Principle: The Swedish Experience', in A. Flinn and H. Jones (eds), *Freedom of Information: Open Access, Empty Archives?* (Routledge): 113–25.

Piotrowksi, S. J. (2010) 'The Operationalization of Municipal Transparency: Primary Administrative Functions and Intervening Factors', *Transparencia y*

Privacidad, 1: www.transparenciayprivacidad.org.mx/numero_1/articulos_1_
in.html.

Public Accounts Committee (2012) *Implementing the Transparency Agenda,*
HC 102 (The Stationery Office).

Roberts, A. (2010) 'A Great and Revolutionary Law? The First Four Years of India's
Right to Information Act', *Public Administration Review,* 70/6: 925–33.

Roberts, A. (2012) 'Transparency in Troubled Times', 10th World Conference of
the International Ombudsman Institute, Nov., Suffolk University Law School
Research Paper 12-35. Available at SSRN: http://ssrn.com/abstract=2153986
or http://dx.doi.org/10.2139/ssrn.2153986.

Vleugels, R. (2011) *Overview of All FOI Law around the World: 2011 Update:* www.
llrx.com/features/foilawsoverview.htm.

White, N. (2007) *Free and Frank: Making the Official Information Act Work Better*
(Institute of Policy Studies).

Winnett, R., and Rayner, G. (2009) *No Expenses Spared* (Bantam Press).

Worthy, B. (2010) 'More Open But No More Trusted? The Impact of FOI on British
Central Government', *Governance,* 23/4: 561–82.

Worthy, B. (2012) 'A Powerful Weapon in the Right Hands? How Members of
Parliament have Used Freedom of Information in the UK', *Parliamentary
Affairs* (Dec.).

Worthy, B. (2013) 'Freedom of Information and the MPs' Expenses Scandal', in J.
Hudson (ed.), *At the Public's Expense? The Political Consequences of the 2009
British MPs' Expenses Scandal* (Hart).

Worthy, B. and Bourke, G. (2011) *The Sword and the Shield: The use of FOI by
Parliamentarians and the Impact of FOI on Parliament* (Constitution Unit).

Worthy, B., Hazell, R., Amos, J., and Bourke, G. (2011). *Town Hall Transparency?
The Impact of FOI on Local Government in England* (Constitution Unit).

4

Valuing Transparency in Government and Media

Patrick Birkinshaw

Introduction

In this chapter I undertake to assess the role and contribution that transparent government and transparent media play in normative theories of democracy. What are the contending values that make different degrees of transparency desirable in government, and in journalism? I take normative theories of democracy to mean a democracy in which all are treated with dignity and given equal protection and advancement in the actions and policies of governors – no group or individual is unjustifiably discriminated against. This is a vision of democracy in which human rights are protected by an independent judiciary; a vision of democracy that is not based on mathematical calculations and counting of hands but one in which the protection of fundamental rights is a central part of the democratic ideal. In what follows, I will suggest that 'democracy' and human rights protection are not simply features of our existence in Leviathan – our public life as shaped by political institutions. A major objective is the extension of transparency and human rights protection to cover powerful actors in the private sector. These are ongoing developments, although I have been writing on them for many years. The actors include the press and media. But it is a subject that spans the vast network of public–private partnerships, offloaded government, and world-dominating power centres such as multinational banks and transnational corporations. We need protection from predators as well as Leviathan.

Responsible journalism has an essential role in advancing democracy, transparency, and human rights. But journalism and the press can abuse their position. The answer does not lie in freedom of information (FOI) legislation for the press. Information or opinion that the press communicates may need to be subject to ways of assessing its reliability and provenance. FOI gives us the information a government possesses, regardless of its accuracy. If government is using inaccurate information, we pass judgement. The press and media are largely privately owned and are seeking to influence and persuade. Tests to establish reliability, bias, and special interest are central here to transparency. Unjustified invasions of privacy and sheer distortion are commonplace. When abuse takes place there need to be effective and enforceable codes of conduct and systematic redress mechanisms. I return to this theme below. But the crucial point is that effective investigative journalism is essential in exposing corruption and abuse, in bringing sunlight to dank worlds. This point screamed out from Jimmy Savile's paedophiliac depravations at the BBC and other public institutions over many years.[1] Surely investigative journalism missed its role in not exposing this wrongdoing?

Openness, transparency, and democracy

Democracy was regarded as the reason in the UK for not introducing a Freedom of Information Act. Our system of government was based on *representative* government, a sovereign Parliament and ministerial responsibility presiding over an anonymous civil service – there was no need for FOI. We had no strict separation of powers, and government was through Parliament and answerable to Parliament. In this system MPs were kings, not citizens. The UK was not, quite simply, the USA.

Without FOI, the UK was notoriously secretive – a feature of government inherited by Westminster-style governments around the world. Information by government was disclosed on the basis of: is it kind, is it wise, is it necessary? There was an absence of open participatory mechanisms. There was enforced deference through ignorance.

Without access to information, preferential conduits were established, most notably around the lobby system, the development of government communications and lobbying networks, and informal means to maintain confidentiality such as the D Notices for the press and media as well as legal ones under the Official Secrets Acts. I return to government proposals for lobbying below.

Reliance upon the 'Westminster system' of governance began to wear embarrassingly thin when Westminster models around the globe adopted FOI regimes – 1982 was a pivotal year. From the 1980s we saw UK reforms removing unnecessary secrecy (much still remained), allowing access to information held by public bodies and enhanced transparency. The crucial change was FOIA in 2000, coming into effect on 1 January 2005, to give access to information held by virtually all public sector bodies. The White Paper in 1997 trumpeted Prime Minister Tony Blair's adulation of FOI. The cynicism of government and a war in Iraq based on fabricated intelligence produced a different response from Blair in *A Journey* (2010). It is a response which echoes in certain quarters in the present government as we shall see.

The FOIA does not stand alone. It comes with a variety of information rights in various laws, some of European provenance. It was part of a package of constitutional reform which stands as a legacy to Blair's governments and includes the Human Rights Act 1998 (HRA), which is now increasingly providing fundamental rights to information, as we shall see, as well as a right to privacy in the form of private and family life. A veritable industry has been built up based on rights of access to information which includes documents. Under FOIA in the region of 100,000–125,000 requests are made each year for information, to well upwards of 100,000 bodies (Information Commissioner 2009 estimates). Public authorities have to provide appeal mechanisms where requests are refused. There are well over 20 exemptions from access – some absolute and others qualified because the public interest has to be considered. Some bodies are excluded from the law: the Queen and the Security and Intelligence Services. An independent Information Commissioner (IC) polices activities, advises generally on information rights and practice, and deals with complaints. Further appeals go to the (now retitled) Information Tribunal, and appeals to the Upper Tribunal and then the higher courts. It is all producing a robust jurisprudence in which judges on the whole have displayed a positive approach to openness.[2]

Now transparency is *de rigueur*. What does transparency mean? It means opening to exposure and scrutiny processes of power and decision-making. How transparent is the UK government? FOIA, sections 35 and 36, protect Cabinet (meetings of government) discussions and decision-making. Section 36 includes disclosure that would 'otherwise prejudice, or be likely to prejudice, the effective conduct of public affairs'. Under the FOIA, section 53 allows for a government veto – an undertaking was given that it would be subject to Cabinet consultation. The veto had been invoked six times by November 2012. The minutes of three Cabinet meetings have been subject to a veto. These included the Cabinet discussions on commencing hostilities in Iraq. Nothing sensational was to be disclosed threatening collective government and its responsibility. Rather, disclosure would have exposed the paucity of discussion on this vital question of life and death. Why, one may ask, does Tony Blair hate FOIA so? A veto prevented disclosure of the National Health Service reforms transition risk register – the tribunal ruled in favour of non-disclosure of the strategic risk register in the Department of Health (EA/2011/0286-7, *Dept of Health v IC* (5 April 2012)). The Commons Justice Committee, in its post-legislative review of FOIA, has not recommended that Cabinet discussions be protected by an absolute exemption but has dropped the hint that the veto power and public interest should protect that which needs to be protected (HC 96 I, II, III (2012–13)); the committee found that the FOIA was 'working well' and represented a 'significant enhancement of our democracy' (the government response is Cm 8505, November 2012). To his credit, David Cameron, the UK prime minister, has supported FOI and extended it. But there are constant rumours of change: especially on charging and making Cabinet minutes subject to an absolute exemption. The Justice Committee report found little evidence of a 'chilling/freezing effect' on advice and deliberation (HC 96 I–III (2012–13)).

We have Secretary of State for Education Michael Gove's departmental efforts to evade FOIA by using personal email accounts – it is still official business, reports the IC in February 2012. There is the whole national security network and security, intelligence and international communications. As I write, the Justice and Security Bill (now enacted) seeks to introduce secret trials and closed material procedures covering such information which a defendant will not be able to see and the press will not be able to report upon. It is not clear when 'gisting' – giving an outline of the case against a terrorist suspect – will be required. Parliament is making secret what the courts ruled could not be secret because of the affront to fair procedure. The bill removes the Norwich Pharmacal procedures in cases involving sensitive information – that is, that received from foreign powers or deemed protected by national security will be unavailable.

When the coalition government came to power in 2010 the emphasis shifted to 'transparency' – one felt that non-statutory informal methods would assist advances in 'transparent government'. Informality has a formidable heritage in the UK where non-legal codes and practices brought about 'open government' rather than full-blooded statutory provisions. Would non-statutory measures replace FOIA? In fact FOIA has been extended by reforms. But the future seems all non-statutory in relation to transparency.

In its 2012 White Paper the government stated: 'The UK Government is recognised as being one of the most open in the world' (Cabinet Office, 2012: 31). It currently co-chairs the Open Government Partnership.

> *There is nothing easy about transparency. The formative years of open government will be tricky. But the prize is effective, personalised, 21st century democracy. It's a more prosperous United Kingdom where the public services on which we all rely are strengthened and improved. ... The future will be Open. (2012: 6)*

The future will see: 'a truly transparent society, with the power where it belongs, in the hands of the people of this country' (2012: 45). Data should be publicly provided free or at a fair price where costly or fairer to the taxpayer (2012: 12).

The White Paper continues: 'We are at the start of a global movement towards transparency – and the UK is leading the world in making data more freely available' (Cabinet Office, 2012: 5). 'Transparency is at the heart of our agenda for government' (ibid.). There is no reference in the paper to the reform of the Official Secrets Act! There will be further publication of spending and almost 9,000 datasets released on www.data.gov.uk covering education, transport, crime, and justice (Protection of Freedoms Act 2012, s. 102(2)(c) amending FOIA, s. 11). Local crime statistics, sentencing rates, school results (whether the cross-bar on grading is raised or not), hospital infection rates, and general practitioner (family doctors) outcomes will be published (Cabinet Office, 2012: 5–6).

As well as publication schemes, all 'departments' have published their first ever Open Data Strategies, including commitments to publish more data. The Treasury will produce in machine-readable format data relating to management and use of EU funds in the UK (Cabinet Office, 2012: 17). Sport England engage in data sharing with sports facilitators in the private sector. Plans include encouraging 'IT systems ... supported by transparent contracts' (ibid.). The National Audit Office reports on IT procurement have shown abysmal waste. The Cabinet Office has produced *Contracts Finder* (contractsfinder.businesslink.gov.uk). The Open Data Institute will seek to unlock the UK's economic capabilities (Cabinet Office, 2012: 16).

Rights to privacy will increase in this brave new world and will be in at the beginning of discussions leading to publication of new datasets. A privacy expert will be appointed to the Public Sector Transparency Board. All of this is developing as the EU proposals for review of the Data Protection directive are taking shape. 'We don't want to use legislation too readily' (Cabinet Office, 2012: 13) but will consult. The White Paper alerts us to the use of social media by the public sector. There will be widespread cooperation with 'developers of data' – third parties (p. 18) and the Open Business Forum. The latter is a business-led working group which will bring together leading companies and organisations to look at how businesses can be more transparent and help consumers and investors to differentiate between them, without adding any further burdens. It will promote employment among youth and apprenticeships. This all sounds like corporatism, the networking of private and public powers and offloading of governmental powers. The state never disappears; it merely reformulates. The problems remain.

While governments have protected the sensitivity of Cabinet proceedings and risk registers, the White Paper states: 'as part of our drive to make policy making more accessible, we are going to open the development process for the upcoming code of practice on FOIA [s. 45] up to the public and offer an opportunity to shape the guidance on datasets using a crowdsourced wiki' (Cabinet Office, 2012: 12). The code should include details of terms governing disclosure of information in contracts between public and private bodies. An Open Data User Group will advise the Data Strategy Board on prioritisation of data release. A Public Sector Transparency Board will attempt to make data accessible and reusable. Academic publicly funded research will be more freely available through a Research Transparency Sector Board. (I should perhaps add that universities have shown themselves to be too often less than transparent in reports of the Information Commissioner and Information Tribunal hearings.) A new array of quangos (non-departmental bodies) and public–private sector compenetration is in the making.

Freedom of speech and information, transparency, and the press and media

I think that for the press the major preoccupation is being allowed to report without hindrance. President Roosevelt described in 1941 the 'first freedom, freedom of speech and expression'. The important aspect of transparency and the press comes with our rights to see how government works and to read reports on the accurate records of lobbying between business and press barons, government, regulators, or police. These have featured in FOI requests. Much of the press is not so high-minded. 'If the internet or social media can do it then why not us?', we heard concerning the naked romp pictures of Prince Harry in August 2012.

The right to press freedom comes with our right to be protected from unjustifiable intrusion and with adequate, independent, and effective forms of regulation and redress. Six years after *What Price Privacy?*, the Information Commissioner's report on the trade in confidential personal data, blagging[3] penalties have not been increased by Parliament. This failure and the generally little-heeded attention and coverage of the *Guardian* necessitated a judicial inquiry by Lord Justice Leveson into a plurality of abuses covering phone-hacking, as well as police and press and government relationships. The inquiry was set up under the Inquiries Act 2005 by the Prime Minister, who appointed Leveson LJ as its chair. The formal title was *An Inquiry into the Culture, Practices and Ethics of the Press* (see Leveson, 2012–2013). Leveson is a Court of Appeal judge. I address his major recommendations below. At the heart of these concerns is the future regulation of the press in a manner that protects the independence of the press and the highest ethical and professional standards. I want to concentrate on two points here. The first is that, in a modern democratic society, a free and independent press is essential. ('Free of whom?', 'Independent of whom?', one must ask.) So is an informed public. The second is that a right to freedom of speech (FOS) has to be balanced against a right to privacy. Witness Lord Bingham, former Law Lord and Justice of the Supreme Court, on the first:

> *The fundamental right of free expression has been recognised at common law for very many years: … The reasons why the right to free expression is regarded as fundamental are familiar … Modern democratic government means government of the people by the people for the people. But there can be no government by the people if they are ignorant of the issues to be resolved, the arguments for and against different solutions and the facts underlying those arguments. The business of government is not an activity about which only those professionally engaged are entitled to receive information and express opinions. It is, or should be, a participatory process. But there can be no assurance that government*

is carried out for the people unless the facts are made known, the issues publicly ventilated. Sometimes, inevitably, those involved in the conduct of government, as in any other walk of life, are guilty of error, incompetence, misbehaviour, dereliction of duty, even dishonesty and malpractice. Those concerned may very strongly wish that the facts relating to such matters are not made public. Publicity may reflect discredit on them or their predecessors. It may embarrass the authorities. It may impede the process of administration. Experience however shows … that publicity is a powerful disinfectant. Where abuses are exposed, they can be remedied. Even where abuses have already been remedied, the public may be entitled to know that they occurred. The role of the press in exposing abuses and miscarriages of justice has been a potent and honourable one. But the press cannot expose that of which it is denied knowledge. (R v Shayler [2002] UKHL 11 at [21])

Wonderful, but rhetoric until 2000! Despite the high value placed by the common law on freedom of expression, it was not until incorporation of the European Convention into our domestic law by the Human Rights Act 1998 that this fundamental right, which has qualifications *prescribed by law* and which *are necessary* in a democratic society,[4] was underpinned by statute. Article 10(1) of the Convention provides:

Everyone has the right to freedom of expression. This right shall include freedom to hold opinions and to receive and impart information and ideas without interference by public authority and regardless of frontiers …

We had never seen the need to guarantee freedom of speech by law; we had not been outraged by prerogative power in the way the Americans had and which led to the First Amendment. I recall the words of horror of the senior judge Lord Bridge in *Spycatcher* in 1987 at the muzzling frenzy of then prime minister Margaret Thatcher (*A-G v Guardian* [1987] 3 All ER 316 at 346f–j). Nor, I hasten to add, are we still subject here to an almost unbridled form of prerogative that we witness in the USA in the continuing existence of Guantanamo. The press in the UK did not benefit from access laws or freedom of speech laws. Prior restraint, residuary liberties, and widespread laws of contempt and defamation probably did more than their fair share to encourage furtive practices in journalism and titillate a captious audience – we see the result in the Leveson Inquiry. I have heard of prosecution decisions involving publication being taken according to the length of the law officer's foot. The Crown prosecutor of *Lady Chatterley's Lover* (Mervyn Griffith-Jones QC) was asked how he made decisions to prosecute for obscenity. 'I'm not a literary man', he said. 'I don't read much. I read whatever the Director of Public Prosecutions sends me and if I get an erection, we prosecute' (Sedley, 2011: 395). What was the test for contempt?

In terms of reporting information, the press has availed itself of FOI and has become an enthusiastic supporter (Hayes, 2009). The basic approach to balancing the public interest in exemptions was set out in the *Evening Standard* case (EA/2006/0006 *DFES v IC & Evening Standard*). There is popular press and media use of FOI, despite its not being a hot news item. Disclosures have involved extraordinary rendition (EA/2011/0049–51 *FCO v All Parliamentary Group on Extraordinary Rendition* (3 May 2012)) and a secret code on the role of the 'Crown' and Prince Charles in advising on legislation affecting their interests.[5] Some details of phone calls between Tony Blair and George W. Bush on the war on Iraq were disclosed (EA/2011/2255, 0228 *S. Plowden and FCO v IC* (21 May 2012)). Information came out on Iraq. Information was not protected on public interest grounds on meetings between the Department for Culture, Media and Sport and the BBC concerning the BBC licence fee. Section 42 information (legal privilege) was protected and non-disclosable (EA/2012/0018 *A. Crawford v IC* (10 July 2012)). But the BBC itself was given a protection from FOIA for information covering 'journalism, art or literature'. This is frequently successfully invoked and included information about *Democracy Live* (*Todd v IC and BBC* (1 May 2012)).[6] Requests may be refused but we still learned via a journalist's request of automatic, number-plate recognition cameras (16,000,000 'reads' per day in the UK from about 5,000 such cameras): EA/2010/0174 (7 June 2012).

I will show why I believe FOI and FOS to be inseparably linked below. The HRA has introduced FOS as a legal right and not just an afterthought of liberty into UK law. The senior judge Lord Steyn's judgment in *Re S* (below) gave an early indication of the importance of FOS and court reporting and the balance to be arrived at between Article 8 rights to privacy (private life[7]) and Article 10 rights to freedom of speech. There are numerous judicial benedictions of the importance of a free press in a rights culture – and no case has explained more emphatically how that culture must be taken on board where the rights under Articles 8 and 10 clash than that involving Max Mosley – former boss of Formula One motor racing – and his hired female playmates (*M. Mosley v Ass News* [2008] EWHC 1777 (QBD)). There is no public interest in prurience.

Despite the fact that special safeguards were built into the Act under s. 12 to safeguard FOS and prevent gagging writs, these are widely reported to have reappeared in privacy actions – the super injunction. Parties have even tried to injunct reports of parliamentary proceedings. The Master of the Rolls and Head of Civil Justice (a senior judge) reported on this (Master of the Rolls, 2012). The pragmatism of English judges has, however, been less inclined to protect sources of information for journalists (like 'forbidden fruits' of illegally obtained evidence), despite the 'chilling effect' this may have on FOS. It is a good instance of how the European Court of Human Rights at Strasbourg stands as a necessary reminder of national shortcomings (*Financial Times v UK* [2010] EMLR 21, esp. para 70).

In order to enhance journalism the Data Protection Act (DPA) protects processing for 'special purposes', meaning journalistic, literary, and artistic purposes. A data subject is virtually deprived of the Act's protection. Leveson was critical of the extent of journalistic protection.[8] Blagging is still not effectively outlawed. However, for investigative journalism the Police and Criminal Evidence Act may offer scant protection from power's all-intrusive grasp.[9]

Balancing freedom of expression, defamation and privacy

Evidence to the Leveson Inquiry identifies the role of the press both as an agent for accountability, openness, and democracy in which freedom of speech is essential; and as purveyors of idle and salacious gossip where freedom of speech and unrestrained journalism can do untold harm and help establish huge and corrupting wealth and power (Leveson 2012–2013, Introduction, paras 1–13).

The courts have become more sensitive to the public benefits of free press reporting on matters genuinely in the public interest. Witness former senior judge Lord Hoffmann dealing with the public interest immunity from defamation in press reports:

Until very recently, the law of defamation was weighted in favour of claimants and the law of privacy weighted against them. True but trivial intrusions into private life were safe. Reports of investigations by

> *the newspaper into matters of public concern which could be construed*
> *as reflecting badly on public figures domestic or foreign were risky. The*
> *House attempted to redress the balance in favour of privacy in* Campbell
> v. MGN Ltd. *(2004) 2 AC 457 and in favour of greater freedom for the*
> *press to publish stories of genuine public interest in* Reynolds v. Times
> Newspapers Ltd *(2001) 2 AC 127. (*Jameel v Wall Street Journal Europe
> Sprl *[2006] UKHL 44 (para 38))*

This was given emphatic support in *Flood*.[10] Privileges in defamation are
strengthened but then privacy protection becomes more widely invoked
by media lawyers. There is an unavoidable balance to be made between
FOS and privacy. Lord Steyn set the balance clearly:

> *The interplay between articles 8 and 10 has been illuminated by the*
> *opinions in the House of Lords in* Campbell v MGN Ltd *[2004] 2 AC*
> *457. …What does, however, emerge clearly from the opinions are four*
> *propositions. First, neither article has as such precedence over the other.*
> *Secondly, where the values under the two articles are in conflict, an*
> *intense focus on the comparative importance of the specific rights being*
> *claimed in the individual case is necessary. Thirdly, the justifications for*
> *interfering with or restricting each right must be taken into account.*
> *Finally, the proportionality test must be applied to each. For convenience*
> *I will call this the ultimate balancing test. This is how I will approach the*
> *present case. (*In re S (A Child) *[2004] UKHL 47-16: reports of a murder*
> *trial in which the mother had murdered a sibling of* S*)*

It involves a two-stage process – is Article 8 engaged and how is it
balanced with Article 10 rights? But much 'personal information'
involves 'processing of data' – terms of legal art. A down-to-earth (and
modified) illustration of the test was set out by the information tribunal
(EA/2011/0173 *J. Morley v IC*). Privacy is starting with a tailwind. The
request was for disclosure of names of youth councillors involved in a
planning (zoning) decision and involved consideration of s. 40(2) FOIA.

> *This does* not *mean, however, that one starts with the scales evenly*
> *balanced. Although a consideration of fairness requires other interests to*
> *be taken into account, where section 40(2) is engaged, the data subject's*
> *interests are clearly paramount. We note that the continued primacy of*
> *the DPA, notwithstanding the passage and implementation of freedom*

of information legislation, was strongly emphasised by Lords Hope and Rodger in Commons Services Agency v Scottish Information Commissioner *[2008] UKHL 47 (paragraph 7). (para 22)*

Crucial at this stage is Sched 2 Condition 6 DPA which involves a three-part test for 'processing of data' to allow access by a requester. First, is there a legitimate interest in disclosure of personal data? Second, is such disclosure necessary to promote that legitimate (public) interest (para 25)? In *Corporate Officer of the House of Commons v Information Commissioner*, 'necessary', in the context of condition 6, 'was taken to reflect the meaning attributed by the European Court of Human Rights when justifying an interference with a Convention right, namely, that there should be a "pressing social need" and the interference should be "both proportionate as to means and fairly balanced as to ends"'. Third, would such disclosure cause unwarranted interference with the interests of the individual whose data is in issue? Even where disclosure is necessary, it is only permissible if it would not cause such interference (para 84). Condition 6 was satisfied in relation to those youths who had otherwise published their names on Facebook and whose names also appear in the minutes in the possession of the Council. Names of youth councillors that were not made public were protected – because of their youth and their desire to remain anonymous. If their names were in publicly available minutes then surely they should be identified?

The rule of law and press regulation

FOI includes getting to know the information that is used to make decisions upon which our lives depend. It is about me as a 'belonger', not an outsider. It is also about accountability. We think of the rule of law in terms of government – Leviathan. It is also, as former senior judge Stephen Sedley reminded us, about Jaws – rapacious corporations (Sedley, 1999). The excesses of banking and sections of the press have brought home the truth of that desideratum; making power wielders accountable is really what the modern embodiment of the rule of law is. That power may be public or private, or a mixture of both. There is nothing new about private control of government or public–private partnerships. The problem is how one balances accountability and transparency with freedom of speech and privacy. The principles of freedom of expression, accountability, and the rule of law are integral to the principle of democracy and they are beyond question (*R (B Mohamed) v SoS FCA* [2010] EWCA Civ 65 para 41). Government and press relationships should be open and on the record. But government should be the subject of FOIA not the press – unless the latter has become a state organ. Whereas for government FOIA is a central feature of transparency, transparency for the press means that there are effective means to ensure professional and ethical conduct and to provide just redress. Individual privacy should be protected unless a clear public interest overrides privacy.

Ministers have expressed concern about statutory regulation of the press. Leveson (2012–2013) opted for a system of self-regulation and he spelt out how an 'independent' body, 'established and organised' by the press, would be appointed. Although expressed as a new form of regulation it would not be a statutory regulator. The body would have a majority of non-press members and no present editor could sit on the body and nor could members of government or Parliament. I would go further than Leveson and say there should be no civil servants or other state-sponsored individuals as members. The chair, I would add, should not be a former editor. Leveson recommended an independent appointments panel with the possibility of one serving editor and a majority of non-press members. It could comprise some 'distinguished public servants' experienced in making independent appointments. The self-regulatory body, he continued, would set standards through a code and in its governance and compliance. It would clarify the 'public interest'.[11] A Code Committee would contain editors who would have an important but not decisive role. The body would hear complaints against members and order appropriate redress and encourage newspapers to settle complaints internally. It would have powers of investigation into serious or systemic breaches. The body would provide a 'fair, quick and inexpensive' arbitration process as an alternative to courts to deal with civil claims against its members. The issue of injunctions would remain with the courts.[12] Contractual whistle-blowing provisions would be strengthened. The cost should be met by the industry. Whatever the outcome of the recommendations, the era of self-regulation and a toothless and supine watchdog (the Press Complaints Commission) must be brought to demise.

Leveson has suggested statutory back-up but not statutory bodies or codes. Legislation would be confined to processes for recognising and validating a new regulator. It would *not* create a *statutory* regulator with powers to prevent publication or compel publication. The verifying and auditing body he recommended would be Ofcom, the communications regulator, provoking criticisms of regulation creep.

Leveson stated in his opening remarks that the focus of the Inquiry was 'the culture, practices and ethics of the press' in the context of the latter's relationship with the public, the police, and politicians. 'All of these matters overlap, and my goal must be to consider what lessons, if any, may be learned from past events and what recommendations, if any, should be made for the future, in particular as regards press regulation, governance and other systems of oversight.' The fear, and it is understandable, is that too powerful a regulator will stifle independence or, in time, it may seek to foster restraints on speech – it will become a *de facto* licensor. I do not envisage a licensing system; history shows how pernicious these have been. The role of any regulator will essentially be to produce a fair and balanced code and to provide an *effective* system of redress. Freedom of speech must be protected as the greatest public interest. Leveson recommended a legal duty in the legislation for government to protect the freedom of the press. But the innocent and the weak also need protection. A recent report from the Reuters Institute for the Study of Journalism (Fielden, 2012) has described the variety in arrangements for regulating the press in a number of countries. My firm belief is that the corporatist 'last chance saloon' arrangements that we adopted in the UK are long overdue for major reform. Binding parties to contracts as per Lords Hunt and Black is not the answer. In 2012 the Press Complaints Commission acknowledged the need for major change, although change was dependent upon the recommendations of Leveson's Inquiry and the government's response. The government's position, with significant press support, was against a statutory body to verify self-regulation. Its preferred option was to have such a body set up by Royal Charter relying upon the prerogative power of the Crown in the hope of ensuring independence. In UK constitutional usage it will simply be government by another name. The BBC is established under Royal Charter. By the summer of 2013, no official response to Leveson had been agreed by the government. As information began to emerge to the effect that, as the Privy Council operates under the advice of ministers, ministers could more easily amend the rules of a body established under charter than under statute, the choice of a regulator by power of a Royal Charter came under question. Press proposals for self-regulation by the press with a reduced role for the state were to be considered by the Privy Council, along with an alternative proposal which had the backing of the three main political parties.

I would argue that a degree of parliamentary underpinning is necessary, together with industry and independent membership and an independent chair, effective powers of enforcement and redress, and compulsory membership. Leveson's recommendations omit or amend some of these features. Leveson recommended such an underpinning but not compulsory membership. By 'compulsory' I mean that the standards and enforcement mechanisms will not be optional. Any press outlet will have to comply with a code in which freedom of speech is guaranteed, together with privacy and redress. Leveson's solution was that the arbitration service he suggested for civil claims should have attractive financial incentives in relation to litigation costs for both the press and litigants suing the press. Those not subscribing would lay themselves open to exemplary damages for breaches of civil law. Press and media regulation should be separate, I believe, although the verifying role of Ofcom arguably confuses this. However, in case the 'last chance' recommendations to avoid statutory regulation are not accepted by the press, Leveson suggested back-up provisions which included Ofcom as a 'backstop' regulator. Any 'regulation' for 'new' media will have to await greater global cooperation than exists today but like many I am wary of attempts to rein in or own the web. I see no reason why major players should not be invited to join, remembering the unattractive consequences of exclusion.

One further point concerns the duty on the press to tell the truth. The hostility of sections of the British press to Europe is infamous, but much of it built on complete distortion of the truth (Leveson, 2012–2013: vol. 2, pp. 687–8; Spencer, 2012). The National Union of Journalists and Press Complaints Commission codes seek to ensure accurate, fair, and undistorted information. There is no effective mechanism to provide this where no privacy or reputation rights are involved. One may say that the marketplace of ideas and free speech will guarantee the truth. The problem here is that, and as Leveson shows, the market has lacked pluralism. There is no duty to correct errors, to make the communications more reliable. Leveson recommended that the self-regulating body should have power to direct the prominence and placement of corrections and apologies.

I return to a point made at the beginning of this chapter. Transparency for the press does not entail a FOIA. What are required are means to assess the accuracy and reliability of information. What financial arrangements have been involved in obtaining information? Leveson recommended that sources and source material should be made public where information is in the public sphere, but I would add that confidential sources must be protected according to the criteria set by the European Court of Human Rights (*Financial Times v UK* [2010] EMLR 21, esp. para 70). I would add that the financial interests of newspaper owners, editors, and senior journalists should be made public. Their lobbying with political actors should be on the record. Any reforms coming from Leveson should not end up providing the enforcement but not the safeguards for a free and plural press. Leveson was adamant that the legislation he recommended would guarantee the freedom of the press.

Lobbying

A way to the nerve centre of power comes through lobbying. Given the emphasis on transparency in the White Paper (Cabinet Office, 2012), how do proposals for lobbying compare? A statutory register of lobbyists – the banks and press barons have been spectacularly successful in lobbying – was a 2010 coalition commitment (Cm 8233). More than three years later, a government bill was introduced (see below). The shortcomings in the proposals have been identified by the Political and Constitutional Reform Committee (P&CR) (HC 153 (2012–13)). 'Defining the activity of lobbying is fundamental to defining who is a lobbyist. The Government's consultation paper fails to do so' (p. 3). The government did not intend to publish details of meetings between ministers and lobbyists; departmental websites already do so, the committee exclaimed in disbelief! Nor did the consultation paper recommend a regulatory code.

P&CR's preferred option was one that encompasses the government's proposals for a statutory register of third-party lobbyists, including disclosure of client lists, and whether or not the lobbyist is a former minister or senior official, but includes the following additional features: a broadened definition of a lobbyist, to include anyone who lobbies professionally in a paid role (thus in-house lobbyists, trade associations, trade unions, think tanks, campaign groups, and charities may be required to register); disclosure of the issues being lobbied on; disclosure of when lobbying services have been provided on a pro bono basis; a statutory code of conduct or a hybrid code of conduct (whereby organisations and individuals must indicate that they have signed up to their industry's relevant code of conduct, so it is clear where complaints can be addressed); and incorporation of published data on whom ministers are meeting (HC 153 (2012–13), para 53). In some cases less information on meetings with lobbyists was being published now than under the previous government (Department of Energy). 'We strongly recommend that Departments publish the date and topic of a meeting with Ministers and officials' (HC 153 (2012–13), para 83; see whoslobbying.com). A government bill on lobbying introduced in July 2013 concentrates on a register for 'consultant lobbyists'.

Leveson recommended that political parties publish a statement on the approach they adopt to relationships with the press and other initiatives to enhance transparency for meetings and communications. It sounds somewhat anodyne. But a sting was attached:

> The open forum which the Inquiry has sought to provide … has inevitably taken place against a background of a continuing conversation between press and politicians to which the Inquiry and the public have not been party. This has not happened under the sort of conditions of transparency which I have concluded to be an essential component for restoration of public trust and confidence … (2012–2013: para 137, executive summary)

Reporting closed justice in a transparent democracy

The war on terror has generated important case law on judicial assistance in reporting cases. *Binyam Mohamed* before the Court of Appeal dealt with an action against the Foreign and Commonwealth Office for documents coming from US intelligence and government (*R (B Mohamed) v SoS FCA* [2010] EWCA Civ 65. M wished to sue the Crown for its involvement through its servants in torture; the action was settled but led to an aborted judicial inquiry and the Justice and Security Act). The documents revealed torture and the involvement of British intelligence officers. The case eventually turned on whether certain paragraphs in a judgment should be shown to M. Apart from M's personal interest in seeing the full and complete reasoning of the court, there was considerable discussion about the principle of open justice generally, and as it might affect the media. Justice must be done between the parties. The public must be able to enter any court to see that justice is being done in that court and that a judge is conscientiously doing his best to do justice according to law.

> For that reason, every judge sitting in judgment is on trial. So it should be, and any exceptions to the principle must be closely limited. In reality very few citizens can scrutinise the judicial process: that scrutiny is performed by the media, whether newspapers or television, acting on behalf of the body of citizens. Without the commitment of an independent

media the operation of the principle of open justice would be irremediably diminished. (2013: para 38)

In litigation between the executive and any of its manifestations and the citizen, the principle of open justice represents an element of democratic accountability, and the vigorous manifestation of the principle of freedom of expression. Ultimately open justice supports the rule of law itself. 'Where the court is satisfied that the executive has misconducted itself, or acted so as to facilitate misconduct by others, all these strands, democratic accountability, freedom of expression, and the rule of law are closely engaged' (para 39). The media must be free on what to report. This reflects the 'diversity of the media' and 'symbolises its independence'. The court was of the firm view that the investigative role of the media exists independently of the principle of open justice, and that the right of the media to enlist the assistance of legislation like the Freedom of Information Act to acquire access to information is 'similarly distinct'. Neither diminishes the principle of open justice (para 40). The media is a facilitator not a driver:

> It is, of course, elementary that the courts do not function in order to provide the media with copy, or to provide ammunition for the media, or for that matter private individuals, to berate the government or the opposition of the day, or for that matter to berate or laud anyone else. They function to enable justice to be done between parties. However where litigation has taken place and judgment given, any disapplication of the principle of open justice must be rigidly contained, and even within the small number of permissible exceptions, it should be rare indeed for the court to order that any part of the reasoning in the judgment which has led it to its conclusion should be redacted. As a matter of principle it is an order to be made only in extreme circumstances. (para 41)

The open justice principle is not diminished by official avenues of enquiry or criminal proceedings – but there are limits imposed by the *sub judice* rule. 'These are distinct elements of our arrangements which serve to ensure that the rule of law is observed, but they do not impinge on the principles of open justice' (para 42).

One should note how at first instance the judgment recorded the absence of a 'systematic archive' for closed evidence and an absence of access to any records of closed procedures ([2009] EWHC 2549 Admin and [2009] 2973 Admin). The difficulties of compiling accurate law reports in secret proceedings was addressed ([2009] EWHC 2549 Admin). The development of the common law has depended upon open, independent law reporting (para 117). Suggestions included the Crown advocate preparing a summary of the main legal submissions by the parties to be disclosed to the law reporters. Skeleton arguments (redacted where necessary) should be made available to law reporters. In the previous proceedings in this case, counsel made these available, but this was the exception rather than the rule. The court should record in its open judgment the legal submissions made. A schedule should be kept of open material so that reporters knew what they were entitled to receive. Better notice should be given and a clear record kept of which part of the hearing was open and which part closed. Procedural rules would have to be introduced accordingly.

Applications may be made to open other closed judgments (or parts of them) or for their release into the public domain on the expiry of a period of time, in the same way as public records are released into the public domain. 'As far as we have been able to ascertain, there is no systematic archive of closed judgments in a registry at the Royal Courts of Justice or a procedure for their release either on application or after a fixed period of time' (119).[13] Open justice is a vital component of the rule of law.

FOI as a human right?

Is transparency a human right? I think, despite its universal buzz-phrase adoption, it is too vague to be a human right. Freedom of information is such a right, I have no doubt. The United Nations subscribed to freedom of information in its famous Resolution of the General Assembly of 14 December 1946: 'Freedom of information is a fundamental human right and is the touchstone for all freedoms to which the United Nations is consecrated' (G.A. Res 59(1) at 95 UN Doc A/64). The right was concerned with freedom of speech. But what is the point of my having a right to say anything if it is badly informed? As FOS has long been seen as the lifeblood of democracy, FOI is assuming a similar position. Samuel Brittan of the *Financial Times* thought I had gone too far in an earlier essay of mine (Brittan, 2006) – just days before the decision in *Reyes* (*Claude Reyes v Chile* Report no. 60/03IACHR) and since then *Tarsasag* (*Tarsasag a Szabadsagjogokert v Hungary* (2009) ECHR 618 and *Kenedi v Hungary*

(2009) ECHR 786; former case law emphasised the right to pass on information rather than the right to receive and get access to information: *Leander v Sweden* (1987) EHRR 43). These latter cases ruled that Article 10 and its analogue in the American Charter of Human Rights did give a fundamental right to documents held by public bodies.

In *Tarsasag*, before the Court of Human Rights at Strasbourg, the right was operative where a state body had a monopoly holding on archives and these were required for the legitimate needs of an NGO. Its right to freedom of speech was denied by refusal. Previously, Strasbourg had ruled that only Article 8 gave a right to information, then Article 2 and Article 6. The impact of the right to information has been felt within domestic case law and is dramatic. There are several cases where the English court of appeal has acknowledged the impact of Strasbourg case law in *Tarsasag* and other cases in reading down the Human Rights Act (*Kennedy v IC* [2011] EWCA Civ 367; *A v Independent News and Media Ltd* [2010] EWCA Civ 343). The reservations of senior judge Lord Brown in *Sugar* should be noted (*Sugar v BBC* [2012] UKSC 4). BBC exclusions for journalism could not be defeated by a fundamental right to information. The exclusion was there precisely to protect the BBC's freedom of speech. Should there be a right of access to information held by the press? Despite their power and influence I have answered 'No'. Leveson believed the exclusions protecting the press as data controllers under the DPA went too far.

A recent case from the information tribunal displays and works through these principles of *Tarsasag* (EA/2011/0112 and 13 *I. Cobain v IC and CPS* (8 Feb. 2012)). This concerned a request by a journalist (Cobain) to obtain records held on Nick Griffin, leader of the right-wing British National Party, and a criminal trial in which he was convicted for racial hatred under public order legislation. The tribunal ruled that the provisions of the DPA scheds 2 and 3 (the latter concerning 'sensitive personal data') had not been interpreted properly in some cases. Furthermore, s. 32 FOIA, which makes an exemption for court documents, had to be read in the light of ECHR jurisprudence. In its report the Tribunal concluded that, whilst there was no general right to receive information under Article 10, the scope of the right had broadened since earlier case law (*A v Independent News and Media Ltd* [2010] EWCA Civ 343 at paras 41–2).[14] Having taken account of arguments as to information monopolies and considered the relevance of Cobain's role as an investigative journalist, the Tribunal concluded that the conventional interpretation of s. 32(2) was an interference with Cobain's rights. In doing so it was plainly influenced by the readiness of the Court of Appeal to adopt recent developments in Strasbourg jurisprudence (in *Kennedy* and *A*, above). The tribunal in *Cobain* agreed. Does Article 10 concern a right of access to information where that information is held by an organ of the state, subject to the conditions described in Article 10(2)? The tribunal noted the impact of *Tarsasag* and *Kenedi* in the Court of Human Rights and how these had focused on receipt (and access to) information under Article 10. The theme of access to information had been emphasised in UK courts as well as at Strasbourg, especially where the press was concerned.

> Kennedy *involved a thirty-year restriction on all information lodged with the inquiry, however trivial or harmless. The report had no difficulty in concluding that it was grossly disproportionate and achieved no reasonable balance of interests. In our judgment, such a restriction on any information lodged with a court and continuing decades after any appeal process is exhausted fails the tests of proportionality by a similar margin. (para 61)*

In *Kennedy*, s. 32(1) could be read down in a way which was consistent with Article 10. Limiting the restriction in Article 32(1) so that it ends once a reasonable time has elapsed after the exhaustion or evident abandonment of the available appeal process would avoid a breach of Article 10 (*D. Kennedy v IC* EA/2008/0083 (18 Nov. 2011; case after remittal by Court of Appeal)). 'Reasonable time' is not a precise term.

Conclusion

Democracy is a protean concept. FOS and FOI and the rule of law are essential features of democracy. None of them comes unpacked. We have moved to transparency whereby the processes of decision-making are exposed so that those who wish to follow a process of decision-making and participate may do so. Democracy has become more participatory. It may be in the process of becoming more *personalised,* as the June 2012 White Paper suggests. I have an uneasy feeling that personalising democracy *undermines* democracy as a societal and indeed global activity – that balance between collective welfare and private interest. This chapter has raised a good many difficulties in the clashes between freedom of information, freedom of speech, privacy protection, transparency within government and press, press regulation, and information as a human right. Difficulties will always be there.

Let me sum it up by saying I do not want to be dominated by unaccountable power. I want to know on what basis governors decide to act in the public interest and I want the press and media to assist in that vital right. I want a press and media that are free and independent but not free and independent to abuse their powers oppressively. As an individual I also want my integrity and private life protected. I want the law to ensure these rights and safeguards.

Notes

1   Jimmy Savile was a very popular TV presenter for the BBC for over forty years. Disclosure of his serious abuses only became public after his death.

2   The UK has a developed tribunal system covering many areas of administrative law and employment law. The tribunal structure was revised by the Courts and Tribunals Act 2007 bringing far greater coherence and independence to tribunals which are now split into First Tier Tribunals (first instance) and Upper Tribunals (appellate). The Courts and Tribunals Service provides administrative support in one integrated agency of the Ministry of Justice for courts and tribunals. For cases involving the press and legal disputes, e.g. freedom of speech, privacy or defamation, the court to hear such cases is the High Court Queen's Bench Division. Judicial review cases are heard by the Administrative Court of the High Court. Appeals from the High Court and Upper Tribunal go to the Court of Appeal and from that court to the UK Supreme Court. The Supreme Court replaced the Appellate Committee of the House of Lords in 2009. Reference is also made to the European Court of Human Rights which adjudicates claims under the European Convention on Human Rights which is a treaty to which the UK is a signatory. Most of the important provisions on human rights under the Convention are incorporated into UK domestic law by the Human Rights Act 1998 and are justiciable before domestic courts.

3   Obtaining personal information by deceit. DPA, s. 55, contains several lawful and public interest defences to obtaining, disclosing etc without consent. See Leveson, 2012–2013: vol. 3, ch. 5.2 pp 1065 et seq.

4   In Art. 10(2) the qualifications are: the interests of national security, territorial integrity or public safety, the prevention of disorder or crime, the protection of health or morals, the protection of the reputation or rights of others, preventing the disclosure of information received in confidence, or for maintaining the authority and impartiality of the judiciary.

5   FS50425063 21 Aug. 2012. See *R. Evans v Information Commissioner* [2012] UKUT 313 (AAC) where the Upper Tribunal ruled that correspondence with Prince Charles held by a department should be disclosed which was followed by a ministerial veto. The information would now be subject to an absolute exemption. The issue of the veto was upheld by the High Court in *R (Evans) v Att Gen* [2013] EWHC 1960 (Admin).

6   The UK Supreme Court has emphasised the importance of this exclusion from the Act for the BBC and the balance between FOI and FOS: *Sugar v BBC* [2012] UKSC 4.

7   8.1. Everyone has the right to respect for his private and family life, his home and his correspondence.

      8.2. There shall be no interference by a public authority with the exercise of this right except such as is in accordance with the law and is necessary in a democratic society in the interests of national security, public safety or the economic well-being of the country, for the prevention of disorder or crime, for the protection of health or morals, or for the protection of the rights and freedoms of others.

8   The important point assisting media and press on the DPA was decided in the Court of Appeal [2002] *Campbell v MGN* EWCA Civ 1373 and was not overturned on appeal. See the critical analysis of Leveson, 2012–2013: vol. 3, ch. 5.2, pp. 1065 et seq, 1111–13. This concerned journalists etc. as data controllers, i.e. holders.

9   The Official Secrets Act 1989 was invoked to obtain evidence from journalists reporting the allegations of police corruption in the hacking episode with a view to bringing charges against the journalists. A widespread outcry helped cause the prosecution to desist: *Guardian*, editorial, 18 Feb. 2013.

10   *Flood v Times Newspapers Ltd* [2012] UKSC 11 – a case extending the public interest defence for responsible journalism. The Defamation Act 2013 contains important liberalising reforms to defamation law including a public interest defence.

11   See CPS, 2012 on DPP guidance on the public interest.

12   Human Rights Act, s. 12, seeks to protect the press from prior restraint. Max Mosley's complaint was that he should have been given warning of the publication by *News of the World* to allow an application for an injunction. The respondent usually has to be notified, with provisos, where an applicant is seeking an injunction restraining a publication. The Court of Human Rights did not uphold Mosley's complaint: 'having regard to the chilling effect to which a pre-notification requirement risks giving rise, to the significant doubts as to the effectiveness of any pre-notification requirement and to the wide margin of appreciation in this area, the Court is of the view that Article 8 does

not require a legally binding pre-notification requirement': *M.Mosley v UK* App 48009/08 (10 May 2011). The House of Commons Culture, Media and Sport Committee (2009–10) recommended a requirement of prior notification should 'normally' be in the Editors' Code subject to public interest exceptions.

13 See the Lords Constitution Committee on the absence of records of the use of Closed Material Procedures under 'other legislation' (HL 18 (2012–13), para 34).

14 See *R (Guardian News Ltd) v City of Westminster Magistrates' Court* [2012] EWCA Civ 420 para 88: 'I base my decision on the common law principle of open justice … the development of the common law did not come to an end on the passing of the HRA', per Toulson LJ.

References

Blair, T. (2010) *A Journey* (Hutchinson).

Brittan, S. (2010) 'Review of *Transparency: The Key to Better Governance* C. Hood and D. Heald eds (2006) ch. 3', *Financial Times*, 9 Oct.

Cabinet Office (2012) *Open Data: Unleashing the Potential*, White Paper, Cm 8353 (The Stationery Office).

CPS (2012) *Guidelines for Prosecutors on Assessing the Public Interest in Cases Affecting the Media* (CPS): http://cps.gov.uk/consultations/media_guidelines.pdf.

Fielden, L. (2012) *Regulating the Press: A Comparative Study of International Press Councils* (RISJ).

Hayes, J. (2009) *A Shock to the System: Journalism, Government and the Freedom of Information Act 2000* (RISJ).

House of Commons, Culture, Media and Sport Committee (2009–10) *Press Standards, Privacy and Libel*, 2nd Report of Session 2009–10, HC 362-I (The Stationery Office).

House of Commons, Justice Committee (2012–13) (HC 96-I, II, III). *Post Legislative Scrutiny of the Freedom of Information Act 2000.*

Leveson, Lord Justice (2012–2013) *An Inquiry into the Culture, Practices and Ethics of the Press*, House of Commons Paper HC 780 I-IV (2012–13), *Executive Summary* HC 779 (2012–13): www.official-documents.gov.uk/document/hc1213/hc07/0780/0780.asp.

Master of the Rolls (2012) www.judiciary.gov.uk/Resources/JCO/Documents/Reports/super-injunction-report-20052011.pdf.

Sedley, S. (1999) *Freedom, Law and Justice* (Sweet & Maxwell).

Sedley, S. (2011) *Ashes and Sparks* (Cambridge University Press).

Spencer, J. (2012) *Cambridge Yearbook of European Legal Studies*, 363.

5

Transparencies

John Lloyd

Journalists see themselves as highly moral actors, and they pursue their moral mission by attempting to make events and characters more transparent, more open to public inspection and judgement. But they see themselves as such in different ways – most obviously so in countries, such as the UK, where there is a strong tabloid press. The 'Sunday-best' or liberal journalistic mission is to provide accurate information and informed analysis; to investigate what appears to be unexplained or suspicious in public life; and to make what is significant interesting to as wide an audience as possible. The tabloid version concentrates on the private lives of the well known, both celebrities from the worlds of entertainment and sport, and prominent public figures in politics and other fields. Their assumption is that private, especially sexual, life is more interesting to their readers and their claim is that private behaviour is a moral test of the leaders and role models of society, and a reliable index of how they will act in public. Broadcasting, especially that regulated by the state and paid for in some form by the public, tends to follow the first model, though increasingly it partakes of the second. As all of these news providers experience falling audiences and revenues, the internet – the main culprit for the mainstream's woes – now becomes the medium for journalism, and it is as yet unclear how journalism, and its versions of transparency and of holding power to account, will fare in this medium. This chapter is an effort to give some pointers to what is presently unknowable.

The Sunday-best/liberal model journalists define their place and role in society as being both a record of and a check on the activities of, in ambition at least, all other institutions, especially those of politics. This is most strongly articulated in the American tradition, and most practised in American journalism: but European journalism, especially the British, has developed or adopted similar approaches. Much continental European journalism had retained a strong attachment to a more literary, reflective style of writing: Geraldine Muhlmann (2011) notes that in journalistic cultures such as the French, German, and Italian, self-critical journalists lament that they do not produce literature and have instead condemned themselves to a more degraded occupation, like a character in Alexander Pope's *Dunciad*. She chides them for letting this self-imposed stigma hinder them in the task of producing good, fact-rich news and analysis – what journalism can and should do. In fact, however, the would-be literati are dying out, or confined to the cultural pages: in most Western cultures, journalists see their normative task as investigation and revelation, including aspects of what had long been considered private life.

The norm has spread. Russian journalists, when freed from the Soviet injunction to produce journalism in the Party's interest, saw a belated holding to account of politics as their main aim in life: an aim, however, now severely constrained by the present administration. Chinese journalists also work under strong constraints, but from the commercialisation of the media under the Deng Xiao Peng reforms from the late 1970s onwards, the greater freedom accorded to journalists has resulted in the rapid creation of a practice of investigative journalism, with notable breakthroughs which have both shamed and angered the authorities. Haiyan Wang, a former investigative reporter on the *Southern Metropolitan Daily* of Guangzhou, wrote (in the *Financial Times*, 15 July 2012):

> *There have been many examples of successful investigative reporting. The much-cited 'landmark' success was the exposure of the death of Sun Zhigang, a graduate who came to the southern city of Guangzhou in March 2003. He was picked up, put in a detention camp and beaten to death. I remember the excitement of my colleagues on Guangzhou's* Southern Metropolitan Daily, *the paper most committed to investigative journalism in China, when it reported the case – which in the end led to the abolition of a bad law. They predicted it would be a 'turning point' in often timid Chinese journalism, and believed that investigative reporting could be a powerful engine of social change.*
>
> *There have been other examples – revelations of tainted milk, workers held in slave-like conditions, villagers compelled to relocate. The media managed to expose the real death toll, which the government had tried hard to cover up, during the 2003 outbreak of the Sars virus.*

In India, the explosive growth of the news media, especially on the many all-news TV channels, has given the country's journalism a new self-confidence and authority. Shekhar Gupta captures this, writing in the *Indian Express* (8 September 2012) about the loss of awe on the part of his Indian colleagues for Delhi-based foreign correspondents, whom they now see as doing the same job in the same ways:

> *the growth of India's own journalism, particularly in the electronic media, has liberated us from our dependence on foreign media ... as democracies grow, evolve, deepen and mature, their reliance on the international media for news about themselves declines. It follows that the clout of the foreign press corps in their capitals also declines accordingly. That is exactly what has happened in New Delhi through two decades of reform. The political class, the bureaucracy and even Indian journalists no longer hold in awe the bureau chiefs of the* BBC, CNN, The New York Times, Time, The Guardian, *even* The Washington Post. *They are fellow journalists covering our country, rather than super-powerful and super-connected foreign journalists who set the agenda for us ...*

This assumption that journalists have both the right and the duty to be investigators of the world's governments, corporations and other centres of power has become the norm, or at least the ideal, almost everywhere: the 'almost' is necessary to recognise that the authorities in societies like North Korea, Cuba and Turkmenistan, along with a number of countries in the Arab world and in Africa, still so tightly control their journalism that little but the official line is permitted to be published. Where more freedom exists, the model reached for is the 'American'; the rubric under which journalists profess to work is 'We hold power to account', even if the honest reporter in authoritarian societies would add the rider '(when power allows us)'.

I should add a rider too. Most journalists, everywhere, don't spend their lives investigating the inner workings of power: they do routine reporting, together with lifestyle, gossip, sport, and cultural pieces. They rely far more than they care to admit on the productions of public relations companies and divisions. But the ideal, even if never actually attempted, is to develop an independent voice and presence which can, where called for, challenge, illuminate, and expose individuals and centres of power – with the express intention of improving society by doing so. James S. Ettema and Theodore L. Glasser (1998) put it thus:

> *Whether the ideal of an adversarial press manifested itself as healthy scepticism or exaggerated cynicism, whether it reflected journalists' commitment to their constitutionally sanctioned duty or merely their psychic baggage, this ideal has long endured as the ethos of American journalism. It may be true that investigative reporting, despite flashes of high visibility, has appeared infrequently on America's front pages. It may also be true that only a minority of journalists expressly adopt an adversarial role. But it is probably just as true that an advanced attitude 'has always lurked in the psyche of American journalists'. The notion that the press should be a relentless adversary of the powerful – 'a lifeline of democracy in reporting upon the use, misuse and abuse of power' – has deep roots in American journalism.*

Ettema and Glasser limit their observations to the US – where journalism has, indeed, some of the deepest roots (Britain's are older, though less robust). But the approach has become universal. Its attraction is in part idealistic: and many journalists are impelled into their profession under the impulse of a strong civic sense, similar to that which leads people to join NGOs, or the United Nations, or radical political groups. Ettema and Glasser (1998), again, write that:

> *in deciding where, as one reporter phrased it, the 'curative powers' of journalistic scrutiny are to be brought to bear, and in working to establish the evaluative standards that are to be used, investigative journalism contributes to the process by which the moral order may be reinforced but may also be altered, if only a little.*

This urge – to serve morality and effect beneficial change – has dangers attendant on it: but it is, at least potentially and at times actually, among the most powerful antidotes to the workings of power, especially where it succeeds in being read or heard or seen in authoritarian societies – powerful, at least, when the exposures gained by journalism are effective, and curative action follows.

Morally charged journalism became universal as an ideal by the end of the twentieth century. It held out a certain version of transparency: that is, to discover the truth, especially about the workings of powers – governmental, corporate, military – which exercise a profound effect on public life and on private lives. It had worked out a rough workaday ethic, which has tended to depend heavily on the end of any journalistic inquiry as a retrospective justification for the means: successful exposure of a wrong expunged the notion that the route to it may have been reprehensible, devious, or even criminal. The actions of the *Daily Telegraph* in 2009 in publishing a full account of expenses and allowances claimed by members of the UK parliament involved paying a reported £110,000 for a computer disk (Tryhorn, 2009): no prosecution was initiated (the Metropolitan Police declined to pursue one, saying it would not be in the public interest).

Journalists had pitted themselves, with some success (and many setbacks), against authoritarian leaders – and continue to do so. But where journalism operates more or less freely, its underpinnings began to shake, and now are shaking violently. Authoritarian leaders are one thing: the internet is another.

The liberal version of journalistic transparency described above was journalism in its respectable guise, most evident in US journalism, from small city dailies through to the descendants of the nineteenth-century magazines which had pioneered long-form narrative journalism – these descendants including the *Atlantic*, *Vanity Fair*, and the *New Yorker* with the news magazines *Time*, *Newsweek*, and *US News and World Report*. It was transparency with conditions and limits: the most pervasive limit was the journalists themselves, through which the narrative was mediated. They set the implicit and explicit conditions within which the story would be told – conditions deriving from a century's experience, discussion, and teaching, in journalism school classrooms and on the newsdesk, of the proper way to inform the audience of events of public interest.

In the ideal and often the practice of the liberal version, facts were checked carefully; comments – save in exceptional cases – were balanced; private life was carefully segregated from public life and only brought into the story when the private could be plausibly shown to bear on the public. In this version, journalism was a serious business, a civic matter, a practice which had to have rules and assume virtue on the part of the journalists, because to hold power to proper account could only be done if the journalism claiming to do so made a proper account of *itself*. That meant a certain transparency in work methods: sources had to be met or called and persuaded to be on the record; interviews were formal, thorough, and sometimes multiple; notes were kept and were available for senior editors to examine; and the reporter had to show that he or she had no membership or allegiance which would compromise the reporting.

The allegiance was to the story, and through the story, the truth, as far as it could be told. Few journalists working within this model were naïve enough to believe that the whole truth could be told: but they, or their editors, were wise enough to understand that only with a belief that the truth about events existed, and was ideally available were there space enough and time, did journalism have a meaning.

The claim of transparency which this version made is long past its high noon. Opinions differ as to whether or not it is dying, or even dead: I do not think it is either, but it is certainly losing ground. In part, this is because it is losing markets and money, and thus power: liberal journalism depends for its success on retaining powerful institutions which command audience and/or elite respect. Newspapers in all Western societies are declining in circulation and in revenue; these include newspapers which have gained wide acclaim for their ability to investigate and reveal a wide range of issues in the public interest – as the *Washington Post*, the *Guardian*, *Le Monde*, *Dagens Nyheter*, *La Repubblica*, *El Pais*, and others. The newspapers which continue to have a business model robust enough to fund many foreign bureaux and reporting in depth are the business papers with a global reach, as the *Financial Times* and the *Wall Street Journal* – where the customers are willing to pay premium prices for accurate news and analysis. The decline of the general newspapers weakens the liberal approach to news: and makes space for a different, even radically different, take on both transparency and the public interest, and the links between the two.

The liberal version has always had a semi-licensed jester in its company. That is the tabloid press; as it developed in the twentieth century, it became a medium less for 'serious' news (which many popular papers had carried, at some length, into the 1970s) and instead developed extensive reporting on the celebrity world, on the affairs of the famous and on television; as well as extensive coverage of sports. Politics were usually reported either through the prism of scandal, or polemically: tabloids as Britain's *Sun* and *Daily Mail* and Germany's *Bild* use their high circulations to promote strong, often abrasive campaigns against trends, policies, and individuals in politics which are likely to appeal to their readerships' sense of outrage.

Britain is the tabloid capital of the world. Of the 9 million copies of newspapers sold every day of the week (including Sunday), 7 million are tabloid – a group which is led by the *Sun* and the *Daily Mail*, with the *Daily Mirror*, the *Daily Star*, the *Daily Record* (Scotland only), and the *Daily*

Express; all have Sunday equivalents. British tabloids see themselves, and have been regarded by others, as highly influential politically and socially – an assessment they share with *Bild,* and to a lesser degree with Sweden's *Espressen* and *Aftonbladet*, respectively right and left-wing tabloids. *Bild* is closest to the *Sun* (though it carries more 'straight' news), in that its support is for parties of the centre right or centre left is not consistent. Like the Rupert Murdoch-owned News International, the UK company which brings together the *Sun, The Times* and the *Sunday Times* (the *News of the World* was closed as a result of the hacking scandal), the Axel Springer group decides which party or parties to support on the group's executives' and editors' view of their policies and leadership. The need, on the part of politicians, to woo the newspaper and the groups' executives and proprietors is thus more urgent than those whose commitment to a political camp is steadier. Even there, however, politicians are aware they cannot take commitment for granted in a much more fluid political time: the tabloids of the left, such as the Swedish *Aftonbladet* and the British *Daily Mirror*, and those of the right, such as the Swedish *Espressen* and the British *Daily Mail*, must also be wooed. Peter (Lord) Mandelson, a former director of communications for the Labour Party and a senior minister in successive Labour administrations from 1997 to 2008, argued (in his witness statement to the Leveson Inquiry in 2011) that this wooing was now a large and inevitable (and unwelcome) part of politicians' task:

> *Ever since the growth of democracy and expansion of the franchise in the 19th century the media have become the principal vehicle for mass communication between those who seek to govern and the electorate. If politicians could directly communicate en masse they would happily do so. They do not want to be under an obligation to the media but, in a democracy, popular elections require mass communication, and as the media in the UK are not owned or controlled by the state, this means that politicians must develop some sort of relationship with commercial and independent media. They must remain, at the least, on neutral terms with private proprietors, editors and journalists whose views and prejudices are continuously mixed in with their professional and ownership roles and who represent a powerful and unelected force in society. (Mandelson, 2012)*

Other countries have tabloids, but they are usually not seen – and do not see themselves – as important to the country's politics. However, they can play a role – probably increasing – through expanding the coverage of politicians' private lives: and where they find a scandal, they will sometimes see that scandal pass into the domain of 'straight' political news reporting, with large effect. The US *National Enquirer,* though much diminished in sales, effectively ruined the political career of the Democratic presidential candidate John Edwards when, in 2008, it unmasked an affair he had with film-maker Rielle Hunter, and claimed he had fathered her child: Edwards, who at first denied it, later admitted the affair but denied that the child was his.

Also in 2008, the *Enquirer* broke the story that the daughter of the then Republican Party's vice presidential nominee, Sarah Palin, was pregnant out of wedlock; and alleged that she had had an affair with her husband's business partner, Brad Hanson. The allegation, which was denied by both Palin and Hanson, was later repeated in a biography of Palin (McGinniss, 2011) – which added the detail that she had had a one-night stand with a basketball player, Glen Rice, while both were at college (and unmarried). The Republican presidential candidate John McCain threatened legal action against the *Enquirer* on the story, and a spokesman for the paper replied that:

> The National Enquirer's *coverage of a vicious war within Sarah Palin's extended family includes several newsworthy revelations, including the resulting incredible charge of an affair plus details of family strife when the Governor's daughter revealed her pregnancy. Following our John Edwards' exclusives, our political reporting has obviously proven to be more detail-oriented than the McCain campaign's vetting process. Despite the McCain camp's attempts to control press coverage they find unfavorable,* The Enquirer *will continue to pursue news on both sides of the political spectrum. (Hamden, 2008)*

This statement appears to put the *Enquirer* on the same level as the mainstream news media in the matter of holding power to account. There was, reportedly, some discussion that the *Enquirer* should be nominated for a Pulitzer Prize for the revelations, though that didn't happen.

The *News of the World* phone-hacking scandal, which resulted in the appointment of an inquiry under the Appeal Court judge Sir Brian Leveson, revealed not just a widespread culture of criminal behaviour, blackmail, and distortion; it also illuminated the close and anxiously cordial, even intimate, relationships British political leaders sought to develop and maintain with editors, senior newspaper executives and owners. The assumed power of the tabloids to influence public opinion meant that those who controlled them were continually and eagerly wooed: even the grossest insults and distortions visited upon individual politicians, their parties, and policies would be quickly forgiven in the search for favourable coverage when it mattered. Chancellor Gordon Brown and his wife Sarah suffered the shock of seeing their baby son's condition, cystic fibrosis, displayed on the front page of the *Sun* – a story which, it later appeared, had been given to the paper by a member of the local health service, though whether or not for payment has not been established. Yet Brown, when prime minister, attended the second marriage of Rebekah Brooks, former *Sun* editor and then chief executive of News International, the *Sun's* publisher; and Sarah hosted Brooks for overnight stays at Chequers, the prime-ministerial country residence. Asked about this during the Leveson Inquiry, Brown said: 'Sarah is one of the most forgiving people I know … we had to get on with the job of doing what people expected' (Leveson Inquiry, 2012b).

The incident highlights two things. First, that 'what is expected' is that prime ministers abase themselves before the power of the tabloid press. Second, that tabloids had a radically different view of transparency than that of the upmarket press as well as broadcast news and current affairs. It is *that* idea of transparency which is becoming much more influential and widespread than the liberal model.

Tabloid editors, giving evidence at the Leveson Inquiry, were often contemptuous of the liberal, anti-tabloid consensus of which they believed Lord Leveson, and his advisers, were a part. Among the most outspoken was Kelvin MacKenzie, former editor of the *Sun*. Asked by the chief barrister for the Inquiry, Robert Jay, for his criteria in judging a story's truthfulness, MacKenzie said that 'Basically, my view was if it sounded right, it was probably right and therefore we should lob it in' (Leveson Inquiry, 2012a). (This was said in the context of a discussion about a story which he ran on the singer Elton John which had been checked but proved to be wrong, and which cost the newspaper £1m in damages.) Previously, in a 2006 interview in the *Press Gazette*, MacKenzie said that 'when I published those stories, they were not lies. They were great stories that later turned out to be untrue – and that is different. What am I supposed to feel ashamed about?' (*Press Gazette*, 2006).

These were 'great stories' because they usually concerned allegations about the sex habits of the famous: the story about Elton John had included some unsavoury allegations which Elton John vehemently denied – allegations which, true or not, would of course attract mass attention because of John's fame. MacKenzie, and all tabloid editors, know that what attracts mass audiences above all else is a series of short narratives about celebrity figures – and thus known to a mass audience – behaving in a scandalous way.

The claim of transparency here is that behaviour which reveals moral, or immoral, choices is more revealing of character and of the state of society than any other revelatory journalism, or is at least on a par with it. Sexual gossip is interesting for most people – much more interesting than the often complex explanations of how corruption works. But to add to their traditional boast that they create popular newspapers while their denigrators create unpopular ones, they add another: that they, too, hold power to account. When the British journalist and former Conservative activist Paul Staines founded his Guido Fawkes website in 2004, his express intention was to publish stories which, he believed, hypocritical and collaborationist political reporters and commentators would not. The stories which have attracted most attention have been sex scandals, some – as the affair which Labour Deputy Prime Minister John Prescott had with his social secretary – becoming major stories in the mainstream media.

This version of transparency believes that the public has a right to know the private behaviour of the political class – and of those prominent in every sphere of public life. The moral claim for this is two-fold. First, prominent people are regarded as role models, and thus all aspects of their behaviour should be made public, since people should not be deceived about their reasons for modelling themselves on these figures. Second, insofar as public censure is attracted to those who are revealed to have adulterous affairs, or other behaviour considered deviant or reprehensible, this is beneficial because it has the effect of deterring others from following their example. The rationale which speaks more to the ethics of journalism makes the claim that human actions cannot be neatly divided between public and private. This is because the way in which men and women conduct themselves in private says much about the way in which they act in public ('if he will lie to his own wife why should he not lie to the electorate?'); and because an adulterous affair undertaken by prominent men and women, especially in politics, can be shown, or claimed, to have public consequences – as the affair conducted by Prescott with his social secretary used his government-funded flat, and was claimed to be an abuse of public property.

The 'Mosley orgy' is a good illustration of the role-model argument. In March 2008, the *News of the World* printed pages of text and photographs, and released video footage, of Max Mosley, president of the Fédération Internationale de l'Automobile, the governing body for Formula One racing, engaged in sado-masochistic sexual acts with five sex workers, simulating (according to the paper) Nazi fantasies. This had wide resonance, since Mosley's father, Sir Oswald Mosley, had been the pre-war head of the British Union of Fascists, and a keen supporter of Adolf Hitler and Benito Mussolini (who funded the BUF). Mosley denied the Nazi theme. In July 2008, he won a High Court legal case against the *News of the World* for invasion of privacy. The presiding judge, Justice Eady, said that 'I see no genuine basis at all for the suggestion that the participants mocked the victims of the Holocaust.'

Mosley was (and remained: motions for his resignation as head of the FIA were defeated, though he later retired, in late 2009) a public figure, albeit well known largely within the world of motor racing. He had paid for what is still widely regarded as 'perverted' sex; and thus it could be claimed he had shown himself to be a poor role model.

The argument that private life should be observed and revealed is not wholly confined to the tabloids. One of Britain's foremost and successful investigative reporters, David Leigh of the *Guardian,* speaks strongly to the view that public and private cannot be separated. Leigh believes that privacy and private spaces often mask activities and policies which can become public in a malign fashion. For the powerful, he believes, the division between public and private is often non-existent: and thus to stop at, say, the bedroom door is as potentially disempowering of a thorough investigation as stopping at the boardroom door.

> People are entitled to know whom Peter Mandelson [who is gay] is sleeping with, if only on the grounds of pillow talk – just as you should know whom a heterosexual person is married to, so that you can see if they are getting preferential treatment because of who their partner is. (Cited in Whittle and Cooper, 2008)

He also points to the need for investigation of sexual affairs, especially of politicians.

> It is in the public interest to know if the sexual partner is of the same political view as the politician; and if the affair may lead to public

malfeasance. The classic was David Blunkett (a former Labour home secretary) carrying on with Kimberley Fortier (chief executive of the right-of-centre Spectator *magazine) where the first reaction in the* Guardian *was – 'oh, this isn't in the public interest; who he has sex with is his business'. This turned out to be wrong; not only was he sleeping with someone of violently different political persuasion – which raises questions of hypocrisy – but he was allegedly doing favours for her nanny and whatever because he was smitten with her. Then there was a whole set of issues over whether he had fathered her child. So the first impulse to say 'leave it alone' was wrong. (Ibid.)*

The mighty engine of human prurience was and remains the largest part of tabloids' business model. Especially when a scandal which breaks in the tabloids or gossip magazines becomes an issue which garners widespread interest and claims to raise questions about the right of the person(s) at the scandal's centre to continue in their role, Sunday-best journalists put on their overalls and get involved. At the same time, the tabloid model does pay some mind to the Sunday-best public sphere, covering politics and foreign affairs and business – though very briefly and often for a polemical purpose.

The decline of the business models for news in the press (nearly always privately owned) and commercial television is usually experienced by mainstream journalists, and by many in the academy and in public life, as a disaster. In a long piece in the *New Republic* the Princeton sociologist Paul Starr (2009) wrote that:

> whether the Internet will ever support general-interest journalism at a level comparable to newspapers, it would be foolish to predict. The reality is that resources for journalism are now disappearing from the old media faster than new media can develop them. The financial crisis of the press may thereby compound the media's crisis of legitimacy. Already under ferocious attack from both left and right for a multitude of sins, real and imagined, the press is going to find its job even more difficult to do under economic duress. And as it retrenches in the face of financial pressures, (Tom) Rosenstiel (director of the Pew Centre's Project for Excellence in Journalism) says, 'More of American life will occur in shadows. We won't know what we won't know.'

This is still the position of many in mainstream journalism everywhere: the relatively rapid hollowing out of institutions which seemed both solid and democratically essential continues to shock.

Nevertheless, for journalists who see their trade as one which is democratically essential, the loss of the carrier of the results of their engagement cannot be the end of the matter, even if it means for many the end of a career. New ways have to be found and are being found to carry on with the mission. The internet has, after all, brought millions more readers – even if often fleeting and casual – to newspapers' websites, and offers a technology which has created a seemingly infinite capacity for providing detail and illustration of what before was, even for lengthy pieces, necessarily limited, and confined to print with a few photographs, usually of bad quality. The internet destroys jobs – no question of that – but it does not destroy either the trade or its Sunday-best purpose.

In a much quoted blog, Professor Clay Shirky (2009) wrote that, when a revolution like the internet happens,

> the old stuff gets broken faster than the new stuff is put in its place. The importance of any given experiment isn't apparent at the moment it appears; big changes stall, small changes spread. Even the revolutionaries can't predict what will happen … And so it is today. When someone demands to know how we are going to replace newspapers, they are really demanding to be told that we are not living through a revolution. They are demanding to be told that old systems won't break before new systems are in place. They are demanding to be told that ancient social bargains aren't in peril, that core institutions will be spared, that new methods of spreading information will improve previous practice rather than upending it. They are demanding to be lied to. There are fewer and fewer people who can convincingly tell such a lie.

Three years and half later, and still no one can predict what will happen. There have been many journalistic experiments, of which very few make money and many rely heavily on sponsorship by wealthy individuals or foundations. YouTube, which now may, or may not, make a profit (Google, which owns it, doesn't break down its figures to show the various operating divisions' profit or loss) has lost many millions of dollars, and survives by being enfolded into the golden embrace of Google.

Is YouTube journalism? Yes. Much of what it does is what journalism does: it makes available very large numbers of significant events, speeches, incidents, and performances which make the news – as, recently, the ludicrous and malignant film *Innocence of Muslims,* which caused riots and death throughout the Arab world and the Muslim diaspora. Like journalism, it will depend for its business model – if it has, or is ever to have, a business model which turns in a profit – on attracting large numbers of views for entertainment, sensation, and gossip. But also displayed will be many thousands of pieces which, like the *Innocence of Muslims,* graphically display what the origin of a particular series of events is, or what effects significant events have caused.

The inclusion of YouTube into the ambit of journalism illuminates something of what the internet might do – be doing – to and for journalism. Journalism carried on the internet will be required to play to its strengths, as it did when it took the form of periodical publishing on paper. Paper, when allied with modern printing technology, had formidable strengths: it was portable, and thus could be carried and read at intervals; the content could be rapidly printed in millions of copies and transported and sold in a variety of outlets – supermarkets, small shops, kiosks, single vendors, vending machines – because of the relative compactness of the product; it allowed journalists to give news a hierarchy and a defined place – big news on the front page, sport pages at the back, leaders and opinions in a defined op-ed area; items could be clipped, retained, and used as reference. Once printed, it was a closed world: that's the way things were, as far as the *Wall Street Journal* or *Bild* were concerned, until the next issue.

The form of the newspaper made journalists into powerful gatekeepers, allowing this in and keeping that out; and to be judges of the prominence and completeness of any given piece of news or opinion. The form in which they published their work was a major source of their power – so long as their newspaper commanded either a large circulation, or influence among different types of power establishments, especially those of politics – since within the closed world of the newspaper, criteria of content, style and prominence were at the discretion of the editor and staff, under the more or less active influence of the proprietor. The technology did not determine the content, but the popularity which the newspaper enjoyed, made possible by mass production and bulk transportation techniques.

Broadcast news, on radio and now much more powerfully on television, shares this aspect with newspapers and news magazines. A bulletin, which contains many fewer words than even a tabloid newspaper, is a sketch of what are considered to be the main news events then current: however well chosen, accurate or relevant, there can be no alteration until the next bulletin. The long-serving CBS broadcaster

Walter Cronkite underscored the finality of news bulletins when he began saying 'that's the way it is' at the end of his newscast. In an interview in his retirement, Cronkite revealed that the then president of the CBS news division, Richard Salant, had objected to the sign off, which Cronkite had not cleared with him: he said, according to Cronkite, that 'you are telling people that's the way it is; but we can make mistakes – it's not necessarily the way it is'. Cronkite said that he realised he was right – 'but by then it had caught on' (Archive of American Television, 2013).

Both newspapers and broadcast news, by the way in which they are produced and distributed, say, implicitly – 'that's the way it is'. What will the internet permit – or dictate – in journalism? The following are some indications.

It already makes specialised journalism much easier. Robert H. Giles, the curator of the Nieman Foundation at Harvard, gives the example of an online journal called *Circle of Blue,* published in three editions and translated into eleven languages by a network of scientists, journalists, and designers, and updated weekly: it reports on the global freshwater crisis. It is, he writes (2010):

> one of many news gathering experiments that are changing the face of journalism. As journalism quickens the pace of its move to the web, Circle of Blue is filling a niche by providing specialized content that is considered essential by an audience of shared interests but that can't be found in such detail anywhere else. In many ways it is reflective of a shift in how we define journalism, or at the very least, in how we go about producing and sharing it.

The internet allows such narrow-casting because its distribution costs are negligible, the members of the interested community will spread the word on its existence, and it encourages interaction within a knowledgeable circle (and thus much of its content is from its readers). This is, of course, about as far away from a general newspaper as it is possible to get and still be journalism: but to get specialised information, especially on the political scene, was and is one reason for buying a serious newspaper. However, even the most serious will cater only occasionally, and relatively shallowly, to a real enthusiast's interests. The internet permits much greater depth: it disaggregates wherever it goes.

It blurs lines which print, more or less, made clear. Newspapers tend to be opinionated, but are not generally written by activists. *Circle of Blue* is produced by journalists and scientists: but, on the evidence of reading a few editions, it appears they think, broadly, alike: climate sceptics won't get much space. The contributors are activists as well as professionals – in the sense that they put their skill as journalists and scientists at the service of a particular point of view which is – in the case of many ecologists – passionately held, which sees the course pursued by most governments as dangerous, and which usually includes a series of proposals for ameliorating the crisis which they forecast. Activism has taken to the internet, since it offers its many forms so much – cost-free distribution, interactivity, information on meetings and demonstrations. The cross between activism and journalism is an old one, but it can be taken to a much higher level on the internet.

The interactivity which the internet allows has led many journalists to argue that the figure of the journalist-as-authority is on the way out. In a lecture titled, tellingly, *Does Journalism Exist?*, Alan Rusbridger, editor-in-chief of the *Guardian* and the *Observer*, argued (2010):

> that there is now an acute tension between a world in which journalists considered themselves – and were perhaps considered by others – special figures of authority. We had the information and the access; you didn't. You trusted us to filter news and information and to prioritise it – and to pass it on accurately, fairly, readably and quickly. That state of affairs is now in tension with a world in which many (but not all) readers want to have the ability to make their own judgments; express their own priorities; create their own content; articulate their own views; learn from peers as much as from traditional sources of authority. Journalists may remain one source of authority, but people may also be less interested to receive journalism in an inert context – i.e. which can't be responded to, challenged, or knitted in with other sources.

This is what Rusbridger calls *authority v involvement* – the second challenging the first so effectively that the old concept of journalistic authority – we know, you don't – is now being demolished.

Professor Jay Rosen of New York University wrote (2011) that:

> routines drive what happens in journalism, and … these routines ultimately served the demands of a particular production cycle: the daily newspaper, the 6 p.m. broadcast, the monthly magazine. Ideas about what journalism is – and even what it can be – get frozen within these routines

> as they become second nature to the people who have mastered them
> ... But that was during the era of heavy industry. The lighter, cheaper,
> and less restrictive publishing tools that we have today can free the news
> system from its production gods. The new gods are the users themselves,
> and what they find useful for staying informed and participating in public
> life – you know, getting things done. Which is why I've said that the
> simplest way to add value in journalism is to save the user time.

Journalism on the internet thus has no choice but to become more self-consciously provisional than it was before: open not just to correction, but to endless development, revision, and reformulation. In that sense, the first thing it does for the mission for transparency which journalism has asserted for itself is to make journalism itself more transparent.

The defining feature of net journalism is, however, its drive towards a particular version of transparency, one which takes at least as much of its inspiration from the tabloid as the liberal newspaper tradition, but which is much more linked to the enabling features of the technology and to the bias towards radical openness which has been and remains the animating spirit of the internet and of its main innovators for whom – especially the people at Google – openness is a crucial part of the business model.

The most popular elements in tabloids are celebrity, scandals, and sex: the web is replete with these, and makes them immortal (and global) with a click. In 2012 the capture of shots of the Duchess of Cambridge – wife of the UK's Prince William, eldest son of Prince Charles – sunbathing topless with her husband in a private garden, showed how rapidly pictures can be put before billions of people – published in a French magazine, *Closer* (now served with an injunction), then in an Italian magazine, *Chi*, then in an Irish tabloid, the *Irish Daily Star*, and now available everywhere on the internet. As the editor of *Chi*, Alfonso Signorini, put it, 'it is a journalistic scoop ... surely its unusual to see a future Queen of England topless? I think it's the first time in history, so it deserves an extraordinary edition' (*Huffington Post*, 2012).

Signorini is right: the publication and global dissemination means that the pictures of the Duchess, and (likely) future Queen, do constitute an enormous scoop: after the publication, the fact that millions have seen her nearly naked will for many years condition the way in which she is and will be received and perceived as Queen. Traditionally – and even now – royalty wears the most gorgeous clothes in a demonstration of power and wealth meant to overawe subjects: the Duchess has been undressed, and can never be fully clothed again. The costumes of power will be much more provisional than they have been on the present Queen, whose body has always been properly covered even in her youth and young womanhood. But the market for such images has been and remains very large: Max Clifford, an expert on and consultant to celebrity, reckons (*The Economist,* 2012) that the photographer who took the images stood to make £1m – though probably made less, because of the ban on their reproduction which the couple obtained in the French courts. Yet, as *The Economist* comments, the web both ensures vast audiences and a shrinking reward: the fact that the pictures can be seen, almost simultaneously with their publication, for nothing, reduces their value.

The narrative of politics has been the major one in the liberal version of the news, which sought to give a coherent account of politics and policies domestically and abroad – following, necessarily, at least the main bones of the political issues of the day. The tabloids, increasingly, have used politics and politicians much more instrumentally, seeing them either as a potential source of scandal – sex, corruption, obvious incompetence – or polemically, as figures who could be held up as an example or, more often, trashed.

The liberal approach to political news and comment shares – using less specialised language – much of the approach to politics which animates political scientists, advancing in comment and editorials a heavily ethical, policy-based, and rational approach, usually quite far from the personalisation of the tabloids. In an essay which combined scholarship with pathos, the former Canadian MP, and minister of communication in 1985, now Professor of Public Policy at the University of Ottawa, Richard French (2012), writes that real political life is far from the academy's conception of it – since it is too fragmented and conflicted to benefit from more than a fraction of scholarly advice. French, in fact, comes close to endorsing a representation of politics in the media which is more tabloid than liberal:

> in contrast to the expository style taught to generations of undergraduates, analogy, narrative, ambiguity, ridicule and obloquy, and a measure of hypocrisy are likely to dominate political discourse. In a complex, rapidly evolving and demanding world … it is prudently rational for citizens to assess character and personality as well as, and often rather than, policy.

As an observer of character and personality, the internet is infinitely better even than tabloids – since it can mobilise and inspire legions of citizen-snoops who will post on the internet whatever gossip and episodes featuring leading political figures they can find – usually that which is damaging to the politician. In mid-September 2012, Mitt Romney was suffering under a revelation that he had apparently damned nearly half the population of the US as hooked on the drug of welfare with a 'victim' mentality – the revelation coming from a video shot at a private fundraising event, leaked and uploaded on the internet, and thence to broadcast news and newspapers. The gaffe was, as such gaffes usually are, more important to political and media circles than to the majority of citizens who pay politics a dwindling amount of attention. But it is held to confirm a trend where the Republican challenger trails, not greatly but consistently, behind President Obama. This is said to be largely because of repeated 'gaffes' – many of which, as the comments on welfare, are exposed through the internet. The internet has greatly increased the sense which men and women in public life now all have, and complain of (usually after leaving office), of being surrounded by a thousand unforgiving eyes, and one false move can mean a crisis, or even oblivion.

The WikiLeaks affair, which saw thousands of State Department cables released through newspapers which collaborated with the WikiLeaks site, founded and run by Julian Assange, has not revolutionised (or dispensed with) mainstream journalism, as many advertised it would do: but it has encouraged and given (mainly by Assange) a strongly moral purpose to the act of 'whistle-blowing' – divulging as many pieces of confidential information as possible. In Assange's (2006) view, this would progressively disable governments, which he sees as conspiracies against the people: in mainstream journalism, such publication is seen to be in the public interest because it will deepen public understanding of the governing process (as, in fact, many of the WikiLeaked documents did).

The work of WikiLeaks has been disrupted but continues: in the past two years the site has released material on the security company Strafor and a cache of emails from Syrian government and military figures, which showed the Italian engineering company Finmeccanica and the US public relations company Brown Lloyd James to be actively employed by the Assad regime while it tried to suppress the uprisings in various parts of the country. The emails were obtained by the 'hacktivist' group Anonymous, which hacked into Syrian government computers and downloaded, over several weeks, millions of emails, then passed them to WikiLeaks: the latter then organised their publication by newspapers in Germany, Italy, Lebanon, and Egypt. Anonymous says that it accessed and distributed the emails in order to assist the courageous freedom fighters in Syria –

a further instance of the coming together of activism and journalism, rendered easy by the internet.

As the citadels of the liberal version of journalism continue to struggle for survival – included among these, papers of great distinction, as the *Washington Post*, the *Guardian,* and *Le Monde* – the question of the survival of serious journalism backed, as serious journalism must be, by a relatively powerful institution remains unanswered. The internet will give serious journalism a home – it already has – but not a business model for much of it: yet in what it does offer, one can glimpse an emerging, much more fragmented, journalistic world, in which the lines and inhibitions of the liberal press are swept away in favour of relentless revelation in the name of a more transparent society. At times this will serve the public purpose, as did the release of the WikiLeaks cables – once redacted and set in context by the collaborating newspapers, much to Assange's later disgust. At other times it will deepen the extent to which celebrated, and many uncelebrated, figures are revealed, usually to their disadvantage. How public life adjusts to this new turn of the revelatory screw will be a matter of great interest and importance.

What will this mean for the assumed corollary of transparency – accountability? For the liberal – or for that matter the tabloid – version of transparency to have an effect publicly, the claimed wrongdoing must be seen to be so, by society at large, the authorities, and the perpetrators. Through the news media, they are being held accountable to the law, or to the regulations which govern their public life, or to a (usually implicit) moral code. Both the perpetrators and society at large have to feel they should be accountable for proven lapses; if they don't, then transparency and holding to account serves no useful social purpose. Journalism becomes merely the product of a section in society, disregarded by the rest – a fate which it suffers in many societies, such as Russia and even Italy.

Where there is accountability, however, it is in part because large institutions of the media world have decided that the lapse is serious, and agree to cover it seriously and over some time. Because they have (had) power and prestige, and (probably) a track record in producing broadly accurate news and investigations, and because they are a respected or at least feared element in the polity, a serious lapse, when apparently proven or admitted, is followed by some form of punishment, often self-administered (such as resignation).

Will this happen when we pass to the internet? As in everything net-ish, we don't know. Paul Starr (2009) is pessimistic:

When they were financially strong, newspapers were better able not only to invest in long-term investigative projects but also to stand up against pressure from politicians and industries to suppress unfavorable stories. As imperfect as they have been, newspapers have been the leading institutions sustaining the values of professional journalism. A financially compromised press is more likely to be ethically compromised.

And while the new digital environment is more open to 'citizen journalism' and the free expression of opinions, it is also more open to bias, and to journalism for hire. Online there are few clear markers to distinguish blogs and other sites that are being financed to promote a viewpoint from news sites operated independently on the basis of professional rules of reporting. So the danger is not just more corruption of government and business – it is also more corruption of journalism itself.

This *is* a danger: but it is not fate. However, journalists must first of all ensure that it is not.

References

Archive of American Television (2013) "'That's The Way It Is:" Cronkite First Anchored "CBS Evening News" 50 Years AGO', 16 Apr.: www.emmytvlegends. org/blog/?p=5780.

Assange, J. (2006) 'State and Terrorist Conspiracies', *me @ iq.org*, 10 Nov.: http:// cryptome.org/0002/ja-conspiracies.pdf.

The Economist (2012) 'Breast Behavior: How Technology and Regulation are Changing the Economics of Nude Royal Photos', 22 Sept.

Ettema, J. S., and Glasser, T. (1998) *Custodians of Conscience* (Columbia University Press).

French, R. (2012) 'The Professors on Public Life', *Political Quarterly*, 83/3: 532–40.

Giles, R. H. (2010) *New Economic Models for US Journalism* (Daedalus).

Gupta, S. (2012) 'National Interest: The Foreign Hand-writing', *Indian Express*, 8 Sept.

Harnden, T. (2008) 'Sarah Palin Affair Rumours Are False, Says John McCain's Team', *Daily Telegraph*, 4 Sept.: www.telegraph.co.uk/news/newstopics/uselection 2008/johnmccain/2680018/Sarah-Palin-affair-rumours-are-false-says-John-McCains-team.html.

Huffington Post (2012) 'Kate Middleton Topless Photos: Chi Magazine Editor Alfonso Signorini Defends Publishing Pictures', 17 Sept.: www.huffingtonpost.

co.uk/2012/09/17/kate-middleton-topless-chi-defends-publishing-pics_n_1890604.html.

Leveson Inquiry (2012a) 'Transcript of Morning Hearing 9 January 2012': www.levesoninquiry.org.uk/wp-content/uploads/2012/01/Transcript-of-Morning-Hearing-9-January-2012.pdf.

Leveson Inquiry (201b) 'Transcript of Morning Hearing 11 June 2012': www.levesoninquiry.org.uk/wp-content/uploads/2012/06/Transcript-of-Morning-Hearing-11-June-2012.pdf.

Mandelson, P. (2012) 'Witness Statement to Leveson Inquiry and Answers to Listed Questions by the Rt Hon Lord Mandelson', May: www.levesoninquiry.org.uk/wp-content/uploads/2012/05/Witness-Statement-of-Lord-Mandelson.pdf.

McGinniss, J. (2011) *The Rogue: Searching for the Real Sarah Palin* (Crown Publishers).

Muhlmann, G. (2011) *Journalism for Democracy* (Polity).

Press Gazette (2006) 'Kelvin MacKenzie: Old Mac opens up', *Press Gazette*, 11 Oct.: www.pressgazette.co.uk/node/35890.

Rosen, J. (2011) 'What I Think I Know about Journalism', Apr.: http://pressthink.org/2011/04/what-i-think-i-know-about-journalism.

Rusbridger, A. (2010) *Hugh Cudlipp Lecture,* January, London College of Communication.

Shirky, C. (2009) 'Newspapers and Thinking the Unthinkable', Mar.: www.shirky.com/weblog/2009/03/newspapers-and-thinking-the-unthinkable.

Starr, P. (2009) 'Goodbye to the Age of Newspapers', *New Republic*, 4 Mar.

Tryhorn, C. (2009) 'Telegraph Paid £110,000 for MPs' Expenses Data', *Guardian*, 25 Sept.: www.theguardian.com/media/2009/sep/25/telegraph-paid-11000-mps-expenses.

Wang, H. (2012) 'The Return of Activist Journalism in China', *Financial Times*, 15 July.

Whittle, S., and Cooper, G. (2008) *Privacy, Probity and Public Interest* (RISJ).

6

Transparency and Public Policy: Where Open Government Fails Accountability

Sarah Cohen

Five years ago, some journalists hoped that the decades-long battle for open and accountable government was shifting their way. New laws in the UK, India, Latin America, and emerging democracies codified the value of transparency and officials accountable to the people. In the US, a new president promised a focus on openness. Local officials such as San Francisco's mayor and Washington, DC's chief technology officer were creating publicly available data centres on their city websites in response to civic hackers and open government movements.

Those moves were not, in retrospect, harbingers of more accountability or access to the government records. Yes, they offered public officials new outlets for their public information campaigns and offered consumers easy access to information that help them navigate their lives. But the promised reinvigoration of transparency for the purpose of monitoring powerful institutions – accountability – has not materialised.

The Obama administration, at the cusp of its second term, has instituted policies that shield information from the public and routinely demands high fees for records related to stories or investigations it deems un-newsworthy. For example, the nonprofit Investigative Reporting Workshop was asked to pay $10,000 for records concerning contracts and loans awarded under the American Recovery and Reinvestment Act because the department concluded its work was unlikely to shed light on government operations.

The lesson is that we cannot depend on this or any other government to voluntarily and proactively share the artefacts of governing – the emails, calendars, contracts and other documents – needed to hold it accountable (see Cohen, 2011).

The US Freedom of Information Act and its cousins, then, represent the modern vehicles for citizens and journalists to obtain the information needed to learn what the government is doing in their names and with their money. According to one of the first FOIA-related cases to reach the Supreme Court, the purpose of the law is 'to ensure an informed citizenry, vital to the functioning of democracy, needed to check against corruption and to hold the governors accountable to the governed' (*NLRB v Robbins Tire & Rubber*, 47 U.S. 214 (1978)).

But certain records that are widely acknowledged as public in the spirit of FOIA remain locked within virtual and physical cabinets. Few public officials make their desk calendars public, despite repeated rulings at the federal level that they are open for inspection. Obtaining basic spending documents, such as contracts, grants and purchase orders, is usually a two-year effort, thanks to provisions that the recipients can review the documents and censor information they consider sensitive. Even basic records that most cities have long ago released remain almost impossible to obtain elsewhere.

The *New York Times* has been litigating access to lists of crime incidents in New York City for nearly three years (*The New York Times Company et al. v The City of New York Police Department*, Supreme Court, New York County, Index No. 116449/10). At issue: whether residents have the right to know what crimes have been reported in their city. Despite the lack of data, reporter Joseph Goldstein wanted to test a tip that police were routinely 'downgrading' incident reports.

Goldstein obtained detailed reports of just 100 crimes in the city and set about following them through the system, from victim to prosecutor. He wrote (2012): 'There were a number of instances in which the police report seemed to portray a less serious account of the crime than the district attorney, or a victim, subsequently provided.' They included two gunshot victims whom police said had scraped themselves while fleeing from a street shooting and an incident that the police classified as a misdemeanor but the district attorney later prosecuted as attempted rape.

There is no way for the *Times* to do a more wholesale audit of police crime data, even though whistle-blowers have gone on the record to describe the pressure to downgrade crimes in the city. These reports are locked in internal databases available only to the department. The *Times* lost its lawsuit in 2013.

This is not just a statistical quibble. Without the data, residents have no way to know the crimes reported in their neighbourhood or the reason for a pool of blood on the sidewalk. Victims of downgraded crimes might never see their cases pursued when the official reports describe them as minor transgressions or accidents. Police fail to pursue criminals who remain free to reoffend.

Secret or sanitised crime data is not limited to New York City. The public crime reports in Los Angeles have been so riddled with errors that the *Los Angeles Times* found crimes that centred around City Hall (Welsh and Smith, 2009). The problem stemmed from an error introduced by a contractor hired by the city to make a public version of its in-house database. Inside the department, police knew the real locations – it was only members of the public who couldn't find them.

Both of these crime examples suggest three areas in which the underlying attitude and frameworks clash between journalists and others who try to monitor institutions and even the most sincere open government programme. These perspectives are what Beth Noveck (2011) has called the 'reformers', who seek openness for the purpose of accountability, and the 'innovators', who view open government as a way to foster partners in furthering its mission and its work.

Other public officials have been more blunt. A long-time UK official who served both in the legislature and as an appointed official once put it this way: 'Freedom of information is for oppositions. Open government is for governments', suggesting that open government policies geared toward gathering information and leveraging expertise – and toward releasing documents and data – are used most often to further the government's agenda rather than allow independent examination.

Ownership

In American-style democracies, citizens own the government and are responsible for its actions. In turn, records created in the course of business belong to the public, not an agency. This issue of ownership lies at the heart of many disputes over access and accountability. If the public owns its records, and the government is simply a custodian, then the government is obligated to share them unless it has a powerful and legal reason why it can't. Most officials turn this presumption upside down – they try to determine what they are obligated to release, not what they must keep secret. It reflects a natural bureaucratic anomaly: officials don't get fired or fined for keeping information secret, but are severely punished for releasing too much.

The confusion over ownership permeates every level of government. In September 2012, a Federal Communications Commission spokeswoman told me that records available on its website one-by-one in a difficult form 'are not available to the public' in any other way, even though it has an internal database of the documents and an index to them available to those inside the agency. My reaction was typical of most reporters: rather than FOIA the records and begin an extended negotiation, I took them off the website using a computer programme. A beat reporter would instead have appealed to regular sources. Many avoid FOIA at all costs, knowing the requests are often irrelevant by the time an agency addresses them.

Ownership is also at the heart of schemes to privatise public information. In the 1990s, a series of lawsuits from New York to California determined that Geographic Information Systems – among the most complex and expensive records to compile, but essential for the efficient operation of sewers, traffic lights, and property sales – had to be considered a public good, and could not be traded for exclusive access to the contractor that created them.

But these lines of ownership are being blurred again. Montgomery County, MD, struck an exclusive deal with a vendor that gave away the public's rights to crime incident databases. Challenge.gov, a clearinghouse for projects that might create an interesting or useful application for the public, sometimes allows preferred access to government records to its winners, effectively closing out others.

In each of these cases, the agencies have decided that employees, vendors, contractors, and grantees are the owners of the data. Once the public doesn't own the records, there are no guarantees that the information it needs to be self-governing will be available.

Purpose of disclosure

The Obama administration has articulated three objectives of trans-parency: accountability, collaborative government and participative decision-making. Add to that a less frequently mentioned objective: helping private organisations create businesses by creatively distributing records the government wants the public to have.

Weather records are perhaps the most obvious form of government information that meets all of the goals. The public has access to all of the forms that the government collects; by publicising the information, government gets to foster and tap hurricane experts and other specialists; companies make it available in engaging and useful ways; and the private sector takes some of the burden off government agencies to warn and prepare for potential disaster. Now the federal government and some local agencies are taking the weather analogy further, by giving away statistics on health indicators, snow plough locations, power outages, and similar records of use to residents and businesses.

The similarity among these records is that they represent information that government officials want the public to have. They include car seat and safety ratings, nutritional information, and statistics on obesity and heart disease. Sometimes selectively releasing information to researchers meets the agency's goals more efficiently. For years, the Department of Health and Human Services allowed researchers and consultants to buy a Medicare claims database for nearly $100,000 a year. They, in turn, used it to document aggregate problems in the system, notably spending patterns that couldn't be explained by the health of the seniors in certain regions nor the quality of care.

In 2011, the department released its storehouse of datasets to the public. Those datasets contained compiled data, not the original billing records needed to hold the programme accountable. It also launched contests for developers to use the data. One contestant created a game for kids to learn about health risks. Another built a website that let users compare health indicators across counties.

But when the *Wall Street Journal* and the Center for Public Integrity sued the agency for access to the billing records at a more affordable fee, they took a very different approach. In 'Secrets of the System', the *Journal* documented egregious examples of suspected fraud (Schoofs and Tamman, 2010). One doctor billed the federal government $1.2 million in one year for physical therapy, more than 24 times the typical doctor's income from the programme. Another had a tell-tale pattern of unusual treatments and soon had his privileges revoked. More recently, the Center has documented patterns in medical billing that have raised costs for taxpayers.

This example suggests that, while there may be good reasons for an open government initiative to publicise and improve government services and consumer information, it rarely advances accountability.

Original or useful?

In 2006, Congress directed the federal government to create a comprehensive database available to the public on contract and grant payments across virtually every agency. The Federal Funding Accountability and Transparency Act was a bipartisan bill sponsored by Sen. Barack Obama, an Illinois Democrat, and Sen. Tom Coburn, an Oklahoma Republican. That bill created usaspending.gov, which, at first glance, seems to document in excruciating detail all of the money the government has paid to private entities.

It might. But there's no reason it would. In fact, usaspending.gov furthered an arcane process of reporting transactions. Most agencies have two systems. One is real – employees order goods, award grants, process invoices, and otherwise manage their budgeted money. The errors are rare and caught by recipients who don't get paid or by auditors who have to balance the books each quarter. But this isn't what the public gets to see. Once they have finished their transactions, employees re-enter the information in a standardised form into the second system, which exists for the sole purpose of making it public. It has no effect on the agency or its operations. At worst, this process would hide fraud or overbilling. At best, it has no natural audit trail and no natural predators. Sunlight Labs, a Washington nonprofit organisation that advocates open government, has documented billions of dollars of mistakes in that public system (Sunlight Foundation, 2010).

A focus on easy-to-use and easy-to-update databases and data feeds may have turned the accountability function of transparency on its head. Instead of getting real records, investigators are stuck with data systems and compilations that are distantly derived from the original source. It should be easier to get the real records, the administrative artefacts, of everyday governing. If there are policy and public information campaigns, then let those agencies create them, even if they continue to outsource them to volunteers using carefully curated datasets that are designed to enhance the message.

Culture

As a reporter at the *Washington Post*, I had experience with three very different cultural attitudes to openness and the ownership, purpose and form of public records discussed here.

Virginia law lays out pages of specific documents that are unavailable to the public. But everything else is, in theory, available and local and state officials usually provide the documents within a week. Maryland is known as a more liberal state, but also one with a paternalistic streak ('Mommy Maryland' to some). Its public records law looks like it would allow for widespread access. But I only succeeded once or twice in actually obtaining records from the state because of its provision allowing officials to decide when it is in the public interest to do so.

Then there was the District of Columbia, which for many years seemed to keep no records, nor know where they would be held if they had. DC, in fact, may provide the most illustrative case of the clash between open government and accountability. A *Washington Post* editorial recaps the recent situation there: 'Two members of the D.C. Council have resigned in disgrace; a third's chief of staff was convicted of taking a bribe … a fourth reported suspected embezzlement from his campaign fund; and the mayor is believed to be under federal investigation' (*Washington Post*, 2012). The city's reaction was not to release records, but to complain that reporters and others were asking for too many. The mayor wanted to limit the kind and volume of records that could be requested.

But across town from the city council is the chief technology officer, who has a different take. In its much vaunted open government programme, the city allows residents to watch the progress of snow ploughs and monitor the status of the frequent power outages in the city, something that neighbouring Maryland has resisted as a security threat, claiming that snow plough drivers might be attacked if residents knew where they were working.

It is paradoxes like these that help make citizens more informed than ever and still in the dark about their governments.

References

Cohen, S. (2011) 'Ensuring Transparency and Accountability in the Digital Age', testimony before the Senate Judiciary Committee, 15 Mar.: www.judiciary.senate.gov/pdf/11-3-15%20Cohen%20Testimony.pdf.

Goldstein, J. (2012) 'Police Reports Suggest Officers May Sometimes Portray Crimes Less Seriously', *New York Times*, 16 Sept.: www.nytimes.com/2012/09/17/nyregion/misdemeanor-or-felony-new-scrutiny-of-how-police-reports-classify-crime-in-new-york-city.html.

Noveck, B. (2011) 'What's in a Name? Open Gov and Good Gov', *Huffington Post*, 7 Apr.: www.huffingtonpost.com/beth-simone-noveck/whats-in-a-name-open-gov-_b_845735.html.

Schoofs, M., and Tamman, M. (2010) 'Confidentiality Cloaks Medicare Abuse', *Wall Street Journal*, 22 Dec.: http://topics.wsj.com/subject/S/secrets-of-the-system/6281.

Sunlight Foundation (2010) 'New Analysis from Sunlight Identifies $1.3 Trillion in Broken Federal Spending Data', 8 Sept.: http://sunlightfoundation.com/press/releases/2010/09/08/new-analysis-sunlight-identifies-13-trillion-broke.

Washington Post (2012) 'The Public's Right to Know in D.C.', editorial, 30 June: www.washingtonpost.com/opinions/the-publics-right-to-know-in-dc/2012/06/30/gJQALLbTEW_story.html.

Welsh, B., and Smith, D. (2009) 'Highest Crime Rate in LA? No, just an LAPD Map Glitch', latimes.com, 5 Apr.: http://articles.latimes.com/2009/apr/05/local/me-geocoding-errors5.

7

Truth Vigilantes: On Journalism and Transparency

Philip Bennett

At 10:29 a.m. on 12 January 2012, Arthur S. Brisbane, the public editor of the *New York Times*, strolled casually into a minefield. Brisbane posted an online query asking readers whether the *Times* should be a 'truth vigilante', deputising reporters to 'challenge "facts" that are asserted by newsmakers they write about'. The question, Brisbane wrote, went to credibility: 'Is it possible to be objective and fair when the reporter is choosing to correct one fact over another?' (Brisbane, 2012a). Could reporters really be accountable for settling an endless caseload of boundary disputes between fact and fiction, dispensing frontier justice at internet speed?

Instantly, Brisbane's invitation raised an army of vigilantes, though not the kind he had had in mind. He was ridiculed on Twitter, mocked in comments on the *Times* site, and his question singled out by critics as damning evidence that the old, sacred oaths of journalism – 'to be objective and fair' – stood in the way of telling the truth. Wasn't the failure to challenge falsehoods and verify the facts a root cause of the mainstream media's galloping irrelevancy? If you couldn't count on reporters to sort truth from lies, and speak plainly about how they performed the operation, what was the point? Why even ask such a question?

By late that afternoon, Brisbane was in full retreat. In an updated post, he lamented that he had been misunderstood. He appended the response from one unhappy reader, who also happened to be the editor of the *Times*. 'Of course we should and we do' challenge news-makers on the facts, wrote Jill Abramson. 'The kind of rigorous fact-checking and truth-testing you describe is a fundamental part of our job as journalists' (Brisbane, 2012b).

The dust soon settled, but the arguments behind the skirmish are still sharp. Coverage of the 2012 elections was full of accounts of frustrated truth-testing on the campaign trail. The issue fuels blogs (and the posts of a new public editor at the *New York Times*). Despite being 'fundamental' to reporting, fact-checking in many papers remains curiously segregated in sidebars, a special category away from the main news. On 13 September 2012, for example, a *Times* news story let pass unchallenged the claim by Mitt Romney that President Obama has 'apologised' for US actions in the Middle East – one of the precise cases cited in Brisbane's original post.

Whether transparency and objectivity, or fairness and accountability, are conflicting, perhaps irreconcilable, values are questions that strike at the core of journalism. Digital tools and culture have introduced new ways of uncovering facts and cornering the truth – and for concocting and spreading untruths with intoxicating success. Journalism's mission to hold the powerful to account is in strong demand. But the exercise is also more difficult and fraught with novel complications. Calls for accountability are as much aimed at journalists as coming from them.

This chapter examines some of the ways journalism has dealt with these questions. How have news organisations used digital tools to advance transparency, both internally and in reporting on complex subjects? How might greater transparency change the culture and practice of reporting? What are its limits? Should journalists consider transparency a means or an end? How does it figure among the complex qualities, values, and methods that lead us closer to the truth?

There are a growing number of examples of news organisations using technology to make internal editorial practices and published journalism more accessible to the public. The trend is part of a broad discussion across society about transparency, privacy, and accountability provoked by the revolution in communications and information technologies. News organisations have not led this discussion; so far, journalism has been mostly a subject rather than a source of innovation. But few fields are as directly affected or more important for shaping whether the trends strengthen or weaken democracy.

The one-way mirror

Journalists have had an awkward relationship with transparency and disclosure. They promote and demand it from others. Transparency is cited as a cardinal virtue in credos like Tom Rosenstiel and Bill Kovach's (2007) *Elements of Journalism*: 'Journalists should be as transparent as possible about sources and methods so audiences can make their own assessment of the information.' But in practice reporters and editors have been wary of applying openness too openly to newsgathering or decisions inside newsrooms.

The ambivalence has several sources. Journalists depend for survival on information flowing in their direction. But the success that comes with 'owning a story' gives reporters few incentives to open their notebooks for colleagues, interest groups, or the general public. Traditionally, reserve has been prized as a competitive advantage. Newsrooms are collegial and diverse societies; but they are also hierarchical, where time and production pressures and the potential chaos of many competing points of view invest an editor with benign authoritarian powers to cut off debate and move on.

In some cases, insularity has seemed, oddly perhaps, a virtue – a bulwark helping to ensure the freedom and independence of the press. The struggle over information is often an asymmetrical contest. Government and corporations have ways of controlling information that are stronger and more varied than the tools available to a reporter. Journalists level the field with sources who must not simply be managed but protected, including with guarantees of anonymity. That journalists go to jail rather than name anonymous sources defends a higher principle than transparency. For a generation of editors, stating 'We stand by our story' to deflect criticism did not seem a dodge. It was seen inside newsrooms (and by supportive readers) as courage in the face of powerful interests.

Complaints about a lack of newsroom transparency surfaced even before the word came into fashion. In 1947, the Hutchins Commission, a blue-chip panel convened by Henry Luce to examine the state of press freedoms, found that, 'One of the most effective ways of improving the press is blocked by the press itself. By a kind of unwritten law the press ignores the errors and misrepresentations, the lies and scandals, of which its members are guilty.' Its report concluded: 'If the press is to be accountable – and it must be if it is to remain free – its members must discipline one another by the only means they have available, namely, public criticism' (Commission on Freedom of the Press, 1947).

Such arguments would lead to the first newspaper ombudsmen in the late 1960s. Representing readers, these in-house critics drew back the curtain on editorial practices, especially on scandal. The *Washington*

Post ombudsman wrote an 18,000-word exposé telling readers how Janet Cooke had fabricated stories that won the paper the Pulitzer Prize in 1981. A similar scandal involving Jayson Blair led the *New York Times* to hire its first public editor. More recent occupants have had some of the busiest beats in the business, investigating everything from coverage of weapons of mass destruction and domestic spying to controversies over staffing or money-for-influence 'salons'.

The internet made anyone a potential ombudsman. Media criticism flourished across the web, often gossipy, partisan, or superficial but roughly organised under a banner of accountability. Readers also had new means for communicating directly with reporters and editors, and vice versa. And for the first time, news organisations brought committed advocates of a new kind of transparency inside the perimeter: digital journalists who saw the greatest impact of openness not in self-criticism, but in changing reporting methods, revealing facts behind the stories, and reinventing publishing models.

Derek Willis, a database editor at washingtonpost.com and now a web developer at the *New York Times*, called for sweeping changes in a 2005 series of blog posts called 'Fixing Journalism':

> *Journalism's chief problem is not bias or its delivery method, although both deserve scrutiny. Journalism suffers from an inability to recognize the shifts in ownership of information and from an astonishingly weak response to the changes that have taken place in the way information is gathered and disseminated ... We haven't realized that some fundamental changes – nearly all driven by the Internet and the new ways of organizing information – have taken place in our profession.*

Manifestos from digital insurgents found a cool reception at first in many newsrooms. It was hard to accept that the same technology that was demolishing journalism businesses would also build better journalism (and for tens of thousands of journalists about to lose their jobs, it was too late already). But the new ideas, language, and practices were at heart consistent with journalism's most noble aims. Today, every serious approach to solving journalism's problems involves some kind of openness: wider collaboration, deeper engagement with outsiders, a reworking of how stories are assigned, reported, and written, recorded, filmed, or photographed – how and when they are published and then kept alive. Today, an editor called to defend controversial reporting is unlikely to get away with a simple, 'We stand by our story', and more likely to answer, 'We'll show you our work.'

Watching the breathtaking advance of internet culture can seem like witnessing a race between forces of darkness and enlightenment. The spread of what Larry Diamond has called 'Technologies of Liberation' has connected citizens with each other and with more information, distributed more widely, than ever before. At the same time, we have seen the same technologies strengthen the state, concentrate power, and raise barriers to scrutiny.

For journalism, the internet provides new ways of discovering stories, identifying sources, verifying facts, sorting data, creating maps and graphics, cultivating diverse voices and opinions, and for publishing. It is also an unmatched transmission route for rumours, half-truths, unverified facts, and propaganda – a fog-belching factory of 'truthiness' (Berkman Center, 2012). The internet can reward biased reporting, hair-trigger publication, and superficiality and mask personal, commercial, or ideological agendas. It is an enabler of anonymity, by definition unaccountable. Those who speak of a 'post-truth' era describe how a lie – Obama's 'death panels', the South Carolina governor's imminent indictment – can go viral while journalists and others grope for the antidote.

Although quite different from each other, the rise of WikiLeaks and the British phone-hacking scandal – two of the biggest press stories of the internet age – both revealed disturbing questions about technology, power, and the news media.

The public has responded to the upheaval in news and information by further devaluing the stock they put in journalism. In a survey released in September 2011, the Pew Research Center found the credibility of the press at the lowest point since its first poll on the question in 1985: 66% of respondents said stories are often inaccurate, 77% said news organisations tend to favour one side, and 80% said news organisations are swayed by powerful people and institutions (Pew Research Center, 2011). Alarmingly, the public was evenly split (at 42%) on whether journalism as it is practised today protects or hurts democracy. In the mid-1980s, twice as many people said news organisations protected democracy as said the press hurt democracy.

Some critics say the loss of credibility is due to news organisations that cling to objectivity, a false religion that has lost its power to deceive. 'To borrow a phrase, every editor who is not too stupid or too full of himself to notice what is going on knows that propagating the myth of "objective journalism" is indefensible,' Conor Friedersdorf blogged in the *Atlantic* (Friedersdorf, 2011). In its place, journalists should state their biases up front and let readers and viewers decide what to believe. Media critic Jay Rosen argues (2010) that journalists should abandon the pretence of 'The View from Nowhere', a neutral voice of disinterest. According to his view, they should disclose not just conflicts of interest they might have in a story, but *any* relevant interests arising from their experience, background, or identity.

This is not a new bleat. Four decades ago Tom Wolfe spread the gospel of 'New Journalism' in strikingly familiar language: 'All the old traditions are exhausted, and no new one is yet established. All bets are off! The odds are cancelled! It's anybody's ball game!' (Wolfe, 1973). It's impossible to know if trust in journalism has suffered because the internet eroded the profession's authority and standards, or simply exposed them as hollow and too slow to adapt. Will trust be restored if political reporters disclose how they vote – or reporters on crime, health, and financial beats disclose if they have ever been mugged, hospitalised, or in love with a Marxist? Some simplistic solutions may make the problem worse, or just seem silly.

What is clear, as Rosen and others have sensibly and repeatedly pointed out, is that the ground has shifted. While internal checks on information have decreased (as with the decline of the copy desk), external checks have proliferated. From a scarcity of sources of verification there is now an oversupply. The deeper and faster these trends become, effective tools for vetting, assessing, and deciding what to believe become more valuable.

David Weinberger, a Harvard researcher and technologist, came up with an equation to describe this process: 'transparency is the new objectivity.' He wrote (2009):

> *Transparency – the embedded ability to see through the published draft – often gives us more reason to believe a report than the claim of objectivity did. In fact, transparency subsumes objectivity. Anyone who claims objectivity should be willing to back that assertion up by letting us look at sources, disagreements, and the personal assumptions and values supposedly bracketed out of the report.*

Applying this maxim to newsrooms is still a tense exercise. But momentum is on the side of openness, which now seems a key to survival, to recognising things as they are. In 2012, *Guardian* editor Alan Rusbridger described 'open journalism' as 'journalism [that] is fully knitted into the web of information that exists in the world today'. The *Guardian*'s ten principles of open journalism seem more grounded in how audiences consume news than how journalists generate accountability reporting (the role is not mentioned). But journalism itself is ripe for audit: 'It is transparent and open to challenge – including correction, clarification and addition' (Rusbridger, 2012). The *Guardian* is a pioneer in promoting openness from the inside out. But its message is heard widely, and shared in US newsrooms. Act now, it says, or lose your chance.

Open government and open journalism

On his first full day as president, Barack Obama announced the goal of creating 'an unprecedented level of openness in Government'. The Memorandum on Transparency and Open Government he signed on 21 January 2009 said the effort would be based on three principles: transparency, participation, and collaboration, noting that 'Transparency promotes accountability and provides information to citizens about what their Government is doing' (White House, 2009).

Building an open government is among the most ambitious initiatives of the Obama administration. Four months into his presidency, Obama used a speech at the National Archives to cite transparency as a core principle in his approach to national security and the rule of law: 'I believe in every fiber of my being that in the long run we ... cannot keep this country safe unless we enlist the power of our most fundamental values.' Under the Bush administration, he said, 'we went off course' (Obama, 2009).

Obama launched a broad review of information and secrecy policies. He directed the attorney general to reverse an order by his predecessor that gave wide discretion to deny freedom of information requests. The administration digitised public records, pledged to strengthen legal protections for whistle-blowers, put new controls on the classification machinery that makes secrets, and speed the declassification system that unmakes them. In its first three years, a new government website, data.gov, published 450,000 datasets of public records (data.gov, 2012).

The news media did not merit a mention in Obama's post-inauguration memo. The same was true more than two years later, when the administration released the Open Government National Action Plan.

The plan called for officials to conduct an open door policy with 'diverse members of the public', but not specifically with reporters assigned to cover them (White House, 2011). The thrust of the plan, and the many sets of rules and instructions published before and since, gave the impression that open government would provide the public with direct access to the workings of government, cutting out the middleman.

At least that's how it seemed to many journalists, including press organisations that were surprised to find their advice was unwelcome (Brainard and Russell, 2012). Journalists give the administration mixed grades on transparency. They praise Obama's goals, but say the results fall short and that a different spirit prevails in the agencies. Across the government, access to officials, if granted at all, requires official permissions, the presence of a minder in interviews, routine insistence on anonymity. Advocacy and journalism groups say it was symbolic of the White House's ambivalence that when they gave Obama an award for his support of transparency, the Oval Office ceremony was held behind closed doors and kept off the presidential schedule (Phillip, 2011).

The administration has heralded what it calls 'smart disclosure', the publication of information that can help citizens make better decisions about nutrition, fuel economy, and health. Officials have been less aggressive, or accommodating, in areas that would lead more directly to accountability reporting (White House, 2012).

Reporters covering health, science, and environment – designated as priorities for transparency by the administration – complain especially about lack of access to scientists and researchers responsible for collecting and analysing government data. In a poll on openness by the Columbia Journalism Review and ProPublica, reporters in these areas ranked the Obama administration ahead of the Bush administration, which had been criticised for politicising science. But a third of those responding to the survey rated Obama 'poor' or 'very poor' on transparency (Brainard, 2011).

Holding the administration accountable for its transparency policies can be difficult because, according to advocacy groups, it doesn't release enough information to judge. 'Measuring what it is we actually know about the openness of the American government is not a straight-forward endeavor,' reported a coalition of transparency groups in September 2012. 'Low quality data hinders efforts to monitor the government's compliance with laws, policies and regulations' (OpenTheGovernment, 2012).

For example, the government reported a decline in 2011 in the number of 'original classification decisions', the root designation of newly minted secrets. Yet out of a total of 127,000 classification decisions, only four were reported as having come from the Central Intelligence Agency (OpenTheGovernment, 2012).

The processing of FOIA requests, the most important tool for prying documents from the government, has had a mixed record. In March 2011 the Department of Justice launched foia.gov to track performance. The administration created the Office of Government Information Services within the National Archives to mediate disputes over FOIA requests. But the system continues to labour under a growing backlog, long waits, and rising costs, especially burdensome to individual journalists or small news organisations. The government reported 644,165 new FOIA requests in 2011. It said it released 236,474 documents in full and denied 30,369. The backlog was 83,490. Among the denials were 4,244 requests turned down for national security reasons, an almost 20% increase over 2010 (Lardner and Bridis, 2012).

Transparency on national security has opened a gap between the administration's lofty aims and reality. Obama's Executive Order 13526, revising the Bush era classification guidelines, says: 'If there is significant doubt about the need to classify information, it shall not be classified.' According to the government, fewer overall secrets are being created, and 50 million pages of older secret documents have been processed for declassification over the last two years (with 80% of those released to the public). But that falls far short of Obama's goal of eliminating the declassification backlog of 370 million pages by the end of next year (Aftergood, 2012).

Secrecy watchdogs praise the Obama administration for several milestones: for the first time, the government released total figures for the nation's intelligence budgets and the number of workers inside and outside government with security clearances. Early in his administration Obama released memos from the Bush administration providing legal justification for the administration's detention and interrogation policies.

However, the administration has refused to release documents about its own legal justifications for targeted killings of US citizens overseas. And it has aggressively prosecuted unauthorised leaks of classified information to the press, charging more leakers under the Espionage Act than all previous administrations combined. After condemning the Bush administration's heavy reliance on the state secrets privilege – which allows the government to seek dismissal of court cases on the basis of national security, often without showing evidence – the Obama administration has invoked it in at least eight cases, a blow to transparency and accountability (OpenTheGovernment, 2012).

What are the overall effects of transparency policies on accountability journalism? For some reporters, additional guidelines and rules about disclosure, even under the banner of enhanced transparency, actually exclude them further from the flow of information. They make it more difficult to develop reliable sources willing to speak openly about controversial subjects. Washington seems more dependent than ever on 'access journalism', in which reporters are granted audiences with officials in exchange for anonymity, limits on the field of questioning or other transactions (such as quote approval) that are often hidden from the readers and viewers. Like orchestrated leaking of secrets, these practices are aimed at putting sources in control of a story.

However, the administration's initiatives have given transparency new visibility, and helped raise its profile within newsrooms. There is new competition between the government and news media over credible, clear, and honest disclosure. And there is a new genre of accountability reporting: on transparency. Journalists and a rich array of nonprofit and academic organisations now routinely assess the administration's policies against its promises. Finally, access to large public datasets and strong demand for innovative reporting methods and storytelling forms have given digital journalists opportunities to experiment and growing influence in newsrooms. Data that would not have fit into a newspaper or on television broadcast is living naturally on the web, inspiring new applications, and becoming a promising field for accountability journalism.

New accountability

When the anti-secrecy group WikiLeaks shared hundreds of thousands of classified US military reports and diplomatic cables with several news organisations in 2010, it was a moment of truth not only in the contentious history of publishing national security secrets, but in the relationship between print journalists and in-house digital teams. The technical challenge of making sense of an enormous cache of cables, first for reporting and then for publication, was complicated by sensitive editorial decisions with very high stakes for the newsrooms involved, and the public.

The WikiLeaks story was widely regarded as a watershed in an era of radical, global transparency, in which technology had trumped censors and government control through a system that made possible verifiable anonymous leaks. The legacy turned out to be more complicated. Several news organisations such as Al Jazeera and the *Wall Street Journal* built encrypted, anonymous drop-boxes for leakers. But they have attracted little business, and included vexing legal loopholes. The *New York Times* investigated building an 'EZ Pass for leakers' but has since put the project on the shelf.

But as a model of collaboration between digital and print operations, especially at the *New York Times* and *Guardian*, the WikiLeaks episode marked a maturing of the partnership between hacks and hackers. This partnership is behind the emerging field of computational journalism. It is producing a new model for investigative journalism projects, and was a prominent feature of coverage of the 2012 presidential campaigns.

ProPublica, the nonprofit investigative news organisation founded in 2007, has produced good examples of how to apply principles and tools of transparency to journalism in the public interest. ProPublica has mined government and corporate data, in some cases combined with contributions from the public, to build interactive graphics that track the government's bailout payments and map the $2.5 billion in foreclosure payouts from banks. Its 'Recovery Tracker' is the most comprehensive and accessible analysis of more than a trillion dollars of government stimulus spending (LaFleur, Kokenge, and Nguyen, 2012).

Scott Klein, the editor of news applications at ProPublica, credits open government policies for helping make such enterprising projects possible. 'The attitude for open data has been very useful for many journalists. People [in government] who would have blanched or been shocked by a request five or six years ago for a big data set from journalists' now recognise a new 'zeitgeist'.[1]

But ProPublica does more than build informational graphics and data visualisation. Their ambition is to put databases at the service of storytelling, including readers' own stories. In 'Dollars for Docs', readers can investigate whether their doctors received hidden payments from pharmaceutical companies. In 'Opportunity Gap', ProPublica has combined databases to compare poverty rates in thousands of schools with the availability of advanced academic courses, and readers can search for individual schools (LaFleur et al., 2013).

These are not just wonky sidebars. 'Dollars for Docs' is the most visited page since the launch of ProPublica's website, with almost 5 million page views.[2] These are applications that lead to discoveries and can yield

113

original stories. And they are evergreen, valuable, and relevant for as long as ProPublica choses to maintain them. Projects like these are redefining the lifespan of a story.

ProPublica has embraced transparency as a mission and as a beat. Like the *New York Times*, ProPublica makes its news applications open source and publishes under creative commons. It invites others to 'steal our stories'. And in coverage, it is an unapologetic advocate of journalism transparency. In a project called 'Free the Files', ProPublica revealed lobbying efforts by some of the country's biggest media companies against rules that would require them to post political ad information online, disclosing who bought the ads, how much they paid, and when they ran. The companies lost, and in August the Federal Communications Commission launched a website listing transactions (Elliott, 2012).

To make its own stories more transparent, ProPublica previewed an application that allows readers to see the source for a fact or assertion in a story. When an 'Explore Sources' button is turned on, words in phrases in the text are highlighted in yellow. Clicking on a highlight calls up an annotation from the source document. In a story posted in late 2011, reporter Marshall Allen made more than 500 annotations in 64 documents he uploaded to DocumentCloud (Shaw, 2011).

Some news organisations have for some time presented source materials online, but new digital tools are making them easier to search and understand. The PBS documentary series FRONTLINE published dozens of searchable long-form video and text interviews conducted for its two-hour presidential election film, *The Choice 2012*, which aired in October 2012 (PBS, 2012). Producers and editors at FRONTLINE believe that television is on the verge of a transformation on the scale of the one occurring in newspapers. The advent of internet television and the popularity of tablet computers have opened a wide space for television news and documentary film to create forms of transparency and interaction.

Perhaps the most important success story of collaboration around transparency in reporting is DocumentCloud, the online database for annotating, organising, and sharing documents on the web. The project was developed by the *New York Times* and ProPublica in 2009, with a $719,500 grant from the Knight News Challenge. Today it is used in more than 600 organisations. Reporters and others have uploaded more than 300,000 documents.

DocumentCloud's contribution to transparency has been both internal and external. It has boosted internal sharing inside newsrooms.

Reporters at the *Los Angeles Times*, for example, used the application to organise and share boxes of documents that revealed millions of dollars of corruption and cronyism in the city of Bell, California.

Journalists can still manage DocumentCloud as a private network. But since January 2011, it has been open to public searches. Today, about 200,000 of the 300,000 documents that have been uploaded are available to the public (Knight Foundation). What began as a method for reporters to organise their work is now also a way for them to show their work.

The 2012 election has highlighted two growing and competitive areas of accountability journalism linked to transparency: campaign finance reporting and fact-checking of political speech. Since the 2008 presidential election, the opening of dozens of fact-checking operations has made it a brand of political reporting. Some are based in universities or run by partisan groups, but journalists staff the most prominent, such as PolitiFact, FactCheck, and the *Washington Post* Fact Checker column. 'By almost any measure the 2012 presidential race is shaping up to be the most fact-checked electoral contest in American history', according to a report from the New America Foundation (Graves and Glaisyer, 2012).

It was possible, for example, to watch President Obama's acceptance speech at the National Democratic Convention on nytimes.com next to a scrolling transcript, annotated and fact-checked by *Times* reporters. This was once a practice reserved for the State of the Union address that has now become common. The PolitiFact website is an alternative narrative of the campaign, so revealing in the scale of its corrections that it is hard to imagine an electoral cycle without it.

Fact-checking operations aim not just at correcting the record or holding politicians accountable. They also hold journalists accountable when they repeat unchallenged claims that deeper reporting has found to be false.

Still, databases of verified facts are not in wide use by journalists, and fact-checking remains a specialised genre within journalism. Fact-checking software is under development, although often what reporters check are interpretations of facts, not easily answered as true or false. An MIT researcher is developing 'Truth Goggles', a feature similar to ProPublica's 'Explore Sources', in which readers can highlight and verify facts and phrases by checking them against 5,000 items in the PolitiFact.org database (Nieman Lab, 2012).

Journalists and developers have been busy trying to pry open the black box of US campaign financing. The *New York Times*'s Campaign

API allows users to retrieve data from Federal Election Commission filings faster than was previously possible, within minutes. ProPublica's PAC Track traces spending and fund-raising by Super PACs, groups that can make unlimited expenditures during the campaigns as long as they don't coordinate with candidates. SuperPacApp, created by Glassy Media in partnership with *Newsweek/Daily Beast*, lets voters learn the source of an ad simply by holding up their telephone to the television or radio, and capturing the audio fingerprint.[3]

Reporters at several outlets have done aggressive, thorough reporting, but the campaign finance system has anti-transparency defences. 'Social welfare organizations', called 501(c)4s for their nonprofit tax status, dwarf Super PACs, and are not required to disclose the identity of donors. ProPublica reported that two such groups, Crossroads GPS and Americans for Prosperity, both supporting Republicans, had already spent $60 million in the presidential race, more than all the Super PACs combined (Barker, 2012).

Using social media to create more transparency in reporting and storytelling while ensuring accuracy is still a challenge. But digital tools are helping build narratives that blend disparate sources to reflect unfolding events with urgency, vitality and drama. During the Arab Spring, Andy Carvin, a digital strategist at NPR, used Twitter, Facebook, and YouTube and other eyewitness accounts to build what the *Washington Post* (2011) called 'a vivid and constantly evolving mosaic of the region's convulsions'. *Columbia Journalism Review* asked, 'Is this the world's best Twitter account?' (Silverman, 2011).

These interactive, linked narratives bring immediacy and breadth of experience to current events. They bear the imperfections of social media, including hard-to-verify accounts (and as Carvin documented, full-blown hoaxes). But Carvin showed that verification could take place among trusted sources. There is an appealing and valuable authenticity in the many voices that tell these stories. As Jigar Metha, a former *New York Times* video journalist whose website 18 Days In Egypt used amateur video to create a living, interactive archive of the events, explained, 'We want to use the same tools to tell the story as the story was told to us'.[4]

For Scott Klein, the next step is to produce text stories that are themselves comprised of structured data: 'That's the great beyond'.[5] The same might be said of video and audio that could be searched, shared, personalised, and compared. Matt Waite, the developer of Politifact, has written that the failure to bring experimentation into the heart of journalism's content management systems has slowed and segregated innovation into stand-alone apps. 'All this talk about a digital future, about moving journalism onto the web, about innovation and saving journalism is just talk until developers are allowed to hack at the very core of the whole product,' he wrote. 'To argue otherwise is to argue that the story form, largely unchanged from print, is perfect and to change it is unnecessary. Hogwash' (Nieman Lab, 2011). This is one possible horizon. A fully transparent, living story would introduce journalism in a potent new language.

Caveats and conclusions

Technology did not cause journalism's problems – and it won't rescue it either. Digital tools can make transparency more difficult. Government transparency policies can have the consequence of placing greater control of information in official hands. Important records remain beyond the reach of journalists.

The two biggest news stories of the twenty-first century so far are not encouraging models of transparency in modern life, or journalism. The aftermaths of the attacks of 11 September 2001 and the financial meltdown in the autumn of 2007 have shown the power of secrecy, of dark markets, of the ability to keep world-changing decisions and events invisible to the public for years. It is perhaps not a coincidence that the last decade has been marked by spectacular failures of journalism to peer into the dark, during the run-up to the war in Iraq and (more ambiguously) before the collapse of the financial bubble.

Even when data are available, there are risks of misinterpretation, manipulation, overconfidence, or bias. Information overload can be as harmful to democracy as a lack of information. According to the statistician Nate Silver, 'The numbers have no way of speaking for themselves. We speak for them. We imbue them with meaning ... we may construe them in self-serving ways that are detached from their objective reality.' How to establish best practices for turning data into useful news and information is one of the most important questions facing journalism. As Silver writes, 'Before we demand more of our data, we need to demand more of ourselves' (2012: 9).

We can draw lessons from successes. Dana Priest and Bill Arkin's (2010) meticulous mapping of 'Top Secret America' for the *Washington*

Post demonstrated the virtue of combining a robust database, obtained through open sources, and a veteran reporter. Bloomberg's dogged reporting revealed a secret financial aid programme from the Federal Reserve Bank that made available $7.7 trillion to banks. That scoop, confirmed by documents obtained through FOIA, helped rewrite the history of the financial crisis (Ivry et al., 2011).

Often overlooked in the debate around digital media are the many readers and viewers who do not have access to broadband internet. News organisations that abandon these audiences dilute their public service. A report by Harvard's Berkman Center noted in 2008:

> *The potential to use new technologies to improve on traditional inequalities is not being fully realized, which has consequences not only for the media consumption of marginalized communities, but also for their representation in the broader public sphere. As journalists increasingly rely on online sources, populations or ideas that are absent from the online space may as well be invisible.*

This remains true today. As news organisations have supported literacy, they should campaign to see that audiences are given equal access to the democratising and enriching qualities of reliable and accurate news and information. Such a goal is consistent with a commitment to openness.

Transparency is a powerful tool for accountability, and for service. It should be applied systematically by journalists and to journalism. It should not be seen as a luxury or elective. It should be woven into the fabric of reporting, storytelling, and publishing.

Transparency is a complement to, not a substitute for, getting things right. It is not the whole story, but it allows the public to see the whole story. The most important challenges for journalism in the digital age are to restore its credibility and authority through accurate reporting of the facts, to make that reporting available to wider and diverse audiences, and to earn back the public's trust that it is engaged in an honest search for the truth.

Notes

1   Interview with the author, 11 Sept. 2012.
2   Interview with the author, 11 Sept. 2012.
3   www.superpacapp.org.
4   Interview with the author, 2010.
5   Interview with the author, 11 Sept. 2012.

References

Aftergood, S. (2012) 'Declassification Advances, But Will Miss Goal', Secrecy blog, Federation of American Scientists, 20 July: www.fas.org/blog/secrecy/2012/07/miss_goal.html.

Barker, K. (2012) 'How Nonprofits Spend Millions on Elections and Call it Public Welfare', ProPublica, 19 Aug.

Berkman Center (2008) *News and Information as Digital Media Come of Age*, Dec. (Center for Internet and Society at Harvard University).

Berkman Center (2012) *Truthiness in Digital Media*, symposium, 6–7 Mar.: http://blogs.law.harvard.edu/truthiness.

Brainard, C. (2011) 'Transparency Watch: A Closed Door' *Columbia Journalism Review* (Sept./Oct.).

Brainard, C., and Russell, C. (2012) *Transparency Wars* (Reporters Committee for Freedom of the Press).

Brisbane, A. S. (2012a) 'Should The Times Be a Truth Vigilante?', *New York Times*, 12 Jan.

Brisbane, A. S. (2012b) 'Update to my Previous Post on Truth Vigilantes', *New York Times*, 12 Jan.

Commission on Freedom of the Press (1947) *A Free And Responsible Press: A General Report on Mass Communication* (University of Chicago Press).

data.gov (2012) 'Data.gov Celebrates Third Anniversary': www.data.gov/whats-new.

Elliott, J. (2012) 'Meet the Media Companies Lobbying Against Transparency', *ProPublica*, 20 Apr.

Friedersdorf, C. (2011) 'Stop Forcing Journalists to Conceal their Views from the Public', *Atlantic,* 30 Oct.

Graves, L., and Glaisyer, T. (2012) *The Fact-Checking Universe in Spring 2012* (New America Foundation).

Ivry, B., Keoun, B., and Kuntz, P. (2011) 'Secret Fed Loans Gave Banks $13 Billion Undisclosed to Congress', *Bloomberg News*, 27 Nov.

Knight Foundation (2012) *Experiments in Media Innovation: A Look at the 2009 Knight News Challenge Winners*, Aug. (Knight Foundation).

LaFleur, J., Kokenge, J., and Nguyen, D. (2012) 'Recovery Tracker: How Much Stimulus Funding is Going to Your County?' ProPublica, 1 Oct.: http://projects.propublica.org/recovery.

LaFleur, J., Shaw, A., Coutts, S., and Larson, J. (2013) 'The Opportunity Gap: Is Your State Providing Equal Access to Education?' ProPublica, 24 Jan.: http://projects.propublica.org/schools.

Lardner, R., and Bridis, T. (2012) 'Government Can't Keep up with Information Requests', Associated Press, 11 Mar.

Nieman Lab (2011) 'Matt Waite: To Build a Digital Future for News, Developers Must Be Able to Hack at the Core of Old Systems', 8 Mar.: www.niemanlab.org/2011/03/matt-waite-to-build-a-digital-future-for-news-developers-have-to-be-able-to-hack-at-the-core-of-the-old-ways.

Nieman Lab (2012) 'How to Peek through Dan Schultz's Truth Goggles, the B.S. Detection Software, Right Now', 14 May: www.niemanlab.org/2012/05/how-to-peek-through-dan-schultzs-truth-goggles-the-b-s-detection-software-right-now.

Obama, B. (2009) 'Protecting our Security and our Values', 21 May, speech at the National Archives Museum, Washington, DC.

OpenTheGovernment (2012) '2012 Secrecy Report: Indicators of Secrecy in the Federal Government', 13 Sept. (OpenTheGovernment).

PBS (2012) 'New Full-Length Trailer: "The Choice 2012"', 18 Sept.: www.pbs.org/wgbh/pages/frontline/government-elections-politics/choice-2012/new-full-length-trailer-the-choice-2012.

Pew Research Center for the People and the Press (2011) *Views of the News Media: 1985–2011*, 22 Sept. (Pew Research Center).

Phillip, A. (2011) 'Not a Secret Any More', 31 Mar.: www.politico.com/politico44/perm/0311/not_a_secret_anymore_a00ccd98-0d9e-4822-8936-168f3a51b959.html.

Priest, D., and Arkin, B. (2010) 'Top Secret America', *Washington Post*: http://projects.washingtonpost.com/top-secret-america.

Rosen, J. (2010) 'The View from Nowhere Questions and Answers', 10 Nov.: http://pressthink.org/2010/11/the-view-from-nowhere-questions-and-answers.

Rosenstiel, T., and Kovach, B. (2007) *Elements of Journalism* (Three Rivers Press): www.journalism.org/resources/principles.

Rusbridger, A. (2012) 'Q & A with Alan Rusbridger: The Future of Open Journalism', *Guardian,* 25 Mar.

Shaw, A. (2011) 'Explore Sources: A New Feature to "Show Our Work"', ProPublica, 15 Dec.: www.propublica.org/nerds/item/explore-sources-a-new-feature-to-show-our-work.

Silver, N. (2012) *The Signal and the Noise* (Penguin).

Silverman, C. (2011) 'Is This the World's Best Twitter Account?', *Columbia Journalism Review,* 8 Apr.: www.cjr.org/behind_the_news/is_this_the_worlds_best_twitter_account.php.

Washington Post (2011) 'NPR's Andy Carvin, Tweeting the Middle East', 13 Apr.: www.washingtonpost.com/lifestyle/style/npr-andy-carvin-tweeting-the-middle-east/2011/04/06/AFcSdhSD_story.html.

Weinberger, D. (2009) 'Transparency is the New Objectivity', 19 July: www.hyperorg.com/blogger/2009/07/19/transparency-is-the-new-objectivity.

White House (2009) 'Memorandum on Transparency and Open Government', 21 Jan. (White House).

White House (2011) 'The Open Government Partnership: National Action Plan for the United States of America', 20 Sept. (White House).

White House (2012) 'Informing Consumers through Smart Disclosure', 30 Mar.: www.whitehouse.gov/blog/2012/03/30/informing-consumers-through-smart-disclosure.

Willis, D. (2005) 'The Collaboration Issue', 29 Apr.: http://blog.thescoop.org/thefix/the-collaboration-issue.

Wolfe, T. (1973) *The New Journalism* (Harper & Row).

8

Data and Transparency: Perils and Progress

Jennifer LaFleur

Data analysis is a powerful tool. For journalists, it takes us beyond reporting anecdotal tales to actually analysing the entire population. It is often these stories, based on independent analysis, that make the biggest difference, prompting important changes. That happened when a team of reporters from the nonprofit newsroom California Watch used multiple databases to show that state regulators 'routinely failed to enforce California's landmark earthquake safety law for public schools.'[1] As a result, California lawmakers ordered audits and investigations and the State Allocation Board made it easier for schools to get funding for seismic repairs.

The investigative team at KHOU-TV in Houston analysed water test data acquired under open records laws and found that homes throughout Texas had radiation in their tap water. As a result, multiple radioactive wells in Houston and around Texas were shut down. The EPA, 'which had previously claimed to KHOU that radiological risk from uranium in drinking water was "insignificant", reversed itself', the station reported (khou.com, 2011). And the EPA launched a study of uranium in drinking water.

Los Angeles Times reporters used local salary data, tax data, and other information to reveal corruption in the California community of Bell.[2] The stories resulted in criminal charges against eight city officials, millions of dollars in refunds to taxpayers and improved access to government salary information in California.

Reporters at the *Las Vegas Sun* (2010) showed how preventable infections and injuries were occurring at Las Vegas hospitals and made data about those hospitals available to consumers – information that hospitals tried to keep hidden.

Stories such as these, which are time- and resource-intensive, have become increasingly difficult as newsrooms have downsized. Often the most difficult task is negotiating for records and data. Many newsrooms have less time to spend negotiating for information and little money to wage lawsuits to gain access to information. There are fewer journalists in watchdog roles. Bureaus in Washington, DC, have emptied, as have statehouse bureaus around the country. *American Journalism Review* (2009) found a 30% decrease in the number of statehouse reporters across the country from 2003 to 2009.

Even before the shrinking of newsrooms, acquiring government data was challenging. Whether at the federal, state, or local level, several barriers cropped up again and again, and still do: prohibitive fees for processing information, privacy regulations, privatisation of government tasks, technical difficulties, and laws that don't always provide for access to computerised information.

Fees

In some places, records requesters continue to face per-record charges for databases amounting to thousands of dollars for a single database. When *The Dallas Morning News* sought criminal incident data from the Dallas police department (clearly a public database under the Public Information Act), the estimated cost exceeded $40,000 (see Figure 8.1).

Your request for information pursuant to the Public Information Act has been received by this department, and was forwarded to the appropriate unit. The respective unit has determined that the cost of reproducing the requested materials will be approximately $42,744.00. Below is an itemized list of the estimated cost.

Quantity	Item	Cost	Extended Cost
1,200	Programming Time	$35.62	$42,744.00

Overhead Charge	$0.00	Estimated Total	$42,744.00

Figure 8.1 Dallas police department fees for criminal incident data

After months of negotiating – an unnecessary process that consumed city resources – the newspaper obtained the data for a few hundred dollars, the actual cost to process the request. We were lucky. The Texas Public Information Act is specific when it comes to records charges. In some states, the only recourse a requester has is to file a lawsuit.

When reporters at *The Modesto Bee* tried to get electronic mapping files of voting precincts, the county elections office refused, offering paper or PDF files instead. The officials claimed that, because it took county workers many hours to create the files, the data should be protected work product. Unfortunately for them, California law covers this assertion only if the government workers had created the programming language. In this case, the county used commercial mapping software. The reporters ended up getting the mapping files, but too late to do the story for which they needed them.

Privacy

At the federal level, the most often cited exemptions in denying requests are those related to privacy. Exemption 6 protects personal privacy. Exemption 7, which protects law enforcement investigations, also exempts information that would 'constitute an unwarranted invasion of privacy'. The same issue confronts requesters at the local and state level. When the *San Jose Mercury News* sought a copy of the database listing information on participants in the state's 'Adopt-a-Highway' programme, its request was denied because it infringed on the participants' privacy – even though their names were already displayed on highway signs.

And indeed, privacy has been a difficult barrier to access to information in California. Article 1 of the California Constitution says that among the 'inalienable rights' of its people are 'enjoying and defending life and liberty, acquiring, possessing and protecting property, and pursuing and obtaining safety, happiness, and *privacy*'.

In Texas, a routine request by *The Dallas Morning News* for personnel records lead to a lengthy court battle over access to public officials' dates of births (Drew, 2010). In Texas, agencies must ask the Attorney General's Office if they want to withhold information from a requester. The *News* had requested and obtained the information previously – including dates of birth. But this time, the Comptroller's Office, which held the data, sued the AG. The *News* intervened in the case, arguing that, without dates of birth, it was not possible to correctly identify individuals. A lower court and an appeals court agreed. But the State Comptroller, which held the records, pushed for changes to the law for two legislative sessions. (In Texas the state legislature meets every other year.) In late 2010, the Texas Supreme Court ruled that the information did not have to be released.[3]

What that means is that stories that previously relied on the information won't be possible. Examples include *The Dallas Morning News* investigation into the Texas youth prison system that found 266 employees with criminal records. Another *News* investigation found hundreds of teachers who were registered sex offenders. Dates of birth were the only way to verify the identity of the individual because many people have the same names.

Privatisation

In some states, where government agencies contract with private companies for data processing, information has been withheld because it was not actually in the hands of the government agency. When it comes to federal FOIA, that information should still be public. In other states, courts have said that if the private organisation is doing government business, then the information should still be available.

Some state attorncy generals have said that government records maintained by a private firm should still be public. In many cases, requesters have had to go to court to gain access to such information. In 2001 the Tennessee Supreme Court ruled that private companies doing government functions must make their records accessible. In that case, *The Memphis Commercial Appeal* sought the records of a company that provided child-care for the state.[4]

In some cases, it is not the government entity itself that makes the argument. Private vendors sometimes make it difficult for agencies to get access to their own data. The Reporters Committee for Freedom of the Press (2007) examined a situation in Wisconsin where local communities contracted with a private company to maintain their assessment data. The cities provided a requester Wiredata Corp. with pdfs rather than the data. An appeals court said that was not a sufficient open records response. The Wisconsin Supreme Court ruled otherwise, saying that the cities fulfilled their obligations under the open-records law.[5]

Technical difficulties

Agencies frequently blame their inability to provide electronic records on their computers. Those of us who regularly request data have heard: 'Our database can't do that' or 'It's too complicated'. But in nearly every case in which I encountered similar excuses, in the end, it was possible for someone at the agency to extract the records. Sometimes it required conversations with the IT staff at the agency and sometimes I had to alter a request.

The Kentucky Attorney General's Office issued a 2002 opinion that a computer crash was not a valid reason for denying a request for data: 'The fact that its computer system was "down" … did not relieve the Department of its statutory duty'.[6]

Outdated laws

Some state open-records laws don't address access to electronic records, so interpretation is often left to individual agencies or courts, if the requester has the resources to sue. The New Hampshire open records law allows an agency to provide a printout of a public record rather than the underlying computer file. Courts there have been mixed on whether an agency must hand over a database (Attorney General of the Department of Justice, 2009). California's law was similar until 2001 when it was amended to include electronic information. But requesters still run into difficulties when it comes to specific types of electronic records. In 2011, an appeals court ruled that a public agency did not have to release GIS (electronic mapping) data under the California Public Records Act.[7]

Solutions

None of these are insurmountable problems. An editor once told me not to complain about how she did something without providing another option. So here are my suggestions for improving government transparency, particularly when it comes to data.

Keep promises

On his first full day in office, President Barack Obama issued two memos to agency heads calling for an 'unprecedented level of openness in government' (2009a) and ordered agencies to administer FOIA with the presumption of openness (2009b). He called for OMB to issue guidance to agencies on exactly how to achieve those goals. For open records advocates and journalists who had lived through eight years of proactive secrecy, hopes were high. Four years later, reviews are mixed as to how well the Obama administration has kept the promise of transparency. Clearly, more information is online and agencies have had to better communicate with FOIA requesters.

A series of reports by the transparency coalition OpenTheGovernment.org has found that while expectations have yet to be fully realised, improvements are being made. The group's 2012 report found that agencies processed more FOIA requests than previously, but because the number of requests increased, the backlog actually increased. In addition, national security agencies continue to classify at the rates of prior administrations (OpenTheGovernment, 2012a).

When it comes to data, federal agencies were required to make 'high-value' datasets available on a new government data site. Data.gov had great promise as a one-stop shopping place for government data. But for many journalists, the data they most often use are not on data.gov. One example: the National Endowment for the Arts (NEA) 'high value' dataset on data.gov consists of results from a survey of participation in the arts (see Figure 8.2). Yet, the most commonly used dataset for journalists is *who got the grants*. That information is on the NEA website, but not in an easily downloadable format (see Figure 8.3).

To meet the promises of FOIA by this administration (Obama, 2009b), several agencies still have work to do. A July 2012 report from

Figure 8.2   National Endowment for the Arts' "high value" data

FY 2012 Grant Awards: Challenge America Fast-Track Review Grants

Some details of the projects listed below are subject to change, contingent upon prior Endowment approval.

All grants are for $10,000.

Readers >>

ALABAMA

Magic City Smooth Jazz
Birmingham, AL
To support Jazz in the Park, a series of concerts at W.C. Patton, Ensley, East Lake, and Arthur Shores Parks. Artists will include saxophonists Vann Burchfield and Kenny Williams, as well as guitarists Keith Williams and Roland Gresham.

Marshall County Retired Senior Volunteer Program, Inc.
Guntersville, AL
To support Melodies and Musings - Our Appalachian Legacy, a series of dulcimer workshops targeted to older adults. The lessons will culminate in a public concert featuring the workshop participants, as well as professional musicians including Bill Collins, Steve Eulberg, Heidi Muller, and Butch Ross.

ARIZONA

Borderlands Theater Teatro Fronterizo, Inc.
Tucson, AZ
To support the production of *Agnes Under the Big Top*, a new work by Aditi Brennan Kapil. The work explores the intersecting lives of recent immigrants to this country and

Figure 8.3   National Endowment for the Arts' grants

the Government Accountability Office found that four federal agencies – the Departments of Homeland Security, Justice, Defense, and Health and Human Services – still need to reduce FOIA backlogs, improve FOIA processes, and better use technology.

Know the law

'No' doesn't always have to mean no when it comes to public records requests. In some cases, requesters are told 'no' to make them go away or out of ignorance of the law. One solution is to educate records administrators and public information officers on the state's open-records laws. In Ohio, all elected officials must attend training offered by the state's auditor.[8] In Texas, elected and appointed officials must have open records and open meetings training. They must provide their training certificate upon request.[9]

At the federal level, the US Department of Justice and the Office of Government Information Services conduct training for FOIA professionals within the government. Many public records administrators are members of the ASAP (American Society of Access Professionals), which conducts regular training. The July 2012 GAO study recommended training for FOIA officers to improve processing of requests. In addition, a recent memorandum by the Office of Management and Budget and the National Archives and Records Administration (White House, 2012) called for agency records officers (a new position designated in the memo) to hold the NARA certificate of Federal Records Management Training.

Follow the law

Many state, local, and federal agencies have spent a great deal of time explaining why a particular database could not be released. And while there may be information that must be redacted or the data must be aggregated, in the end, there are solutions to various scenarios. Here are some common problems that requesters encounter.

- 'The database contains personal information.' The solution? First, confirm that it actually does contain such information. Next, confirm that the information is protected by law. If that's actually the case, then tell the agency, 'Just don't provide that field, then.'
- 'We don't have reports with those exact fields.' Communicate. The requester doesn't know what reports are there. The data holder should let them know. It might very well be that they have something that is very close to what is needed.
- 'Providing the information violates FERPA/HIPAA or another privacy laws.' This can be the case even if you are not getting identifiers for the students/patients. The argument is that, with all the other details, you could figure out individual identities. In those cases, most education datasets aggregate the data and mask instances with, say, fewer than five cases.

Build new systems with open records in mind

Any new computer systems should be designed with public information in mind and so that restricted information can be withheld easily if necessary. The memo from the OMB (White House, 2010) calls for federal agencies to use electronic recordkeeping: 'By 2019, federal agencies will manage all permanent electronic records in an electronic format.' While the memorandum calls for electronic record management, it doesn't emphasise that systems should be designed with transparency in mind, except for when it comes to email. The directive calls for agencies to manage email in a way that allows them to 'identify, retrieve and retain the records'.

Some state legislatures have called for data systems designed for public access. When the Arkansas Freedom of Information Act was updated in 2001 to address access to electronic information, it stated: 'Any computer hardware or software acquired ... shall not impede public access to records in electronic form'.[10] In Connecticut, new computer systems purchased by agencies must be designed to promote public access to the information.[11] The Delaware Attorney General has opined that databases should be segregable to permit access to information that is not exempt under the state's open records law.[12]

Keep it simple

Flashy dashboards and fancy graphics are not transparency. Access to information that tells citizens what their government is up to and how their money is being spent is transparency. Providing that information in simple forms – including data in pure, basic formats such as comma-delimited text files – enhances access to information. Even for members of the public, graphic displays of data can be overwhelming. With no offence intended to those geeky mothers out there, I proposed implementing 'the mom test': Before launching fancy dashboards, developers should have their mothers try to use the system. If Mom can't find information, many other people will not be able to find it.

For data requesters, including journalists who want to analyse the data for stories or other purposes, make pure data formats available with documentation on how to interpret the data. Make it clear where that information is. When I do trainings for reporters, I always tell them to look for the 'get the data' link on a website (see The Reporters Committee for Freedom of the Press, 2003).

Improve data accuracy

While we are on the topic of better ways to provide data, agencies should work to improve data accuracy. The condition of government data varies widely. At my end, I do everything I can to 'clean' data before using it. I would hope that government agencies would strive for the same thing. Data are the basis upon which officials govern.

Agencies that blame bad data on the underlying entities that submitted it could do things to better control what goes into the data. When ProPublica obtained data from the U.S. Department of Education Office of Civil Rights in 2011 to build our Opportunity Gap project, we found significant problems in the data: schools with more teachers than students, schools offering more than 1,000 Advanced Placement courses when fewer than 40 exist. Some of these problems could be resolved by putting tighter restrictions on web-based data entry forms. The education data problem from above could be resolved by restricting data entry on number of AP courses to anything between 0 and 40.

Agencies also should provide data quality reports. We know that they often rely on others to enter their data or send their data. The Federal Motor Carrier Safety Administration tracks how well states report their data (see Figure 8.4). This measurement is really important for us to know in analysing and using the data. On its website, FMCSA states: 'With data we can measure the effectiveness of our programs, identify which motor carriers to target for enforcement actions, know which new programs to implement, and what safety areas to address in our strategic planning process'.[13]

The Texas Department of Public Safety issues a similar report when it comes to crime data submitted by counties (the column on the far right of Table 8.1 indicates the percentage of records that are complete).

In a push for better data, the Governor's Office told counties that report less than 90% of their data that they would lose grant money. The political blog Grits for Breakfast obtained the memo and posted it online (Grits for Breakfast, 2012). As a reporter, that tells me that information from Dallas County in the state crime data is incomplete. I might want to get data directly from the county and compare it to the state data.

What we most need to know

Access to government data is essential for citizens to know what their government is doing and how their money is spent. This includes records about licensing, enforcements, inspections, and payments. Spending information is particularly important at a time when budgets are being slashed.

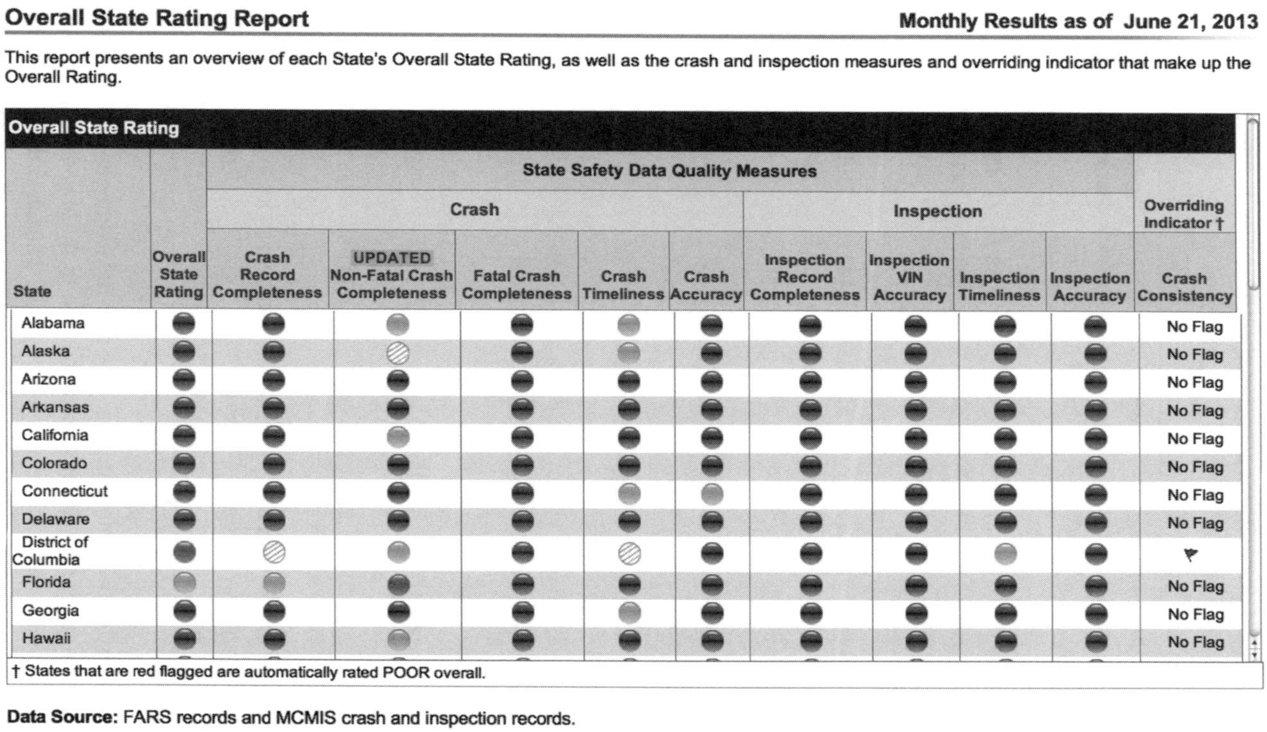

Overall State Rating Report

Monthly Results as of June 21, 2013

This report presents an overview of each State's Overall State Rating, as well as the crash and inspection measures and overriding indicator that make up the Overall Rating.

Overall State Rating

State	Overall State Rating	State Safety Data Quality Measures									Overriding Indicator †
		Crash					Inspection				
		Crash Record Completeness	UPDATED Non-Fatal Crash Completeness	Fatal Crash Completeness	Crash Timeliness	Crash Accuracy	Inspection Record Completeness	Inspection VIN Accuracy	Inspection Timeliness	Inspection Accuracy	Crash Consistency
Alabama											No Flag
Alaska											No Flag
Arizona											No Flag
Arkansas											No Flag
California											No Flag
Colorado											No Flag
Connecticut											No Flag
Delaware											No Flag
District of Columbia											
Florida											No Flag
Georgia											No Flag
Hawaii											No Flag

† States that are red flagged are automatically rated POOR overall.

Data Source: FARS records and MCMIS crash and inspection records.

Figure 8.4 Federal Motor Carrier Safety Administration state rating report

Table 8.1 Texas Department of Public Safety Crime Records Service CCH dispositions associated with reported charges

Adult

Date reported	Reported year	Total charges reported	Charges disposed by prosecutors	Charges disposed by courts	Total disposed	Completeness percentage
Crane						
Jan 2010	2008	100	4	58	62	62%
Jan 2011	2008	121	5	104	109	90%
Jan 2011	2009	116	5	86	91	78%
Crockett						
Jan 2010	2008	173	12	127	139	80%
Jan 2011	2008	211	21	165	186	88%
Jan 2011	2009	292	48	173	221	76%
Crosby						
Jan 2010	2008	133	10	54	64	48%
Jan 2011	2008	158	21	118	139	88%
Jan 2011	2009	179	38	97	135	75%
Culberson						
Jan 2010	2008	89	0	0	0	0%
Jan 2011	2008	217	58	1	59	27%
Jan 2011	2009	122	3	1	4	3%
Dallam						
Jan 2010	2008	351	154	136	290	83%
Jan 2011	2008	301	137	116	253	84%
Jan 2011	2009	280	79	113	192	69%
Dallas						
Jan 2010	2008	71,891	6,636	48,173	54,809	76%
Jan 2011	2008	71,093	6,494	51,434	57,928	81%
Jan 2011	2009	67,269	4,143	45,084	49,227	73%

As part of the American Recovery and Reinvestment Act, President Obama promised that citizens would be able to track every dollar of the stimulus money. And while after some initial glitches federal financial-tracking sites made it much easier to get information about the stimulus and other programs, we cannot track every dollar. The data contains information about so-called prime recipients and, for some programmes, sub-recipients, but money often flows below that level.

For example, weatherisation funds were awarded to states, which then dispersed funds to community action agencies, who then hired contractors to perform work. The stimulus data contains information only on which community action groups got the money, not where the money went after that (LaFleur, 2009). In addition, detailed information on expenditures for programs such as Pell grants and Small Business Administration loans were not included in data on the federal recovery.gov site. Those data are available from usaspending.gov. ProPublica compiles a full dataset each quarter to make it easier for reporters and readers (LaFleur, Kokenge and Nguyen, 2012).

Hidden tricks

While the federal Freedom of Information Act has nine exemptions covering areas such as national security or personal privacy, the third exemption allows for other statutes to be used to withhold information. And there are many of those. A 2011 study by the Sunshine in Government Initiative, which was co-published with ProPublica, found that agencies use more than 240 such statutes to withhold information (LaFleur, 2011). Some of those laws make sense – such as those protecting medical or financial information. Others appear to be outright ridiculous, such as the Watermelon Research and Promotion Act. Another law protects information about the location of caves.

The number of these so-called B3 exemptions is so high because these exemptions were often tucked into other legislation without the public or open-records advocates noticing. But changes to FOIA that went into effect in 2009 require that legislation identify when a B3 will be created. Agencies also must disclose in their FOIA annual reports which of these statutes they use and how often they have used them. The SGI study found the statute most widely used – by 20 agencies – was a law protecting losing contract bids.

In an interview with ProPublica, Patrice McDermott, director of OpenTheGovernment, which pushed for the B3 reforms, explained that while there may be legitimate reasons to withhold certain information, 'blowing holes in the Freedom of Information Act is not the way to do it' (LaFleur, 2011). One recent B3 was pulled back. Financial reforms passed in 2011 by Congress included an exemption to withhold from the public information concerning 'surveillance, risk assessments or other regulator and oversight activities' (ibid.). The exemption became law, but it was later rescinded after it came under fire by transparency groups. In its recommendations for the 113th Congress, OpenTheGovernment.org suggested that oversight and reform committees be more involved in proposed exemptions:

> Because the provision does not amend FOIA directly ... it is rarely referred to Committees with expertise in public access to government information. Any legislation that could alter the public's ability to access records under FOIA should be thoroughly evaluated by experts well-versed in the public's right to know. (OpenTheGovernment, 2012b)

Communicate

While the days of sending a FOIA request to a federal agency and not hearing anything for years seem to be mostly behind us, communication with federal FOIA requesters could be better and more consistent across agencies. Some states require specific communication – such as letting requesters know when the information will be ready. Federal agencies now must provide requesters with a tracking number that requesters can use to check the status of their request. So far, in my experience, most of my responses from federal agencies include a tracking number.

A significant step in the right direction when it comes to communication was the creation of OGIS.[14] Congress established the Office of Government Information Services in the OPEN Government Act of 2007. OGIS was designed as the federal government FOIA ombudsman. While the folks at OGIS say they don't take sides, they do support the FOIA process and have been very helpful to hundreds of requesters in getting agencies talking with requesters. In some cases – particularly with complicated data requests – they have organised conversations between FOIA staff, IT staff, and counsel.

In addition, a new federal site FOIA.gov provides statistics about how agencies have processed their FOIA requests and information for requesters – such as FOIA contacts at agencies.

Our part

Journalists will not solve anything simply by grousing about public records issues. But writing about public records can make a difference. Having written more than 100 columns on public records for *The Dallas Morning News* and the *San Jose Mercury News*, I found that readers actually do care about getting information on what their government officials are doing. When information is being kept from the public, tell them.

In 2011, *The Salt Lake Tribune* did just that. When the legislature attempted to gut Utah's open-records law, the newspaper published dozens of stories and editorials about the proposal (Pyle, 2011). Their work eventually led to a recall of the legislation.

In 2010, *The Washington Post* did an extensive investigation into the way guns move through society. According to the team's submission to Investigative Reporters and Editors, the *Post* 'set out to break the secrecy imposed by Congress and examination of how guns are used in crimes'.

The Sunshine in Government Initiative has done a great job compiling stories that have made use of FOIA.[15] In addition, Investigative Reporters and Editors ExtraExtra[16] often feature stories that have made use of FOIA and state public records laws.

Conclusion

The Obama administration set high expectations with the promises made by the President during his first days in office. And so the administration has been criticised for failing to fulfil those promises. But progress has been made during the past four years when it comes to public data. Clearly some agencies have put more data online, but both the quality and usability of that data could be improved.

The issue is not so much the FOIA law itself, but rather its implementation. Agencies need to develop systems that follow the spirit of openness laid out by President Obama and Attorney General Holder (2009). Agencies must provide FOIA staff with training and resources. And FOIA staff must make the process of requesting records easier, reduce backlogs and set reasonable fees.

Access to data in some categories of records should be revisited. In fact, President Obama's FOIA memo (2009b) would seem to call for it: 'In the face of doubt, openness prevails.' Information that was closed during the Bush administration (Ashcroft, 2001) is important for citizens and journalists. For example, useful details about dam inspections continue to be withheld under post-9/11 protections. As a result, citizens do not know about potential dangers near their homes.

We cannot rely on our law-makers alone to protect our right to know. As journalists, we must continue to request information. We must be sure student journalists learn about open government. And when officials violate transparency, we must write about them to keep government accountable.

Notes

The links in this chapter and examples of public records columns also are available at www.jenster.com/oxford2012.

1   www.californiawatch.org/earthquakes.

2   www.latimes.com/news/local/bell.

3   *Texas Comptroller of Public Accounts, Petitioner, v Attorney General of Texas and The Dallas Morning News, Ltd., Respondents.* [2009] Supreme Court Opinion: www.supreme.courts.state.tx.us/historical/2010/dec/080172.pdf;   Dissenting Opinion: www.supreme.courts.state.tx.us/historical/2010/dec/080172cd.pdf).

4   *Memphis Publishing Co. et al. v Cherokee Children & Family Services, Inc. et al.* [2002]: www.tncourts.gov/sites/default/files/OPINIONS/TSC/PDF/023/Cherokee.pdf.

5   *WIREdata, Inc., Plaintiff-Respondent v Village of Sussex et al.*: www.doj.state.wi.us/dls/OMPR/2010OMCG-PRO/2008_WI_69_WIREdata2.pdf.

6   Kentucky AG Op. 02-149: www.jenster.com/ky_ag_02_149.pdf.

7   www.leginfo.ca.gov/cgi-bin/displaycode?section=gov&group=06001-07000&file=6250-6270.

8   www.auditor.state.oh.us/services/opengov/default.htm.

9   www.oag.state.tx.us/open/og_training.shtml.

10   www.arkansasag.gov/pdfs/foia-ocr.pdf.

11   Connecticut Freedom of Information Act: www.ct.gov/foi/site/default.asp.

12   www.rcfp.org/delaware-open-government-guide/iii-state-law-electronic-records.

13   www.ai.fmcsa.dot.gov/DataQuality/DataQuality.asp?redirect=overview.asp.

14   www.ogis.archives.gov.

15 www.sunshineingovernment.org/index.php?cat=33.
16 www.ire.org/blog/extra-extra.

References

American Journalism Review (2009) 'AJR's 2009 Count of Statehouse Reporters: State-by-State Numbers', Apr./May: www.ajr.org/article.asp?id=4722.

Ashcroft, J. (2001) FOIA Memorandum: www.gwu.edu/~nsarchiv/NSAEBB/ NSAEBB84/Ashcroft%20Memorandum.pdf.

Attorney General of the Department of Justice (2009) 'Attorney General's Memorandum on New Hampshire's Right-To-Know Law, RSA Chapter 91-a', 15 July: www.doj.nh.gov/civil/documents/right-to-know.pdf.

Drew, J. (2010) 'Texas Supreme Court Rules State Workers Birth Dates aren't Public', *The Dallas Morning News,* 4 Dec.

Government Accountability Office (2012) *Report to the House Committee on Oversight and Government Reform on the Freedom of Information Act* (GAO): www.gao.gov/assets/600/593169.pdf.

Grits for Breakfast (2012) 'Most Texas Counties Don't Meet Governor's New Crime Data Criteria, May Lose Grants', 17 Jan.: www.gritsforbreakfast.blogspot. com/2012/01/most-texas-counties-dont-meet-governors.html.

Holder, E. (2009) FOIA Memorandum: www.justice.gov/ag/foia-memo-march 2009.pdf.

khou.com (2011) 'A Matter of Risk: Radiation, Drinking Water and Deception – Part 1', video: www.khou.com/video?id=129195838&sec=548547.

LaFleur, J. (2009) 'Stimulus Weatherization Aid Favors Cold Regions', ProPublica/ *USA Today,* 6 May: www.usatoday.com/news/nation/2009-05-06-weather ization_N.htm.

LaFleur, J. (2011) 'FOIA Eyes Only: How Buried Statutes Are Keeping Information Secret', ProPublica, 14 Mar.: www.propublica.org/article/foia-exemptions-sun shine-law.

LaFleur, J., Kokenge, J., and Nguyen, D. (2012) 'Recovery Tracker: How Much Stimulus Funding is Going to Your County?' ProPublica, 1 Oct.: www. projects.propublica.org/recovery.

Las Vegas Sun (2010) 'A breakthrough in medical transparency', 27 June: www.lasvegassun.com/news/2010/jun/27/complete-guide-vegas-health-care/#axzz2YqXbWLJ6.

Obama, B. (2009a) Transparency Memorandum: www.whitehouse.gov/the_press_ office/TransparencyandOpenGovernment.

Obama, B. (2009b) FOIA Memorandum: www.whitehouse.gov/the_press_office/ FreedomofInformationAct.

OpenTheGovernment (2012a) *Secrecy Report* (OpenTheGovernment.org): www. openthegovernment.org/node/3577.

OpenTheGovernment (2012b) '5 Issues Congress Should Seriously Consider', 14 Sept.: www.openthegovernment.org/node/3582.

Pyle, G. (2011) 'HB477: Utah reacts …', 5 Mar.: www.sltrib.com/sltrib/ blogsdebate/51370959-176/governor-public-records-bill.html.csp.

The Reporters Committee for Freedom of the Press (2003) 'Access to Electronic Records: A State-by-State Guide to Obtaining Government Data': www. jenster.com/elec_access_all.pdf.

White House (2010) *OMB Directive on Open Government*: www.whitehouse.gov/ sites/default/files/omb/assets/memoranda_2010/m10-06.pdf.

White House (2012) *Memorandum for Agency Heads on Managing Government Records Directive* (M-12-18), 24 Aug.: www.whitehouse.gov/sites/default/files/ omb/memoranda/2012/m-12-18.pdf.

9

The Transparency Opportunity: Holding Power to Account – or Making Power Accountable?

Paul Bradshaw

Introduction

Over the past two decades three cultural developments have combined with technological trends to facilitate a significant change in the ways that journalists and, importantly, citizens can hold power to account. Right to information (RTI) laws, public service information (PSI) initiatives, and the open data movement have separately and in combination contributed to a massive expansion of the amounts and types of information available to journalists; the ability to access these; and the techniques, knowledge, and skills needed to do so.

Interviews with 26 journalists involved in data, conducted for this chapter, found an overwhelming agreement that independent and government open data, right to information laws, and APIs (see below) had each changed the way that they held power to account. However, this change has only come relatively recently to the news industry, while transparency initiatives have become complicated by developments in decentralisation, commercial interests, government outsourcing and privatisation, and data quality and choice.

This chapter maps that territory, the ways in which it is being used to hold power to account, and the concerns over weaknesses in the new information environment.

Right to information?

Citizens' right to information in countries such as the US and Sweden has been well established for some time, contributing to a rich history of computer-assisted reporting (CAR), particularly in the US where the passing of the 1966 Freedom of Information Act coincided with curiosity about scientific research methods and the growth of computing power.

In the UK, however, computer-assisted reporting has a much shorter history. The country's own Freedom of Information Act received royal assent in 2000, but was not implemented fully until 2005, leaving it 30 years behind many Scandinavian countries, 20 behind Australia, Canada, and New Zealand, and a decade behind Austria, Italy, the Netherlands, and Portugal. It is not the last country to do so, however, and the organisation Right2INFO.org now counts some 90 nations with right to information laws or regulations, while the movement continues to grow in South America, Africa, and Asia (Right2INFO.org, 2012). On an increasingly globalised stage for politics and business, this is particularly important as journalists can and do use other countries' RTI laws to gain access to information about their own country.

Open data

Alongside this spread of formal legislation there has been a parallel and equally important independent 'open data' movement which sought – and continues to seek – to open up information in the public interest, in much the same way that journalism has, but with the key difference that 'open data' are typically readable by computers, making it easier for humans to combine and interrogate them.

A pioneer in this sphere has been the UK's mySociety, which began in 1998 as Up My Street: a website where members of the public could find out about their local area. In 2000 the team added a facility for users to find out who their local elected representative was and, crucially, how to contact them. Neither initiative was popular with parliamentary authorities, which tried to make things as difficult as possible for the project. But it was with the launch of They Work For You in 2004 – a way to find out about a politician's attendance and voting records – that things really heated up, and the site was threatened by the authorities with legal action for breach of copyright (Brooke, 2010).

The website stood its ground, and the action was never brought. Within a year mySociety's tools were being used in television news coverage of elections, and the site extended into other services, such as making it easy to make and follow FOI requests with What Do They Know.

By 2006 the *Guardian* had launched its 'Free Our Data' campaign to open up taxpayer-funded data to the public. And in 2009 Rewired State held its first 'Hack the Government Day' at the newspaper's offices in Kings Cross. An initiative aimed at gathering developers together in creating applications from civic data, many results touch on areas traditionally covered by the media. The tool helping users clear up local roadkill, for example, fits a role normally performed by the local press. 'Should I Really Buy That?' – a site which tells you if the car you are about to buy is likely to get stolen – would be a feature in any automotive magazine. And 'where's my new house?' shows the number of new houses that could potentially be built on local authority land.[1]

Many of these initiatives rely on the ability to 'scrape' webpages: creating scripts to automatically gather information from them. This might, for instance, involve conducting automated searches on a public database in order to compile the results into a more accessible spreadsheet. Or writing a programme that analyses hundreds of official reports on PDF form, in order to unlock the data within.

Open data events have since multiplied, including the Carbon and Energy Hack Weekend, Young Rewired State, Parliament, Justice and Home Affairs, and Education. Similar 'hackdays' and 'hackathons' ('hack' referring to a quick and often ugly solution to a particular problem) are organised by organisations ranging from technology and news organisations to nonprofits and academic institutions, government itself, and government employees such as NHS worker and software company co-founder Dr Carl Reynolds (NHS Hack Day, 2012). And it should be pointed out that these events are by no means restricted to the UK.

In addition to the websites and apps generated by these events, there have been a number of more substantial independent open data efforts, most notably from former magazine publisher Chris Taggart. Taggart's first open data venture, OpenlyLocal, collected spending and other data from local authorities across the UK from 2009 onwards. The site would eventually include a feature whereby users could select an individual item of spending and automatically generate an FOI request to ask for more information.

As he 'followed the money' he added sister site OpenCharities – data on charity accounts (a major supplier to local authorities) – the following year, and OpenCorporates – company data – the year after that. OpenCorporates now covers company data from across the world. Fellow OpenCorporates founder Rob McKinnon launched Who's Lobbying to open up data on that practice, having already worked for They Work For You New Zealand. Internationally They Work For You helped with the creation of OpenAustralia.org, and inspired the Irish political data site KildareStreet.com. Spain's Voota and Arregla mi Calle are inspired by sister projects They Work For You and Fix My Street.

The public spending project Where Does My Money Go? has also expanded outside the UK, publishing spending data from almost every continent under the name OpenSpending. Meanwhile, data on land deals is collected and analysed by Landportal.info, and in Chile the Ciudadano Inteligente Fundación opened up the Chilean MPs' register of assets and interests by building an open database (finding that 'nearly 40% of MPs were not disclosing their assets fully': Dudman, 2012). The organisation has now launched a database that 'enables members of the public to find potential conflicts of interest by analysing the data disclosed through the members' register of assets'.

This 'crowdsourcing' of data – opening it up to public scrutiny or collaborating with users to collect it in the first place – has also been adopted by projects from Where Are The Cuts? and Voluntary Sector Cuts to the Campaign for Better Transport and ProPublica's PatientHarm community, while the *Guardian* has adopted the same technique to gather data on everything from Olympic ticket allocation and broadband speeds to overcrowding and food banks.

PSI

At the same time as the argument was being made for greater accountability in public data – and citizens empowered by new technologies took the initiative in compiling and publishing that data – a parallel argument was being made for the *economic* benefits of publishing public sector information (PSI).

Due in large part to this argument, in 2010 the major target of the Free Our Data campaign – Ordnance Survey – finally published large amounts of geographical data which it had previously charged for. The same year saw an avalanche of UK data, from local government spending to the central government COINS database, organograms to trace accountability, ICT contracts, and various other sources of data. Many other important datasets, however, such as the Postcode Address File and national Green Belt data (Bowarva, 2012), remain closed to the public.

Since then the pace has not slowed. In addition to more government data being opened in the UK, there has been an increasing dialogue between governments and open data initiatives, along with the significant creation of the Open Government Licence, which offered an alternative to Crown Copyright and assumed by default that users had the right to reuse and share information (Shadbolt, 2010). This was particularly important for those who wanted to scrape public information but who could have been threatened with legal action for publishing their work.

At the launch of a new set of UK government spending data, Tim Berners-Lee was asked what the point of this exercise was. Realistically, who would hold government to account? He replied:

> *The responsibility needs to be with the press. Journalists need to be data-savvy. It used to be that you would get stories by chatting to people in bars, and it still might be that you'll do it that way sometimes. But now it's also going to be about poring over data and equipping yourself with the tools to analyse it and picking out what's interesting. And keeping it in perspective, helping people out by really seeing where it all fits together, and what's going on in the country. (Arthur, 2010)*

In transport and elections, data are now being published in real time, a development which should be of particular interest to journalists focused on contemporary events but which has been largely ignored, particularly by regional newspaper websites where data on issues such as road maintenance and gritting are of most interest.

Many parts of the news industry have at least recognised the importance of data: *Daily Telegraph* trainees attending the Press Association's six-week course now spend three days on data, on top of a pre-existing day on FOI, and the newspaper launched a blog dedicated to data during the 2012 Olympics. The BBC College of Journalism has rolled out an internal training scheme to hundreds of staff. In January 2013 the *Birmingham Mail* launched the first UK regional newspaper datablog in partnership with Birmingham City University and Help Me Investigate

(Reid, 2013), and publishers Trinity Mirror launched a centralised 'data-driven' unit in March 2013 (McAthy, 2013). Talking about the launch, digital publishing director David Higgerson said:

> *There is a massive opportunity for creative, data-savvy reporters to revolutionise part of our industry, using new tools to do what we have always done best – bring important truths to light, hold the powerful to account, and provide vital information to our public in a compelling, easily digestible way. We aim to do just that. [In some cases data may reach across] local geographic borders, so a centralised unit makes perfect sense in terms of generating content and sharing best practice.*

There is also growing interest from magazine publishers including RBI, Centaur, Haymarket, TopRight, and Reed. One magazine executive explained in an interview with the author that a significant driving force behind their interest was competition with blogs: data journalism was seen as a way of differentiating their reporting from that competition.

In an international survey for this chapter of 26 journalists that work with data, over 90% said their employers were increasing the data skills of its workforce, largely through training, but with a significant proportion – 42% – doing so through the creation of specialist positions. In a shrinking workforce, this is particularly significant.

In journalism schools, data journalism has found an integral role at my own institutions – Birmingham City University and City University London – and is taught as part of other courses at many other institutions. The schedules of international investigative journalism conferences have become dominated by sessions on computer-assisted reporting and data journalism, and panels discussing data are a regular fixture at mainstream journalism events. The nature of those students attracted to journalism – arts and humanities graduates; people who are more comfortable with words than numbers – means that opportunities to develop data skills are still not often taken up by a majority. For those that do, however, employment is much more easily found, and in some cases data journalism work as a student has led to a disproportionate number of front-page splashes in national broadsheets.

The data.gov initiatives of countries like the US and UK have spread to Kenya and Russia, and been joined by regional and city-specific data hubs from Calgary and Montevideo to Zaragoza and Victoria. In Spain over 200 participants gathered for the meeting of Spanish open data initiatives Encuentro de Iniciativas Open Data en España, organised by the Spanish Ministry for Industry, Energy and Tourism and the Ministry for Finance and Public Administration, together with the Spanish national data portal, datos.gob.es. Bodies such as the United Nations and World Bank have started publishing open data, and even corporations such as the Italian energy company Enel. And across the EU the Visby Declaration in 2009 noted, among other pledges, that:

> EU member states and community institutions should seek to make data freely accessible in open machine-readable formats, for the benefit of entrepreneurship, research and transparency.
>
> Access to and reuse of public sector information and data should be improved among EU Member States. The domains of data targeted by the Directive on the re-use of public sector information should be enlarged. (European Commission, 2009)

September 2011 saw the launch of the Open Government Partnership, an initiative for 'more transparent, effective and accountable governments' (Open Government, 2011). In June 2012 Norway became the first country in the Partnership to publish its company register as data, being later joined by the UK, while Belgium announced its intention to do the same (Open Corporates, 2012).

The focus has broadened to take in scientific data: in June 2012 The Royal Society published its report *Science as an Open Enterprise*, which noted:

> [The scientific] process must now adapt to two challenges. First, the ready access to data needed for replication and re-use is problematic for modern, massive data volumes. Second, the public interest in access to scientific information conflicts with the implicit assumption of many scientists, that the scientific process involves the specialist, professional scientific community alone, and that any major societal implications should be communicated to public and policymakers as finished, expert conclusions.
>
> The response to both these challenges is 'open science', an ethical imperative for science, whose default position is to make scientific knowledge freely and promptly available to others, whether scientists and citizens, in an accessible and useable form, unless there is an appropriate reason not to do so.

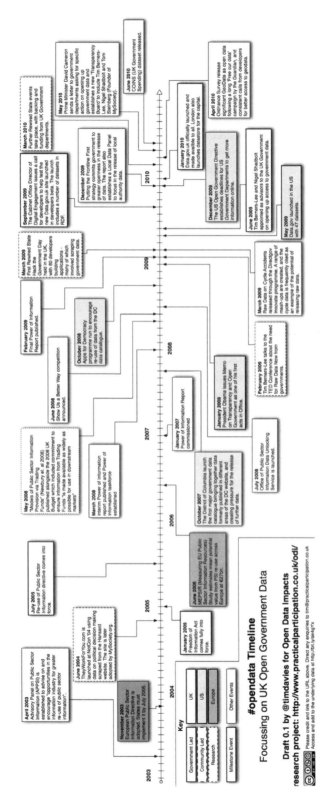

Figure 9.1 Timeline of open government data by Tim Davies, 2010

Source: www.opendataimpacts.net/2010/06/a-timeline-of-open-government-data. Used with the permission of Tim Davies.

This is mirrored by moves by the UK government to release university research data (Cabinet Office, 2012) and wider moves around open access publishing (Finch Report, 2012; European Commission, 2012) – against the opposite movement with regard to the FOI Act (FOI Man, 2012).

And, as an increasing number of commentators argue 'Data is the new oil', open data has started to attract the attention of big corporations. In the UK Microsoft is attempting to get a foothold with its Open Government Data Initiative, part of a wider commercialisation of open data shared by the coalition government, which is helping to fund an Open Data Institute to explore ways of generating revenue from data (Clarke, 2012). The government led its 2011 Autumn Budget Statement on open data (Cabinet Office, 2011), including a plan to share personal medical records with private companies and an emphasis on the need for the Data Strategy Board overseeing the acquisition of data to include 'representatives of commercial re-users'.

The funding of the Data Strategy Board will be reliant upon the profitability of the Public Data Group, which plans to make money from public data. Tim Davies notes a conflict of interest in the arrangement: 'If properly released in free forms, [the data] would likely undermine the current trading revenue model of the PDG. That doesn't look like the foundation for very independent and effective governance or regulation to open up core reference data' (Davies, 2011).

Where are the journalists?

Throughout this summary of data releases and campaigns only one news organisation has been mentioned: the *Guardian*. And journalists are not mentioned at all in Tim Davies's report on the use of open government data. Users of that data, he finds, have been split between 'micro-enterprises and SME business in the private sector, local and national public sector institutions, and academic institutions, with a very limited representation of voluntary sector workers' (Davies, 2011).

But notably, when identifying reasons for using government data, Davies's first set of drivers make it clear that journalism *should* have a role in this sector. In addition to the driver of 'wanting to better understand government and to promote efficiency and accountability', he lists the following impacts of using open government data:

- 'Supporting scrutiny';
- 'Informing citizens as voters';
- 'Informing citizens on specific issues'; and
- 'Supporting campaigning and lobbying'.

However, Davies says that 'Whilst examples of [open government data] use to support scrutiny of formal political processes is apparent, there is more evidence of use supporting co-production of public services between social and commercial entrepreneurs and the state, and of [it] being used to create improved information services for "citizen consumers"'. This absence of the scrutiny role traditionally played by journalists is particularly problematic given that, in formal open data projects such as data.gov.uk, governments 'retain some gate-keeping power by setting the categories and structure in which data is recorded and released'.

While the incoming coalition government in the UK subscribed publicly to the release of datasets on spending, it also announced the abolition of the Audit Commission (Sear, 2012). And in its report on data. gov.uk, the (separate) National Audit Office (2012) highlighted that:

> *While the Government has encouraged greater transparency in local government, it has discontinued many of the existing arrangements for performance reporting. For example, the Government has stopped the National Indicator Set, along with some of its component data collections such as the Place Survey. Existing repositories of comparative data, such as the Audit Commission's OnePlace website, are no longer supported or updated.*

This undercuts the ability of citizens and journalists to hold power to account. When the *Guardian* wanted to test David Cameron's statement that too many schools were using 'Indian dancing' to fill their sports teaching quota, for example, they found that data on sports participation had not been gathered since 2010, when the government discontinued the survey (Evans and Eaton, 2012). When crime data were published on a flashy new government website, the *Telegraph*'s Conrad Quilty-Harper (2011) noted a number of important flaws in the release:

> *No IDs for crimes: what if I want to check whether real life crimes have made it onto the map? Sorry.*
>
> *Six crime categories: including 'other crimes', everything from drug dealing to bank robberies in one handy, impossible to understand category.*

No live data. No dates or times: funny how without dates and times I can't tell which police manager was in charge.

Case status: the police know how many crimes go solved or unsolved, why not tell us this?

Oh and did I mention the site took six months to create and cost the taxpayer £300,000?

An increasing proportion of public spending is also being conducted outside of public organisations – one particularly visible example being the formation as a private company of LOCOG to organise the London 2012 Olympics – while the drive to make those organisations also accountable to the public appears to be not quite so enthusiastic.

And in sectors from healthcare to education, decentralisation initiatives complicate an already difficult environment of data collation: the shift in health spending to a larger number of clinical commissioning groups with fewer resources to deal with FOI requests creates an extra burden on those requesting data; while the introduction of academy schools – which are allocated budgets centrally rather than locally – represents a similar challenge.

As gatekeepers to open government data, the government is also able to choose the priorities for data release. In the UK, then, while announcements were made that welfare and credit will be open to scrutiny (and commercial exploitation), data that scrutinise corporations or government – tax, arms exports, employment law violations – were not mentioned (Bradshaw, 2012). And in the US the Sunlight Foundation noted a similar tendency:

Data.gov started with enormous promise ... As it has evolved, we have gotten a progressively better website: a more attractive design, and somewhat improved organisation of the data sets. But it's still a pretty mediocre data repository and the types of data available remains an enormous concern.

It turns out that the government has some interesting ideas about what counts as 'high value' information. The Department of the Interior seems to feel that population counts of wild horses and burros are 'high value' but records of safety violations like the ones that seem to have led to the Upper Branch Mine disaster are not.

We want to see data that can be used to hold government – and the entities that report to it – accountable. (Miller, 2010a)

Bad data

The Sunlight Foundation's Clearspending website did just that by comparing reports of public spending at different points. In the process they demonstrated a recurring problem with bad data:

> *Just under $1.3 trillion in federal reporting data from 2009 is unreliable.*
> *The data inaccuracies we uncovered account for 70 percent of the total*
> *$1.9 trillion in government spending data reported in that year. Some*
> *of the numbers are too big, some are too small and some are missing*
> *completely, while other spending data entries don't have the detail that's*
> *required or were reported months later than the law demands. (Miller,*
> *2010b)*

Data have become so central to the operation of business and commerce that *data are now becoming the power that must be held to account.*

The plan to release patient data to private companies is just one example of a process that needs to be scrutinised carefully, with many concerns about patient confidentiality and privatisation (Sparrow and Mulholland, 2011), and over the effectiveness of a policy designed to stimulate UK business (Davies, 2011).

Privacy concerns are not limited to government. The midata project launched by the UK government in November 2011 seeks to make it easy for the public to access data held about themselves. But it also raised concerns about who exactly would control that data (Davey, 2011), how it might be enforced, and how standardisation of data formats might be used to share data between companies and government. Similar concerns have been expressed regarding the NHS Information Centre's plans to improve the linking of data across the health service (Laja, 2012). The centre became a non-departmental public body in April 2013.

On many occasions the scrutiny of such data is conducted by non-traditional journalists. In Mexico, for example, blogger Diego Valle-Jones scrutinised official data on drug-related deaths using a statistical technique for identifying potentially fraudulent data (known as Benford's Law) and found some suspicious patterns and omissions:

> *The Acteal massacre committed by paramilitary units with government*
> *backing against 45 Tzotzil Indians is missing from the vital statistics*

database. According to the INEGI there were only 2 deaths during December 1997 in the municipality of Chenalho, where the massacre occurred. What a silly way to avoid recording homicides! Now it is just a question of which data is less corrupt. (Valle-Jones, 2010)

Similar disconnects between data at different points in the system have been identified by the mental health charity Rethink Mental Illness (James, 2012), and Detective Inspector Philip Shakesheff. The latter exposed a 'gap between [local authority] records and police data', as the *Sunday Times* reported in a story headlined 'Care Home Loses Child 130 Times':

The true scale of the problem was revealed after a check of records on police computers. For every child officially recorded by local authorities as missing in 2010, another seven were unaccounted for without their absence being noted.

The number who go missing is one of the indicators on which Ofsted judges how well children's homes are performing and the homes have a legal duty to keep accurate records. (Rayment, 2012)

More broadly, data blogger Tony Hirst (2012) 'followed the data' to identify the practice of 'data laundering in evidence based policy making':

We have some dodgy evidence, about which we're biased, so we give it to an 'independent' consultant who re-reports it, albeit with caveats, that we can then report, minus the caveats. Lovely, clean evidence. Our lobbyists can then go to a lazy policy researcher and take this scrubbed evidence, referencing it as finding in the Deloitte report, so that it can make its way into a policy briefing.

More traditional examples of identifying 'bad data' include the Bureau of Investigative Journalism's (2012) work on unrecorded deaths in police custody, Channel 4 News's identification of the flawed data being used to 'decide our children's future' (Worrall, 2011), the *Guardian's* 'naming and shaming' of opaque government annual reports (Rogers, 2011), and the *Chicago Tribune's* work on police crash reports (Hilkevitch, 2012).

Partnerships between traditional media and other agencies

As more of these stories come from outside traditional media, partnerships are being formed. A front-page *Guardian* investigation into lobbyist influence in the UK parliament, for example, resulted from a partnership with web-scraping site Scraperwiki:

> *Journalists can put down markers that run and update automatically and they can monitor the data over time with the objective of holding 'power and money' to account. The added value of this technique is that in one step the data is represented in a uniform structure and linked to the source thus ensuring its provenance. The software code that collects the data can be inspected by others in a peer review process to ensure the fidelity of the data. (McGuire, 2011)*

And Channel 4's *Dispatches* partnered with the same site to investigate assets owned by the UK government, and brownfield land owned by local authorities (Irving, 2011).

The *Guardian*'s Datablog helps facilitate more ad hoc partnerships, as citizens come forward with datasets they have compiled, and the stories behind them – or investigate datasets provided by the *Guardian* itself. In addition, new data-focused agencies such as OWNI and Dataveyes in France, Effecinque in Italy, Open Data City in Germany, the Bureau of Investigative Journalism and Help Me Investigate in the UK, and ProPublica in the US are also partnering with more established outlets to play to the strengths of each.

The exercise of power

It is important to remember in governments' move to publish 'open' data that control of information still represents the exercise of power, and shifts in that control remain open to abuse, gaming, or spin. Tony Hirst (2011), for example, identifies the potential for data about higher education to be monopolised by one organisation at extra cost to universities, resulting in less detailed information for students and parents. And Oxford Brookes academic Dan Herbert, in analysing the arrival of commercial-style accounting reports for the public sector, argues that it may represent not transparency, but obfuscation:

There is absolutely no empiric evidence that shows that anyone actually uses the accounts produced by public bodies to make any decision. There is no group of principals analogous to investors. There are many lists of potential users of the accounts. The Treasury, CIPFA (the UK public sector accounting body) and others have said that users might include the public, taxpayers, regulators and oversight bodies. I would be prepared to put up a reward for anyone who could prove to me that any of these people have ever made a decision based on the financial reports of a public body. If there are no users of the information then there is no point in making the reports better. If there are no users more technically correct reports do nothing to improve the understanding of public finances. In effect all that better reports do is legitimise the role of professional accountants in the accountability process. (Herbert, 2011)

Like Hirst, he argues that the raw data – and the ability to interrogate them – should instead be made available because (quoting Anthony Hopwood): 'Those with the power to determine what enters into organisational accounts have the means to articulate and diffuse their values and concerns, and subsequently to monitor, observe and regulate the actions of those that are now accounted for.'

The *Manchester Evening News* discovered this when they wanted to look at spending cuts. What they found was a dataset that had been 'spun' to make it harder to see the story hidden within, and to answer their question they first had to unspin it – or, in data journalism parlance, clean it. Likewise, having granular data – ideally from more than one source – allows us to better judge the quality of the information itself.

Three laws of open government data

There is a rich history of governments making it difficult to access data they have published – from publishing as PDFs or even images, to hiding it behind search forms or requiring users to pass a test to access or use it. David Eaves (2009) expresses these problems as the 'Three laws of Open Government Data':

1. 'If it can't be spidered or indexed, it doesn't exist.'
2. 'If it isn't available in open and machine readable format, it can't engage.'
3. 'If a legal framework doesn't allow it to be repurposed, it doesn't empower.'

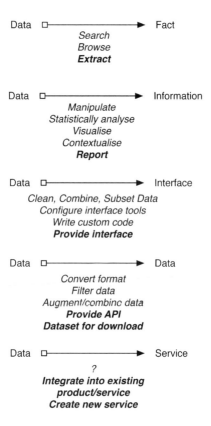

Figure 9.2   Five patterns of data use identified by Tim Davies, 2010

Source: www.opendataimpacts.net/report/wp-content/uploads/2010/08/How-is-open-government-data-being-used-in-practice.pdf. Used with the permission of Tim Davies.

All of these problems can be seen as an attempt to maintain the 'friction' that, according to Chris Taggart, have enabled governments and businesses to operate. Businesses such as real estate, he says, are based on the friction in commerce that has historically required us to use (and stay with) such intermediaries, while friction between countries allowed different companies to dominate different spaces.

Privacy exists because of the friction involved in combining information from diverse sources. And democracies depend on the friction between different arms of government, the friction of organising elections and pushing through legislation.

As friction is removed through access to information, he argues, we get problems such as 'jurisdiction failure' (corporate lawyers having 'hacked' local laws to international advantage), but also issues around the democratic accountability of ad hoc communities and how we deal with different conceptions of privacy across borders.

The role of news organisations and journalists here is contradictory: as actors dealing with information they are capable of reducing the friction between citizens and power, but should also be aware of the shift in power that that represents. Whose 'power' do we hold to account?

Returning to David Eaves's Three Laws, we can see that publishers may be guilty of breaking them also. Journalists, still focused on the 'story' unit that drove analogue media, risk not giving enough weight to the data that lie behind it. An illustration of this can be gained by looking at the five patterns of data use identified by Tim Davies (see Figure 9.2).

Converting data into facts and into information are familiar processes for journalists. But the other three options: converting data into an interface, a service, or indeed more data (for instance, cleaned, converted, verified, or combined), have not been taken up widely in the industry – although there is a clear interest in these areas as the industry looks for new business models. There are some innovative startups attempting to reinvent media models from outside along these lines, such as Rafat Ali's Skift, which warrants describing in full:

> Ali and cofounder Jason Clampet want to collect a vast data library to build tools that would be useful not just to the travel industry but anyone hoping in a car, train or bus to get away. [Skift] would be a media company built on a stable of products, not just content. 'We're starting with what we're grandly sort of calling the world's largest data warehouse of publicly available travel industry data,' he said.
>
> That means things like visit and occupancy information that tourism boards report to the government, departures and delay information from airports, and flight data supplied by airlines to agencies like the FAA. It's the type of information typically hidden away in Excel spreadsheets on seldom visited agency websites. 'We're gonna try and collect it, clean it, normalize it, put it in a dashboard that humans can understand, and then build services on top,' he said. He said they will also create APIs for the travel data they harness on the site.
>
> Ali stresses that as Skift grows they will hire more writers – but the writers will be focused on original reporting, not the things aggregation and

curation can pick up more easily. Ali said curation is still an undervalued asset that can prove useful to content creators as well as their audiences. The day-to-day news of airlines' fuel prices or the ebb and flow of tourism can be aggregated from elsewhere. Ali wants the site to chase the big stories, the airline bankruptcies and innovations in travel tech. (Ellis, 2011)

Initiatives such as these are largely being undertaken by agencies outside of news organisations, from mySociety's various tools to Patient Opinion in health, Tayside police force's own online feedback tool myPolice, the transport-and-property site Mapumental, Placr on public transport operators, Your Taxi Meter on licensing, CycleStreets on public bike hire, and Allotment Data. When compared to these initiatives, it is clear that traditional news media could be doing a lot more on the front of making power accountable in a truly networked, collaborative, service-driven manner.

But it is also not yet clear which business models will support such activity: mySociety supports its work through a combination of external development work and volunteers' efforts, but the schools comparison service Schooloscope is no longer maintained after the founders decided they could not support the costs of updating it. Likewise, parts of OpenlyLocal are now over two years out of date as broken scripts go unfixed. Some, such as Patient Opinion, are nonprofit companies which get their funding from the public sector they gather data on. Many are personal pet projects which rely on a founder's passion and funds and in some ways resemble the hyperlocal scene, with projects generating revenue for the founder indirectly through consultancy and other work.

In traditional media the business case behind data journalism is perhaps clearer: stories created with these techniques typically experience both higher traffic (three-quarters of the *Texas Tribune's* traffic comes through its databases) and time spent per page (the *Guardian's* Datablog posts have a dwell time five times higher than the site average). Costs of newsgathering, production, distribution, research, and development can also be reduced by news organisations who open up their data (the *Guardian*, again, is an exemplar of this with their Datablog photo pool and dozens of online tools built by its community of over 8,000 developers).

APIs

An API (Application Programming Interface) allows developers to get information from a service based on different requests – for example, 'Tell me who is the MP for Bolton North East' or 'Give me all articles by Bob Jones between these dates'. APIs could be key to news organisations' ability to collaborate with citizens and hold power to account in the future, as more and more data can be linked not just through government APIs but also independent open data APIs such as those provided by OpenCorporates; social network APIs which allow you to match public data with your own; and APIs around connected objects – our cars, phones, ID cards, delivery parcels and anything else: the who, what, where, when, and how of journalism.

An early example of how this can play out is provided by ProPublica's news app 'The Opportunity Gap' (Garber, 2011). The traditional news story here is about high-poverty schools having lower access to educational programmes. But the app uses Facebook's API to match open government data to the individual user's social media data. The resulting app tells you how that story plays out with regard to the schools that you attended, and which of your friends have used the app – so you can discuss the story. Holding power to account is just one part of the challenge for journalism: engaging what were once readers – and are now *users* – is the other. This sort of strategy offers new opportunities on both, especially when considered alongside the wider developments around user data, as described by Alan Mutter (2012):

> To date, publishers have applied the same business model to everything from print and the web to the latest mobile and social platforms: Build the biggest possible audience.
>
> This approach, unfortunately, is exactly at odds with the point of Big Data, whose goal is to connect individuals with information specifically tailored to them.
>
> The quicker Big Data applications develop, the faster the large but untargetable audiences traditionally delivered by newspapers will become an anachronism, thus limiting their utility to consumers and value for advertisers.

Two qualities of APIs are particularly key for news organisations: timeliness and personalisation. Needless to say, both also present new

159

dangers. Recently, for example, the operators of the UK Police API emailed all users to say 'a technical problem has prevented police outcomes data for the Metropolitan Police being made available for July 2012 and the June 2012 outcomes data for the Metropolitan Police is incorrect'.

Journalist Alex Howard sees the ownership and control of data as a key issue. 'For lots of types of data – finance, for instance – there are laws that say who can obtain it and who can use it. But new kinds of information don't necessarily have legal and regulatory frameworks' (Bell, 2012).

Summary: Holding power to account – or making power accountable?

The early history of journalism and the press is peppered with figures who helped broaden both the information available to the public, and the independence to report it. In the eighteenth century John Wilkes helped campaign to make parliamentary debates public, contrary to the 'privilege' that ordered that politicians should be protected from the influence of the electorate. William Cobbett took the opportunity to publish debates both contemporaneously and retrospectively, before selling on to Hansard, whose name was in turn used by Parliament itself when it took control of publication of its proceedings. Parliament's own pursuit of mySociety for publishing details of debates would represent a case of history repeating itself, as those in power found themselves making the same arguments against publication as in 1771.

Our ability to hold power to account is reliant on the work of these figures: from Wilkes and Cobbett, to Tom Steinberg of mySociety and Chris Taggart of OpenCorporates. While a great deal of importance is attached to the traditional role of journalists in holding power to account, that exceptional role which involved making power accountable has taken on a renewed significance.

The former may be about using the information in the journalist's possession to ask tough questions of the powerful, but the latter is about making such information accessible in the first place. And in a media environment characterised by increasingly networked, collaborative ways of operating, and business models that are increasingly exploring the possibility of online data services, apps, and platforms, 'making power accountable' – by making information available – assumes a significantly increased importance.

Many of the biggest stories of the last decade – UK politicians' expenses and the warlogs and diplomatic cables released by WikiLeaks at different points in 2010 – have been about this process. Freedom of Information campaigner Heather Brooke's five-year campaign for publication of politicians' expenses was focused on the information, not a particular story. In both cases, a large part of the publication involved providing access to full data.

Significantly, none of those datasets was released in full by government authorities: in the case of politicians' expenses, it was being involved in the 'redaction' (blacking out) of key details as part of official publication that led one disillusioned participant to leak the unredacted version to the *Daily Telegraph*. Even in the US, where public access to information had been established in law a year previously, it was Philip Meyer's collection of his own data on race riots in 1967 that inspired a generation of computer-assisted reporters.

In all these cases, merely having the data was not enough. Writing about this, Tim Davies (2012) highlights the importance of *complementarity*:

> We need not just raw materials, but diverse sets of skills and supply chains, frameworks, cultures and practices … Investors, payment processing services, app store business models, remittance to developers, and often-times, stable jobs for developers in an existing buoyant IT industry that allow them to either work on apps for fun in spare time, or to leave work with enough capital to take a risk on building their own applications are all part of the economic background. Developer meet-ups, online fora, clear licensing of data, no fear of state censorship of applications built and so-on contribute to the social and legal background. These parts of the complex landscape generally cannot be centrally planned or controlled, but equally they cannot be ignored when we are asking why the provision of a raw material has not brought about anticipated use.

Journalists can now access a wealth of official data, can scrape data from digitised sources, crowdsource it from networks, call it from APIs, collect it themselves, or collaborate with other parties who have already done so. As the transparency agenda is coopted and side-stepped, journalists may find it useful to have other means at their disposal, while also maintaining a watch on the role and quality of government data itself. The lack of numeracy in a profession which values itself on its literacy should be of particular concern here. But key above all will be the journalist's role to go beyond the datasets which governments want us to have – data churnalism – and seek the data that answers the questions which need to be asked.

Note

1   http://hacks.rewiredstate.org/events/nhtg12.

References

Arthur, C. (2010) 'Analysing Data is the Future for Journalists, says Tim Berners-Lee', *Guardian*, 22 Nov.: www.guardian.co.uk/media/2010/nov/22/data-analysis-tim-berners-lee.

Bell, E. (2012) 'Journalism by Numbers', *Columbia Journalism Review*, Oct.: www.cjr.org/cover_story/journalism_by_numbers.php?page=all.

Bowarva, O. (2012) 'Green Belt Boundaries for Britain – Open or Closed Data?', 17 Jan.: http://mapgubbins.tumblr.com/post/15993324558/green-belt-boundaries-for-england-open-or-closed.

Bradshaw, P. (2012) 'New UK Open Data Moves: Following the Money and Other Curiosities', *Online Journalism Blog*, 5 Dec.: http://onlinejournalismblog.com/2011/12/05/new-uk-open-data-moves-following-the-money-and-other-curiosities.

Brooke, H. (2010) *The Silent State* (Windmill Books).

Bureau of Investigative Journalism (2012) 'Revealed: Deaths that were Not in Official Report', 31 Jan.: http://www.thebureauinvestigates.com/2012/01/31/revealed-the-dead-not-included-in-the-official-figures.

Cabinet Office (2011) *Further Detail on Open Data Measures in the Autumn Statement 2011*, 29 Nov.: http://www.cabinetoffice.gov.uk/sites/default/files/resources/Further_detail_on_Open_Data_measures_in_the_Autumn_Statement_2011.pdf.

Cabinet Office (2012) *Open Data: Unleashing the Potential*, White Paper, Cm 8353 (The Stationery Office): http://www.cabinetoffice.gov.uk/sites/default/files/resources/CM8353_acc.pdf.

Clarke, G. (2012) 'Open Data Institute Pours Golden £10m Shower on Upstarts', *The Register*, 23 May: http://www.theregister.co.uk/2012/05/23/open_data_institute.

Davey, E. (2011) 'Giving Consumers the Midata Touch', *BIS Blog*, 3 Nov.: http://blogs.bis.gov.uk/blog/2011/11/03/giving-consumers-the-midata-touch.

Davies, T. (2011) 'Evaluating the Autumn Statement Open Data Measures', *Tim's Blog*, 2 Dec.: www.timdavies.org.uk/2011/12/02/3090.

Davies, T. (2012) 'Complexity and Complementarity – Why More Raw Material Alone won't Neccessarily Bring Open Data Driven Growth', *Open Data Impacts blog*, 28 Oct.: www.opendataimpacts.net/2012/10/459.

Dudman, J. (2012) 'Chilean Website Allows Voters to Expose MPs' Conflicts of Interest', *Guardian*, 18 Apr.: www.guardian.co.uk/news/datablog/2012/apr/18/chile-open-government-brasilia-2012.

Eaves, D. (2009) 'The Three Laws of Open Government Data', *eaves.ca*, 30 Sept.: http://eaves.ca/2009/09/30/three-law-of-open-government-data.

Ellis, J. (2011) 'Rafat Ali on Building a Media Company on Top of Public Data', *Nieman Journalism Lab*, 1 July: http://www.niemanlab.org/2012/07/rafat-ali-on-building-a-media-company-on-top-of-public-data.

European Commission (2009) *Visby Declaration*, 10 Nov.: http://ec.europa.eu/information_society/eeurope/i2010/docs/post_i2010/additional_contributions/conclusions_visby.pdf.

European Commission (2012) *Towards Better Access to Scientific Information: Boosting the Benefits of Public Investments in Research*, COM (2012) 401 final: http://ec.europa.eu/research/science-society/document_library/pdf_06/era-communication-towards-better-access-to-scientific-information_en.pdf.

Evans, L., and Eaton, J. (2012) 'How Many Children are Learning "Indian Dancing" in Schools?', *Guardian*, 18 Aug.: www.guardian.co.uk/news/datablog/2012/aug/18/participation-school-sport-coalition-stop-reporting.

Finch Report (2012) *Accessibility, Sustainability, Excellence: How to Expand Access to Research Publications*, Report of the Working Group chaired by Janet Finch (Research Information Network): http://www.researchinfonet.org/publish/finch.

FOI Man (2012) 'Remote Ivory Towers or Engaged with the Modern World? Universities Must Decide', *FOI Man*, 12 Jan.: http://www.foiman.com/archives/456.

Garber, M. (2011) 'ProPublica's Newest News App Uses Education Data to Get More Social', *Nieman Journalism Lab*, 1 July: http://www.niemanlab.org/2011/07/propublicas-newest-news-app-uses-education-data-to-get-more-social.

Herbert, D. (2011) 'Release of Whole of Government Accounts', *Open Knowledge Foundation Blog*, 13 July. http://blog.okfn.org/2011/07/13/release-of-whole-of-government-accounts.

Hilkevitch, J. (2012) 'Chicago Police Crash Reports are Full of Errors, Study Finds', *Chicago Tribune*, 23 Apr.: http://articles.chicagotribune.com/2012-04-23/

classified/ct-met-getting-around-0423-20120423_1_crash-reports-red-light-cameras-data.

Hirst, T. (2011) 'Immediate Thoughts on the "Provision of Information about Higher Education"', *OUseful.info*, 12 July: http://blog.ouseful.info/2011/07/12/immediate-thoughts-on-the-provision-of-information-about-higher-education.

Hirst, T. (2012) 'Sleight of Hand and Data Laundering in Evidence Based Policy Making', *OUseful.info*. 1 Feb.: http://blog.ouseful.info/2012/02/01/sleight-of-hand-and-data-laundering-in-evidence-based-policy-making.

Irving, F. (2011) 'Should Britain Flog off the Family Silver to Cut our National Debt?', *Open Knowledge Foundation Blog*, 14 Mar.: http://blog.okfn.org/2011/03/14/family-silver.

James, V. (2012) 'Freedom of Information and Unusable Data', *New Statesman*, 23 May: http://www.newstatesman.com/blogs/voices/2012/05/freedom-information-and-unusable-data.

Laja, S. (2012) 'Long-Awaited NHS Information Strategy "Could Mean Better Data Linking"', *Guardian*, 3 May: http://www.guardian.co.uk/government-computing-network/2012/may/03/nhs-information-strategy-data-linking.

McAthy, R. (2013) 'Trinity Mirror to Set up Data-Driven "Digital Journalism Unit"', Journalism.co.uk, 25 Mar.: www.journalism.co.uk/news/trinity-mirror-to-launch-data-driven-digital-journalism-unit/s2/a552493.

McGuire, A. (2011) 'Read All About It Read All About It: "Scraperwiki Gets on the Guardian Front Page ..."', *Scraperwiki Blog*, 25 Feb.: http://blog.scraperwiki.com/2011/02/25/read-all-about-it-read-all-about-it-%E2%80%9Cscraperwiki-gets-on-the-guardian-front-page-%E2%80%9D.

Miller, E. (2010a) 'Gov2.0 presentation: An Open Government Scorecard', *Sunlight Foundation Blog*, 7 Sept.: http://sunlightfoundation.com/blog/2010/09/07/gov2-0-presentation-an-open-government-scorecard.

Miller, E. (2010b) 'Clearspending. That's What We Need', *Sunlight Foundation Blog*, 8 Sept.: http://sunlightfoundation.com/blog/2010/09/08/clearspending-thats-what-we-need.

Mutter, A. (2012) 'Big Data is a Big Deal for Newspapers', *Reflections of a Newsosaur*, 7 Aug.: http://newsosaur.blogspot.co.uk/2012/08/big-data-is-big-deal-for-newspapers.html.

National Audit Office (2012) *Implementing Transparency* (The Stationery Office). www.nao.org.uk/publications/1012/implementing_transparency.aspx.

NHS Hack Day (2012) 'NHS Hack Day – Something Important is Happening!', *NHS Hackday Wiki*, 2 May: http://wiki.nhshackday.com/wiki/Press%20Release%2002/05/2012.

Open Corporates (2012) 'The Closed World of Company Data', *OpenCorporates,* 16 Apr.: http://opencorporates.com/downloads/ogp_company_data_report.pdf.

Open Government (2011) Official brochure, *Open Government Partnership*: http://www.opengovpartnership.org/sites/www.opengovpartnership.org/files/page_files/OGP_Oficial_Brochure_1.pdf.

Quilty-Harper, C. (2011) 'Why www.police.uk is Useless – AKA the 'Oh Look Pretty Maps!' Effect', *Daily Telegraph,* 1 Feb.: http://blogs.telegraph.co.uk/news/conradquiltyharper/100074290/why-www-police-uk-is-useless-aka-the-oh-look-pretty-maps-effect.

Rayment, T. (2012) 'Care Home Loses Child 130 Times', *Sunday Times,* 15 Apr.: www.thesundaytimes.co.uk/sto/news/uk_news/Society/article1016904.ece.

Reid, A. (2013) 'Help Me Investigate and Birmingham Mail launch datablog', Journalism.co.uk, 1 Feb. 2013: www.journalism.co.uk/news/help-me-investigate-and-birmingham-mail-launch-regional-datablog/s2/a551945.

Right2INFO.org (2012) *Access to Information Laws: Overview and Statutory Goals*; http://right2info.org/access-to-information-laws/access-to-information-laws-overview-and-statutory#_ftnref7.

Rogers, S. (2011) 'Named and Shamed: The Worst Government Annual Reports', *Guardian* Datablog, 27 Oct.: http://www.guardian.co.uk/news/datablog/2011/oct/27/department-resource-accounts-reports.

Royal Society (2012) *Science as an Open Enterprise*: http://royalsociety.org/policy/projects/science-public-enterprise.

Sear, C. (2012) *Audit Commission: Abolition,* Commons Library Standard Note, 3 July: www.parliament.uk/briefing-papers/SN05681.

Shadbolt, N. (2010) 'New Open Government License', data.gov.uk, 30 Sept.: http://data.gov.uk/blog/new-open-government-license.

Sparrow, A., and Mulholland, H. (2011) 'Cameron Accused of Putting NHS on Sale over Plans for Life Sciences', *Guardian,* 5 Dec.: http://www.guardian.co.uk/society/2011/dec/05/cameron-nhs-sale-life-sciences.

Valle-Jones, D. (2010) 'Statistical Analysis and Visualisation of the Drug War in Mexico', *Diego Valle-Jones Blog,* 15 June: http://blog.diegovalle.net/2010/06/statistical-analysis-and-visualization.html.

Worrall, P. (2011) 'How Dodgy Stats Could Decide our Children's Future', *Channel 4 News FactCheck,* 7 Nov.: http://blogs.channel4.com/factcheck/how-dodgy-stats-could-decide-our-childrens-future/8400.

10

Data, Data Everywhere: Open Data versus Big Data in the Quest for Transparency

Helen Margetts

Contemporary government in the developed world is awash with data. From the mid-2000s, the UK and US governments pioneered initiatives in 'open data', where swathes of government data have been opened up for commercial and public consumption. Such initiatives have obvious potential to go beyond freedom of information legislation to enhance transparency, making 'open book' governance possible for the first time. Meanwhile, across the private sector 'big data' has become the theme of current thinking, with corporations tumbling over each other to produce huge reports and convene conferences on the cornucopia of benefits to be gained in terms of efficiency and quality of policy and operations in public and private sectors alike. Journalists have been innovative in developing the skills and expertise to use both 'open' and 'big' data to open up policy and administration to the public, particularly via creative and illuminating visualisations, and many media outlets now employ 'data editors'.

All these data and techniques to analyse them seem to promise previously unimaginable advances in transparency and openness for government, far beyond what can be achieved with freedom of information initiatives. But open data initiatives have been criticised for resulting in 'dumps' of data for the sake of it, and disappointing in public value terms, with benefits gained more by commercial developers than either policy-makers or citizens. And governments have been far slower than either the private sector or the media world in developing the expertise and skills needed to handle big data, meaning that it has not yet shone the light on government it appears to promise. There seems to be a possibility that public sectors will slip between the 'open data' and 'big data' archipelagos, lagging behind corporations in gaining benefits from big data, yet not making the transparency gains hoped for from open government.

This short chapter articulates the distinction between open data and big data (often conflated by commentators), discusses the synergies and tensions between them, and considers how the merits of each might be better exploited to enhance transparency.

Open data: The road to transparency?

Cross-nationally, a rash of open data initiatives with the aim of opening up public sector datasets for use started from 2009. In the UK, the open data agenda started under the Brown administration of 2009–10, when the Prime Minister appointed Sir Tim Berners-Lee and Nigel Shadbolt as information advisers to 'transform access to Public Sector Information'. The two spoke to the Cabinet and visited all major departments and agencies, persuading them of the importance of opening up datasets where there were no privacy concerns. Datasets freed up in this way were loaded to the data.gov.uk site that by 2012 provided access to over 7,800 datasets. Unusually for an incoming government of a different political party, this agenda was pursued under similar lines under the coalition government in 2010, continuing the programme of data.gov.uk; forming a Public Sector Transparency Board to oversee open data releases across the public sector and founding the Open Data Institute, directed by Berners-Lee and Shadbolt. In June 2012 the Cabinet Office and Transparency Board produced an *Open Data* White Paper, the first chapter of which laid out the government's plans for 'Building a transparent society'. Each government department has now published its first 'Open Data Strategy' and departments are also to set out how they are going to 'stimulate a market for its use' (Cabinet Office, 2012a).

In the US, an equivalent initiative was kicked off by the federal administration of Barack Obama in 2009, with the aim of 'increasing public access to high value, machine readable datasets generated by the Executive Branch of the Federal Government' and seeking to become a 'repository for all the information the government collects'. Beth Noveck, author of *Wiki Government* was appointed as the US's first deputy Chief Technology Officer, as a strong advocate for the open data agenda. From the start, the US open government directive required that all agencies 'post at least three high-value data sets online and register them on the site within 45 days'

(Obama, 2009). In August 2010, a position was posted for 'Evangelist for Data.Gov Open Government', illustrating the almost ideological fervour with which new administrations in the US and UK pursued the openness agenda, at least at the beginning. By 2011, the data.gov initiative had attracted worldwide attention and No. 10 Downing Street had attempted to trump the US by appointing Beth Noveck as the UK government's CTO, as announced in George Osborne's Autumn Statement in 2011 (although this later transmuted into a rather vaguer appointment). By 2012, the data.gov portal contained 378,529 raw and geospatial datasets, with 1,264 'government apps' and 236 'citizen-developed apps'; the appearance of the site and the disparity in these numbers suggesting an imbalance between the amount of data made available and the proportion actually used by citizens.

Similar initiatives have continued across the world, including Australia, Morocco, Canada, the Netherlands, Chile, Italy, Spain, and France, all launching in 2011. From their conception, these initiatives have been considered unequivocally good things, the 'little white bunnies' of administrative reform that policy-makers and academic commentators alike find it hard to question or criticise. But increasingly there seems to be a sense of disappointment in the extent to which open datasets are actually used by citizens, even indirectly through intermediaries, in comparison to their development for commercial gain or scientific endeavour, and the extent to which they have improved transparency. The reasons for this disappointment are varied. First, although for obvious reasons 'open' data to most people is clearly linked to the aim of increasing transparency, it has not always been the primary aim. For example, the aim of the new Open Data Institute (announced by Chancellor George Osborne in his Autumn Statement in November 2011) was to 'stimulate innovation and enterprise', with no particular mention of transparency. Open data is a good label for initiatives that do not necessarily fall within the original spirit of transparency; the open data portals of Bahrain and Saudi Arabia probably fall within this category.

Second, open data can be manifested as a front end or shallow veneer on an otherwise secretive and closed governmental organisation. Datasets released for public consumption do not necessarily either shed light on or improve governmental processes, particularly if there are no feedback loops between the datasets themselves and the agencies which produce them. Indeed, in the UK such feedback loops have not really existed – although there is now an option for the users of the www.data.gov.uk website to notify errors or problems discovered in the data, it is very unclear how they get fed back to the originating agency. Open data does not automatically satisfy the notion of 'open book governance' (Dunleavy et al., 2006), where openness of processes becomes embedded in all administrative operations. As one advocate of open government put it: 'Just throwing data over the transom doesn't change how government works. It doesn't do anything to get anyone to do anything' (Noveck, 2012).

Perhaps the most important criticism of open data initiatives can be levelled at the quality and accessibility of the data. Open datasets are often released in raw form, in forms fairly inaccessible to average citizens, and are prone to error. For example, part of the Transparency Board's work during 2012 was to mandate central government departments to release monthly a dataset of all contracts over £25,000. This sounds like a major opening up of public sector processes to public scrutiny, and in the case of information technology contracts (which according to this author's analysis of the largest datasets represent around 35% of expenditure to outside bodies) could provide the public with information that is important to democratic accountability and government with an understanding of its contract relationships that it does not currently possess. But it has been released in spreadsheet form, with ambiguous column headings and the metadata are of different formats across departments. It is extremely difficult to understand without computerised summarisation – which in turn is difficult to perform, due to the raw nature of the data and the lack of consistency in coding it up. This author wonders if any individual or organisation outside a research team dedicated to investigating such issues has ever looked at it.

Finally, there are concerns that public officials could shy away from some aspects of the openness agenda, given the ways in which such datasets could be used to berate public sector agencies, without an informed evidence base. Government officials may be right to fear the open data agenda with its potential to bring 'severe performance regimes' by highlighting raw variation in the performance of public sector agencies, such as schools, hospitals, and so on, without accounting for the underlying differences in constituency demographics (Shadbolt, 2012). Some commentators have even suggested that open data when transported to some contexts, specifically the National Health Service, represents a revival of New Public Management reform, with its capacity to facilitate marketisation and to provide easily visualised empirically based (although potentially misleading) league tables of hospitals and individual healthcare professionals, and have even associated open data with 'neo-liberalism in practice', arguing that it reinforces relationships between state and private sector actors, and does so by 'weakening the positions of both citizens/patients and clinicians' (Keen et al., 2012: 9).

Data deluge: The era of big data

Meanwhile, as open data initiatives have been getting under way, there has been a concurrent development in the commercial world – a trend towards the generation, analysis, and use of so-called 'big data', the data generated through the use of digital technologies for administrative operations, interaction with customers, and in society more generally. The concept derives from observations of the world's ever increasing technological capacity to store, communicate, and compute information and the fact that the majority of our technological memory is now in digital format (Hilbert and López, 2011). Put simply, now that so much of economic, social, and political life takes place online, social media, websites, sensors, mobile applications, and cameras generate all kinds of non-traditional sources of data which offer new potential for organisations of all kinds to understand their own operations and their relationships with their users. Big data is typically huge, unstructured, real-time and transactional, representing some kind of 'whole population'. What is big enough to be considered 'big data' can vary considerably, but a rule of thumb definition is data too large to be collected, analysed, and managed in a normal desktop computing environment or by commonly used software tools.

Corporations have tumbled over themselves to demonstrate their profile in this 'hot trend in the IT world' (Oracle, 2012). McKinsey, IBM, Gartner, and Oracle are just a few of the firms to produce reports on big data during 2011–12. All advertise a cornucopia of benefits to be derived from big data, particularly increased efficiency, enhanced productivity, improved customer retention, and greater capacity to innovate, all through a more detailed and insightful understanding of their business. Of course, the same corporations are offering 'big data solutions' to both firms and governments, so these reports are geared at establishing their credibility in this latest trend. But there is no doubt that new approaches to generating and analysing huge-scale datasets of this kind offer great possibilities for both efficiency and innovation, even though the billions of dollar estimates of savings for private and public sectors through effective use of big data (see Manyika et al., 2011) may be somewhat over-hyped. Transparency is often mentioned as one of the benefits of using big data, although generally as a spin-off rather than the primary objective.

In spite of all the possibilities for more realistic and efficient policy-making that big data might offer, government has been far slower to enter this arena. In part this might be due to a reluctance to embark on any enterprise that contains the word 'big' and 'government' in the same catchphrase; the phrase 'open government' is a far more attractive and benign mantra for politicians in particular, so government initiatives are less likely to be given the 'big data' label. Indeed in the UK, neither the *Open Data* White Paper (Cabinet Office, 2012a) nor the *Government Digital Strategy* (Cabinet Office, 2012b) makes any mention of big data. In other countries, there has been a much higher profile for big data within government, particularly in the US. In March 2012, the White House released details of a new big data strategy, with over $200 million a year committed to research grants. Although some of the initiatives announced under big data have an open data element, with the White House teaming up with Amazon Web Services to make the 1,000 Genomes Project data (200 terabytes) available to genetic researchers, the emphasis is on research and development, with the expectation of big payoffs. As the Director of the White House Office of Science and Technology put it at the announcement of the strategy: 'In the same way that past Federal investments in information-technology R&D led to dramatic advances in supercomputing and the creation of the Internet, the initiative we are launching today promises to transform our ability to use Big Data for scientific discovery, environmental and biomedical research, education and national security' (Press Release, 29 March 2012). And the departments involved were very much those involved in scientific research, rather than in large-scale interactions with citizens: NSF and the NIH, the Department of Defense, the Department of Energy, and the US Geological Survey. There have also been some notable initiatives at state level, such as the Massachusetts Big Data Initiative in May 2012, investing in research and development with a matching grant programme to investigate how data analytics and applications could improve the efficiency and effectiveness of government programmes and services. But again the initiative was geared at advancing the 'knowledge economy' with no mention of transparency or openness.

The benefits of big data for public policy and the delivery of government services, therefore, are potential rather than observable in practice. But big data has already presented as a new type of data for how we understand society, bringing about a major shift in the way that social science is conducted. Empirical research in the social sciences has hitherto been largely based on surveys; that is, data derived from questioning a representative sample of populations about what they think they did or think they might do. In contrast, big data, derived, for example, from people's digital interaction with organisations or from the use of social media, consists of real-time transactional data about what people really did or think, relating to whole populations rather than samples, bringing social science closer to physical or life sciences. Academic researchers from the US and Europe, from disciplines across the social sciences and the humanities, particularly but not exclusively those focused on some aspect of online behaviour, are starting to generate and analyse big data, with two international conferences in Oxford alone in September 2012 (convened by the Oxford Internet Institute and the Oxford eResearch Centre). Researchers from the physical and life sciences have always worked with big data, and cross-disciplinary teams are forming as social scientists recognise the need to develop new methodological expertise and learn from disciplines such as computer science, physics, and biomedicine.

For public policy, therefore, aimed at changing societal behaviour, big data offer massive scope for understanding people's needs and preferences and what they are willing – or not willing – to do, in terms of civic engagement or complying with legislative change. It makes it possible to understand which incentives will work and under what circumstances and to design policy and administrative change in a way that is realistic and efficient. Also, as governmental organisations become increasingly digital in their operations and interactions with citizens, big data offers great potential for opening up government to public understanding and hence for transparency. Taken to the extreme, if we think of an organisation like Wikipedia, which is entirely digital, then a download of its entire edit history provides the complete transactional history of an organisation, providing a hitherto unimaginable opportunity to understand its governance arrangements (see Loubser, 2010). As governmental organisations increasingly 'become' their web presence and back-end information processing systems (Dunleavy et al., 2008; Margetts, 1999; Steinberg, 2012), such possibilities open up for government also.

As with open data, there are a number of criticisms or concerns that have or can be raised over the trend towards big data. First, it brings ethical challenges; as danah boyd (2010) put it, 'Just because it is accessible doesn't mean using it is ethical'. Big data offers potential to make evidence-based predictions of future trends, in society just as in the natural world. If big data can be used to predict the future, then it can allow probabilistic models of policy-making, based on what will probably happen. Such models raise questions of justice and equity – the identification of crime 'hotspots' so small that we can predict crime there before it happens, for example – what do we do with this information? People living in that micro-local area will have a far higher probability of being arrested than those in other parts of the country.

Another ethical issue provoked by the use of big data is that of privacy. On the one hand, the very idea of big data is that it is so big everyone is anonymous; if you want to hide a tree, do it in a forest. But de-anonymisation through the use of big data or the matching of datasets remains a threat that can work against the use of big data. In 2006, AOL released the search records of half a million AOL search engine users, supposedly anonymised by removing names and IP addresses. Within days, however, the *New York Times* had revealed the identity of one user and more followed. This one example of de-anonymisation has had a dramatic impact on companies' willingness to release data, or even publish the results based on user data, with Eric Schmidt, CEO of Google, announcing shortly afterwards that 'this kind of thing could not happen at Google' and no anonymised log data has been released to the research community since then. Some commentators have even questioned the use of big data for its privacy threats, arguing that aggregating and distributing data out of context is a privacy violation; 'Big Data isn't arbitrary data; it's data about people's lives, data that is produced through their interaction with others, data that they don't normally see let alone know is being shared. The process of sharing it and using it and publicizing it is a violation of privacy' (boyd, 2010).

Furthermore, big data generation analysis requires expertise and skills which can challenge governmental organisations in particular, given their dubious record on the guardianship of large-scale datasets, the management of contract relationships and large technology-based projects, and capacity to innovate with newer media and technologies in comparison with firms, social enterprise, and citizens themselves. Big data usually provides a picture so complex that visualisation has to be part of the narrative, and these skills are difficult to acquire, particularly for governments whose online presence is overwhelmingly presented in text form.

Data journalism: Filling the gap

It is perhaps journalists and media organisations who have done most to overcome this last challenge of using big data, and to further the aims of using these initiatives, big data and open data, to enhance transparency by acquiring some of the skills and expertise to understand and analyse big data. The phenomenon of 'data journalism' involves finding data sources, interrogating them, matching up across datasets, and visualising them. Most major media outlets now employ 'data editors' with particular expertise in this field. The *Guardian*, a leader in the field at least in the UK, produced early in 2011 a kind of 'big' dataset of its own use of big data, showing all the data journalism reported including all spreadsheets, authors, number of comments and retweets, which is now updated every month (*Guardian* Datablog).

In 2012 Google supported the first ever 'data journalism' awards, organised by the Global Editors Network. The winner investigated the FBI's use of informants in terrorism-related cases, revealing a clear pattern on how the FBI generated terrorist plots from sting operations, while the second investigated the reasons behind the correlation between methadone-related deaths and poverty in Washington State. As one of the judges put it, visualisations like these are not only visually compelling and intuitive 'but, more importantly, the visualisation helps to reveal trends and meaning that would not have been possible using traditional narrative techniques' (*Guardian* Datablog, 2012). In general, perhaps journalists more than any other profession have shown a willingness to learn the skills and develop the expertise to present big data in an appealing and useful way, in particular by developing techniques of visualisation that academics tend to lack and government have not begun to contemplate.

Open data versus big data

The concepts of big data and open data are often discussed almost interchangeably. Journalists in particular have been inclined to view all types of data that can fall into the big data category as thereby open, and likewise to see open data as somehow 'big'. One of the leading journalists in the field, the *Guardian* data editor Simon Rogers even conflated the two in the term 'open journalism', in his blog in September 2012.

However, to conflate the two concepts is to miss an important point. Open data is not automatically big data; indeed many of the datasets made available through open data initiatives are actually 'small', in that they represent a sample of what is available or, at least, can be made publicly available. Some of the most fervent advocates of open data have even observed that government agencies break up datasets into smaller components, in part so that they can make more impressive claims about the number of datasets that have been made available (Shadbolt, 2012). Likewise, big data is not necessarily open; it is often proprietary, its use restricted to the organisations that generated it, for example to maintain competitive market advantage or for privacy reasons, as discussed above. Facebook, for example, holds a mass of big data that is extremely closely guarded and is never opened up even to researchers except in the most partial ways. As noted above, open data is generally regarded as somehow 'better' than big data. For example, as the VP of Gartner put, in commenting on Gartner's own big data report in 2012, although 'big data … creates business value by enabling organizations to uncover previously unseen patterns … for clients seeking competitive advantage through direct interactions with customers, partners and suppliers, open data is the solution' (Gartner, 2012). He called for an 'open-data' strategy even for firms.

One way to view the distinction between open and big data is in terms of production and consumption of these kinds of datasets. Open data is in general, not consumed by the same stakeholders as it is produced. It tends to be produced by government agencies, mandated to do so by some central agency, with a vague notion that it will provide public value, either in terms of economic benefits or enhanced transparency. But once it has been released, there are virtually no feedback loops between the data and the agency which released it. So if, for example, developers attempting to work with the data find problems or inaccuracies, there are no ways for them to feed this information back to government. In contrast, big data is something that is 'there' by virtue of administrative operations, and in this sense remains closer to the organisation producing it, and which in general has most to gain from its analysis, in terms of efficient and realistic policy-making and service delivery for example. Such data can highlight important variations in service provision between local deliverers, for example, but in general is less likely to be used in a political way to berate public agencies.

Conclusion: Prospects for transparency

So what have been the real gains in transparency terms from these developments? This short chapter has discussed the most important developments in open data and big data in the UK and US, drawing out the differences and synergies between them. Open data emerges as a reform development with mixed aims and extremely varying results in transparency terms, with a tendency towards politicisation, partly due to the attractiveness of the label for politicians. It may be that big data, with its less explicit transparency aims, and its suitability for rigorous scientific analysis of societal interactions, is the better long-term bet for more substantively transparent government and even 'open-book' governance.

Obviously, there is a large subset of data that is both open, in that it has been produced with the aim of opening up government, and also 'big', in that it represents the whole of population real-time transactional data that can be analysed in a way that makes public organisations both more efficient and more transparent. Such data offer real hope for the future of transparency. But those who produce such data with this aim in mind have also to ensure that it overcomes the hurdles that are discussed above, specifically ethical concerns over equity, justice, and privacy and the strong requirement for government to acquire new skills and expertise in data generation and analysis as well as the kind of visualisation that journalists have started to undertake.

References

boyd, d. (2010) 'Privacy and Publicity in the Context of Big Data', WWW2010: http://futureweb2010blog.wordpress.com/2010/04/29/danah-boyd-privacy-publicity-and-big-data.

Burn-Murdoch, J. (2012) 'Winners of the Inaugural Data Journalism Awards Announced', *Guardian* Datablog, 31 May: http://www.theguardian.com/news/datablog/2012/may/31/data-journalism-awards-winners.

Cabinet Office (2012a) *Open Data: Unleashing the Potential*, White Paper, Cm 8353 (The Stationery Office).

Cabinet Office (2012b) *Government Digital Strategy*, Nov. (The Stationery Office).

Dunleavy, P., Margetts, H., Bastow, S., and Tinkler, J. (2008) *Digital Era Governance: IT Corporations, the State and e-Government* (Oxford University Press).

Gartner (2012) 'Big Data Drives Rapid Changes in Infrastructure and $232 Billion in IT Spending through 2016', 12 Oct.: www.gartner.com.

Hilbert, M., and López, P. (2011) 'The World's Technological Capacity to Store, Communicate, and Compute Information', *Science*, 332 (6025): 60–5.

Horowitz, M. (23 June 2008). 'Visualizing Big Data: Bar Charts for Words'. *Wired Magazine*, 16.07.

IBM (2012) 'What is Big Data? Bringing Big Data to the Enterprise': www-01.ibm.com/software/data/bigdata.

Keen, J., Calinescu, R., Paige, R., and Rooksby, J. (2012) 'Big Health Data: Institutional and Technological Challenges', paper at IPP2012 conference 'Big Data, Big Challenges', Oxford, Sept.

Loubser, M. (2010) 'Organisational Mechanisms in Peer Production: The Case of Wikipedia', D.Phil. thesis, University of Oxford.

Manyika, J., Chui, M., Bughin, J., Brown, B., Dobbs, R., Roxburgh, C., and Byers Hung, A. (2011) *Big Data: The Next Frontier for Innovation, Competition, and Productivity* (McKinsey Global Institute): www.mckinsey.com/Insights/MGI/Research/Technology_and_Innovation/Big_data_The_next_frontier_for_innovation.

Margetts, H. (1999) *Information Technology in Government: Britain and America* (Routledge).

Novek, B. (2009) *Wiki Government: How Technology Can Make Government Better, Democracy Stronger, and Citizens More Powerful* (Brookings Institution Press).

Novek, B. (2012) 'Demand a More Open-Source Government', *TEDGlobal*, 15 Sept.: www.ted.com/talks/beth_noveck_demand_a_more_open_source_government.html.

Obama, B. (2009) *Memorandum on Transparency and Open Government* (White House).

Oracle (2012) *Integrate for Insight: White Paper* (InfoWorld Custom Solutions Group): www.oracle.com.

Rogers, S. (2012) 'Open Data Journalism', *Guardian* Datablog, 20 Sept.: www.theguardian.com/news/datablog/2012/sep/20/open-data-journalism.

Shadbolt, N. (2012) 'Open Data', keynote address to the IPP2012 conference, 'Big Data, Big Challenges', Oxford, Sept.

11

Corporations and Transparency: Improving Consumer Markets and Increasing Public Accountability

Joel Gurin and Beth Simone Noveck

From cuneiform to card catalogues, people have always recorded data. But now we have tools to collect information faster than ever before. The proliferation of data includes statistics collected by governments about the economy, such as unemployment data or data that we supply on our tax returns and patent filings. When the media refer to the era of 'big data', they are including the vast amounts of information we also passively generate. Our mobile phones and cars contain sensors to track and report our location, position, acceleration, and temperature. The smart meters in our homes reveal when we turn on the heat or hot water. Companies increasingly gather data about our shopping and web-browsing habits. The world's storehouse of digital information is growing at the rate of 5 trillion bits per second (Overbye, 2012).

What is revolutionary is not only the quantity of data but also how we can use computers to search, sort, compare, aggregate, visualise, and track data. This kind of analysis can help us understand more about ourselves, our communities, and our environment, realising the benefits of what has been called the quantified self (see quantifiedself.com) and community (Dyson, 2012). But these benefits can only be realised if data are available in a form that computers can ingest and process (see Noveck and Goroff, 2013). Data must be *open* – freely accessible and computable. When data are open, anyone can create sophisticated visualisations, models, and analyses, as well as spot mistakes or mix and mash across datasets to yield new insights.

The ability of third parties to participate is what makes open data truly transformative. When data are open, data stop being just data and become, instead, a catalyst for creative problem-solving and innovation by a community (Noveck, 2012). Governments in several countries, including the United States, have committed themselves to greater transparency and are publishing open data in computable formats online. Open data can have an impact in two often-overlooked areas: it can empower consumer choice and it can increase institutional accountability in the public interest. (Open data is also catalysing new entrepreneurial opportunities and job growth, though we will not focus on the economic impact in this chapter.)

Open data can empower consumers to make more informed decisions in the marketplace. A new policy approach, known as 'smart disclosure', aims to give consumers more complete data about the cost, quality, and safety of the products and services they buy, as well as the labour practices and health and environmental impact of product manufacturers and service providers (see Thaler and Tucker, 2013). (The benefits are still assumed. Because smart disclosure depends on the most recent technology to work, the approach is still fairly new and needs to be further studied.) Smart disclosure is already being used in online and mobile applications to help consumers choose products and services and thus remedy market failures due to insufficient consumer information. Smart disclosure has its roots in behavioural economic theory that better information will lead to better consumer decisions about cars, mobile phone plans, financial services, healthcare, higher education, home energy options, and other services. In addition, the theory holds that informing consumers will make consumer markets more efficient, fostering competition and innovation (see National Science and Technology Council, 2011; Office of Management and Budget, 2011; White House, 2011).

While smart disclosure can be an innovative and progressive approach to consumer protection, it's ultimately limited to consumer product and service markets. Open data can drive accountability about corporate behaviour in ways that go beyond consumer choice, markets, and pricing, when governments also demand that data about corporate ownership and control and corporate activities be disclosed. In the same way that greater disclosure about the workings of government agencies is intended to lead to decreased corruption, there is an assumption that governments can make the entities they regulate more accountable by collecting and disclosing data about them, or requiring those entities to disclose data themselves, particularly if the data is disclosed in standardised and computable formats. A new foundation-backed effort called OrgPedia, which we also discuss in this chapter, is designed to use both government-mandated and other sources of data to make corporate ownership structures more transparent – what we can call organisational transparency. Its goal is to enable regulators, researchers and journalists to hold companies accountable for those actions that are outside the purview of smart disclosure.

Greater transparency is essential to help prevent corporate abuses in the boardroom or the mine. Smart disclosure and organisational transparency can provide investigative opportunities for print, online, and broadcast media, making new kinds of journalistic analysis and reporting possible. With such data tools journalists can pull together information from disparate databases to analyse issues and trends across organisations and sectors in ways never before possible, potentially leading to more effective journalism even in the wake of reduced budgets. However, both smart disclosure and organisational transparency rely on open data to beef up transparency beyond what investigative journalism can do after the fact. These new, tech-enabled transparency practices are intended to spur corporate accountability and also, perhaps more importantly, to improve governmental effectiveness and accountability. Much of the story of corporate malfeasance involves a shared failure between business and regulators who fail to enforce regulations. These new forms of transparency represent experimental techniques for improving the watchdog functions of government (Fung et al., 2007).

With open data about organisations and about the products they produce in computable formats, the hope is that we can develop tools to target scarce enforcement resources. For example, if we can 'see' when a company is engaged in price gouging or can visualise a company's labour and environmental violations on a map, then we can get early warning signs about where oversight is most needed. The hope is that smart disclosure and organisational transparency can result in more effective regulation that may, at the same time, be less burdensome to business than mandated and directive approaches such as rate regulation.

As powerful as smart disclosure and organisational transparency can be, they are not always enough to solve problems that may need stricter regulations. An overreliance on transparency to improve markets and corporate behaviour could lead to an abdication of government responsibility and a privatising of public functions (Slee, 2012). This chapter explores how these new kinds of tech-enabled transparency can best be used to help drive greater accountability in the industries that government agencies regulate, and where the pitfalls are in using them. We also discuss the ways that increased corporate transparency can be used by the media to benefit the public. And we conclude with a discussion of the research now needed to assess whether and when transparency works to produce greater accountability, and what the limits are of this approach.

Smart disclosure: Helping consumers through transparency

Since 2011, President Obama's Administration has taken several steps to promote smart disclosure as a policy approach designed to help consumers make better informed decisions, foster data-driven innovations that benefit consumers, and help create more transparent, efficient markets for goods and services. The Task Force on Smart Disclosure: Information and Efficiency in Consumer Markets was established by the National Science and Technology Council in July 2011 to study this approach. With support from the task force, the US government included smart disclosure in its national open government plan (White House, 2011), and the Office of Management and Budget (2011) released a guidance memo instructing agencies on how to use smart disclosure where appropriate. The task force's report was released in 2013.

Smart disclosure involves releasing data that can fuel the creation of web-enabled tools that benefit consumers. Web entrepreneurs and others are using smart-disclosure data to create online and mobile 'choice engines' – tools that help consumers make important and difficult choices in sectors such as healthcare, education, personal finance, energy, transportation, and telecommunications. Air travel search sites are a prime example of choice engines: they allow consumers to filter data by using information about their preferred airlines, travel times, price range, and other factors, and find a small selection of flights that meet their needs out of hundreds of possibilities. Unlike older forms of product transparency such as food labels, smart disclosure practices focus on creating tools using multiple variables where there is not necessarily one 'right' answer. In other words, in today's complex product markets such as financial products or mobile phones, consumer protecting is not simply about showing the number of calories but showing a range of product attributes, enabling each person to decide what the good or bad choice is for that individual.

Smart disclosure is being implemented in the hope that informed consumers will make for more transparent and efficient consumer markets. For example, when service providers profit from hidden fees, consumers can't accurately compare the true price of different services, and competition suffers. But when consumers can easily assess price and quality, competition becomes more robust, and new, innovative companies can compete more effectively against those that are already established. Smart disclosure can support job creation both by fostering the growth of these new companies and by fostering a growing industry of websites and apps that work as consumer choice engines.

Some smart-disclosure choice engines have created their own databases about products and services – for example, by doing customer satisfaction surveys on insurance companies, airlines, or other service providers (as *Consumer Reports* does), or by scraping information from companies' websites and cell phone bills submitted by consumers (like the American company BillShrink[1]). But government agencies and legislators can support such efforts by mandating the release of consumer-focused data. The best examples are those where the government:

1.   mandates data to be disclosed across an industry (comprehensive);
2.   in standard, computable formats (open data); and
3.   which can be used by government or others to create choice engines and apps (to support informed consumer choice).

In the US, Congress has mandated some forms of smart disclosure and agencies now have smart-disclosure initiatives in several sectors, including the following.

Education

The Higher Education Opportunity Act of 2008 added substantially to the original Higher Education Act of 1965, with several provisions to increase transparency and consumer information on student loans, college costs, and other financial issues (U.S. Congress, H.R. 4137, ss. 110, 111, 112, 120, etc.). To help implement the Act, the US Department of Education now provides government data and online tools[2] to help students and families choose a college and decide how to finance their education. The Department's College Navigator website[3] includes net price calculators that allow prospective students to enter information about themselves to find out what students like them paid to attend each institution in the previous year, after taking grants and scholarship aid into account.[4]

Personal finance

The Consumer Financial Protection Bureau, a new agency created by Congress in response to the financial crisis, is undertaking a number of initiatives to improve transparency both through conventional printed forms and through online disclosure of data. The Bureau's mission, as stated on its website, is driven by the concept of using transparency to empower consumers:

> The central mission of the Consumer Financial Protection Bureau (CFPB) is to make markets for consumer financial products and services work for Americans – whether they are applying for a mortgage, choosing among credit cards, or using any number of other consumer financial products … Above all, this means ensuring that consumers get the information they need to make the financial decisions they believe are best for themselves and their families – that prices are clear up front, that risks are visible, and that nothing is buried in fine print. In a market that works, consumers should be able to make direct comparisons among products and no provider should be able to build, or feel pressure to build, a business model around unfair, deceptive, or abusive practices. (CFPB, 2013)

Healthcare

The Affordable Care Act, the US healthcare reform legislation passed in 2010, established a strong role for consumer choice in healthcare: under its provisions, many consumers will choose and purchase health insurance from state-based exchanges. In a related effort, the US Department of Health and Human Services (HHS) has developed interactive online consumer tools, such as Healthcare.gov and Medicare.gov, which help consumers compare insurance plans and the quality of healthcare providers. The department worked with the health insurance industry to provide information tailored to the individual's needs, including data on the number of applicants denied coverage, which had not been previously available.

Transportation

The Department of Transportation (DOT) has long published data on airlines' on-time performance and consumer complaints against airlines. The DOT also now requires airlines to advertise the full price of flights, including taxes and fees, so that consumers can accurately assess their costs through travel websites and other means. In establishing this rule, the DOT took note of the way that consumers now shop for air travel online, and even estimated the value of time that consumers would save in searching for flights with the new rule (US Department of Transportation, 2011).

Personal data for individuals: Health and energy use

In order to make the best possible choices, consumers don't only need the kind of data about products and services described in these examples. They also need easy access to data about themselves that will help them match their own needs to what's available in the market. Someone purchasing health insurance, for example, will benefit from easy access to his or her medical records in figuring out how to get the best affordable coverage for the kinds of healthcare they use. In the US, the government has launched the Blue Button initiative, which has developed into a public–private partnership where agencies and companies give individuals access to their personal electronic health records (Chopra et al., 2010). The US government has also worked with private energy suppliers to launch Green Button, which is making personal energy usage data available to tens of millions of their customers (Chopra, 2011). Similarly, the UK government's Midata initiative has been working with industry to make data about consumers' energy use and other consumer data available to each individual.[5]

OrgPedia: Organisational transparency in the public interest

Where smart disclosure makes data about services available for consumers to use, OrgPedia – a new resource now in development – will deliver data about for-profit and nonprofit corporations for journalists, regulators, and concerned citizens to use. While smart disclosure is focused on empowering individual consumer choice, OrgPedia is designed to make visible the ownership and control relationship among firms and directors and enable users to mash up data about corporate entities from different sources. For example, OrgPedia will make it possible to learn whether environmental violations at a company's many factories add up to a poor environmental record for the parent company, or whether a company with a history of labour problems has other issues as well. OrgPedia is one of a handful of new efforts designed to increase organisational transparency about finances, governance, structure, and operations of both for-profit and nonprofit organisations. Examples include Open Corporates and Duedil in the UK, and LittleSis and CorpWatch in the US.

The most basic form of organisational transparency – the disclosure of corporate ownership and control structures, which is a prime focus of OrgPedia – could be a major step to increase corporate accountability. There are many examples of corporations that have used complex ownership structures to make it difficult to trace their actions, and their violations of regulations, back to a single corporate source.

One classic example of investigative reporting on corporate behaviour demonstrates why organisational transparency is necessary. A *New York Times* Pulitzer Prize-winning series on McWane, Inc. managed to uncover that 'in plant after plant, year after year, McWane workers have been maimed, burned, sickened and killed by the same safety and health failures. Flammable materials are mishandled; respirators are not provided; machines are missing safety guards; employees are not trained.' Yet the reporters also noted that 'The evidence spills forth from hundreds of regulatory files scattered in government offices around the country – more than 400 safety violations and 450 environmental violations since 1995 alone' (Barstow and Bergman, 2003). What is needed now, and what OrgPedia is designed to provide, is a way to organise such 'scattered' data that makes it much easier to spot, analyse, and report on a company's patterns of regulatory violations and unsafe practices.

Complex corporate structures may have both contributed to the global financial crisis and made it more difficult to solve. An international banking study done after the collapse of Lehman Brothers found that:

The Lehman Brothers group consisted of 2,985 legal entities that operated in some 50 countries ... It consisted of a complicated mix of both regulated and unregulated entities ... [A] trade performed in one company could be

booked in another. The lines of business did not necessarily map to the legal
entity lines of the companies ... Structures of this complexity are common
in large international financial institutions. (Basel Committee, 2010)

Greater organisational transparency can make it easier to spot risky
patterns in investment firms and to help resolve problems quickly when
they arise.

Finally, consumers often care about corporate ownership, especially
when a parent company is taking a position they disagree with. The *New*
York Times reported that consumers protested to Kashi, an American food
company with an 'organic' image, when they learned that Kashi's parent
company, the cereal manufacturer Kellogg's, was lobbying against labelling
foods containing genetically modified organisms. The *Times* quoted a
spokesman for an organic industry group as saying that

Consumers aren't always aware that their favorite organic brands are in
fact owned by big multinationals, and now they're finding out that the
premium they've paid to buy these organic products is being spent to fight
against something they believe in passionately ... They feel like they've
been had. (Strom, 2012)

To increase organisational transparency of all kinds, the OrgPedia Project,
designed by a consortium of leading research universities with initial
funding from the Alfred P. Sloan Foundation, is now being planned as a
'Wikipedia of firms'. It is envisioned as a free and open toolkit that will
enable regulators, researchers, journalists, activists, and investors to map a
company's ownership structure and visualise its financial, environmental,
workplace, health and safety performance firm-wide. It will combine
clearly labelled data from government, such as securities, environmental,
and patent filings, with data from public and private sources, as well as
information contributed and corrected by companies, organisations, and
individuals. By bringing these data sources together, OrgPedia will aim to
create an independent source for comprehensive information about public
and private, domestic and global firms.

OrgPedia is organised around the belief that one of the best ways
to gather data quickly about the 'terra incognita' of companies and
organisations globally is to crowdsource that data, offering incentives such
as challenges and prizes to people to contribute missing information and
rate and rank each other's contributions for accuracy.

OrgPedia is designed to be a downloadable resource for economists, regulators, and researchers. It will make available a rich array of information, including:

- 'business card' information with name, location, and other identifying information about individual firms;
- ownership information about who owns and manages the firm and whom it owns and operates;
- open government data about each corporation, including securities and patent filings and environmental and labour records;
- data from other public and private sources; and
- most importantly, bulk downloads of data across multiple firms and sectors.

OrgPedia will draw on government agencies that collect data through regulatory processes, on information provided by corporations themselves, on private sources of information such as financial databases and news reports, and on members of the public. Like Wikipedia, OrgPedia will use public participation to check and add to data from other sources – and will allow corporations, in turn, to correct inaccurate information about themselves. Unlike Wikipedia, however, OrgPedia will highlight the provenance of each data element so that users can decide for themselves which sources they trust for different kinds of information.

One of the goals of this project is to enable users to analyse issues that cut across an entire industry, in addition to looking up data for individual corporations one at a time. OrgPedia will use linked data to enable users to do mash-ups of different datasets and will provide basic interactive and analytic tools. It will also support the development of new tools through an API that will enable other organisations to import OrgPedia data for their own projects.

OrgPedia and other corporate transparency websites can be used by researchers, journalists, policy-makers, and watchdog organisations. They can also help corporations and investors better understand the business environment in which they operate. These websites enable companies to learn about both competitors and potential partners in their field, and give investors financial data and reputational data to help them determine the potential and risk of investing in a given company.

New government reporting standards will support the development of OrgPedia and similar resources. In the US, the Securities and Exchange

Commission (SEC) now collects and releases data on companies using eXtensible Business Reporting Language (XBRL), a computer language that makes it possible to embed large amounts of data in a form that can be easily searched and analysed with the use of computers. Governments in the United Kingdom, Australia, Belgium, China, Ireland, Japan, Singapore, and Sweden have similar requirements. In South Africa, companies are required to use XBRL to report data on their environmental and social impact in addition to financial data. This type of reporting, known both as ESG reporting (Environmental, Social, and Governance) and 'One Report', is of increasing interest to investors both in the US and abroad (US SEC, 2012; and see Eccles and Krzus, 2010).

The opportunities for the media

Both smart disclosure and the kind of organisational transparency exemplified by OrgPedia represent efforts to apply the technology of big data to the problem of reducing obfuscation – often the result of entrenched legal loopholes – in firm behaviour. Given the lack of transparency there has been in the past, these new forms of disclosure could open up new opportunities for journalists and the media of all types – print, broadcast, and online.

Smart disclosure has the potential to revolutionise service journalism. While consumer-focused reporting has a long history, the increasing complexity of consumer services and issues poses new challenges. In the past, staples of consumer-focused service journalism have included exposing scams, highlighting product-safety concerns, and giving consumers general advice on finding the best deals in airline flights, credit cards, or other services. Today, however, consumer services have reached a level of complexity that demands more sophisticated reporting and analysis. Service plans have become more confusing, whether a consumer is choosing a combination of devices and data plans from a wireless provider or trying to sort out the intricacies of health insurance. As smart disclosure begins to make the markets for consumer services more transparent, a new generation of web-savvy journalists can take advantage of its data and applications.

At a higher level, smart disclosure will make it easier to analyse patterns across an industry and report on the results – for example, by identifying health insurance companies that have the highest rates of denying claims, or credit cards that charge the highest late fees. It can enable journalists to analyse consumer markets and expose industries that rely on hidden fees, confusing terms of service, or other forms of obfuscation to profit from their customers' confusion. Smart disclosure can also reveal problems of quality in healthcare, nursing homes, and other essential services that can have an impact on public health.

Where smart disclosure provides new opportunities in consumer reporting, OrgPedia and similar websites will make possible new journalistic research and reporting on corporate practices. These websites will make it possible both to do research on individual companies' practices – for example, determining whether a company has a record of labour or environmental violations – and to look at practices and issues across an entire industry, such as electronics manufacturing, food production, or financial services. Local reporters, too, will be able to use online resources to investigate local plants and factories, tie them to their parent companies, and identify issues in the context of those companies' overall behaviour. The kind of reporting that the *New York Times* did on McWane, Inc. will ultimately become much easier for investigative journalists around the country to do.

Government agencies are not only the drivers of corporate transparency, they are also critical sources of open data that can be increasingly useful to the media. The report, *The Information Needs of Communities*, released by the US Federal Communications Commission in 2011, cited the potential power of data released by the government. As the report noted, 'The effective dissemination of government-collected information can empower citizens, improve accountability, lower reporting costs, and stimulate entrepreneurship' (Waldman and Working Group, 2011: 345–6).

In both the UK and the US, leading consumer organisations have begun to work on transparency initiatives. These organisations are both advocacy organisations and consumer-focused publishers, and work with government and government data in both capacities. *Which?* in the UK has worked with the government's Midata initiative, and has advised the government on consumer interests and on consumer concerns about access to personal data.[6] In the US, *Consumer Reports* now uses a number of government databases as sources for its evaluation of products and services. For example, the organisation mines data from the National Highway Traffic and Safety Administration to identify car safety problems, and from the National Health and Nutrition Evaluation Survey for issues related to food safety.[7] As data reporting and analysis continue to improve,

CORPORATIONS AND TRANSPARENCY

other consumer publications and media outlets will be able to analyse any number of government data sources in the same way.

As the US and other governments make more open data available, journalists of all kinds, in all media, will be able to use the data in the interest of accountability journalism. By providing a new level of information about consumer services, smart disclosure can change the standard for how government agencies should help consumers, and will make agencies more accountable for promoting consumer protection and empowerment. As described above, federal agencies are already giving consumers more data about important aspects of health, finance, energy, education and transportation. While the responsible agencies have sometimes done this at the direction of Congress, other smart disclosure initiatives have been conceived of and implemented as agency rule-makings or simply as highly effective online tools that agencies can provide. As more agencies use smart disclosure, journalists, as well as consumer advocates, can legitimately ask why those that don't practise smart disclosure are lagging behind.

While we believe that both smart disclosure and organisational transparency will be important tools for journalists, the proof will come as they are put into practice. We look forward to seeing new, creative case studies that demonstrate when and how open data is most effective. In particular, it will be important to see how new tools can make it possible to do classic kinds of investigative projects in less time, at lower cost, and with more comprehensive results than before.

Finally, journalists, advocates, and the public at large will have to determine when open data is enough, and when more direct regulation is needed. Simply telling the public about hazardous products, foods, or drugs, for example, is important, but it would never substitute for recalling them and getting them off the market. In many cases, transparency and traditional regulation need to go hand in hand, and journalists can help keep regulators honest if they rely on open data when they should also be taking direct action.

Toward a corporate transparency research agenda

The John D. and Catherine T. MacArthur Foundation has funded an effort led by Professor Noveck to plan a Research Network on Opening

Government. This pre-network, on which Joel Gurin also served, includes in its scope the research agenda on the impact of open government data.[8]

While corporate transparency may be improving both consumer decision-making and public accountability, research is needed on exactly how effective it can be and under what circumstances. Since smart disclosure and web-enabled 'choice engines' are relatively new consumer tools, there has been little formal research on how much they can help consumers make informed decisions that benefit them. There is also little research on the impact of the kind of corporate transparency represented by OrgPedia and similar websites. Not enough is known about what forms of corporate disclosure are most accurate and useful or, on a technical level, how different kinds of corporate data can best be organised, managed, and analysed.

For smart disclosure, an intriguing and important question is whether, and under what circumstances, transparency can benefit the providers of products and services themselves. It is likely that consumers will reward companies that are transparent about their practices in markets where consumers have especially confusing choices. (For example, some major health insurers are now helping their policy-holders with online tools for choosing healthcare providers with high ratings from their patients and low out-of-pocket costs.) Companies may adopt smart disclosure voluntarily to clean their own house and reduce the risk of more burdensome regulation. And businesses have an interest in smart disclosure when they themselves are consumers of services: there are now online resources that use smart disclosure to help companies manage their pension plans, choose money-saving cell phone plans, and control their health-insurance costs. By assessing the potential business benefits of smart disclosure, researchers could help encourage voluntary disclosure that can be faster and less contentious than a government regulatory process.

Research is also needed on Environmental, Social, and Governance (ESG) reporting, which has become a significant area of interest and concern for investors, social activists, and the leaders of corporations themselves. Much of the drive for this kind of corporate transparency has come from activists who want to use it to improve corporate practices for the public good. For example, the Carbon Disclosure Project collects data provided by corporations about the impact of their operations on carbon emissions, and provides the data to institutional investors who represent more than $80 trillion in assets. Data on corporate activities are also used by investment managers directing socially responsible funds, and, ultimately, by individual investors concerned about the use of their investment dollars. Increasingly, ESG data is being seen as a key measure of corporate leadership and corporate sustainability that should concern even investors who are only interested in a company's financial performance. There is a need for research on how to establish standards for ESG reporting, how to ensure accuracy and usability of ESG data, and how journalists and others can make use of these insights into corporate practices (Eccles and Krzus, 2010).

Another area for research is more technical. We need to research approaches to pattern recognition that can help us learn more from the data that government already collects. Since it is difficult for government agencies to mandate transparency against strong industry opposition, and even more difficult for legislative bodies to enact new mandates for transparency, the best first approach is to make as much as possible of the data we now have. For example, sophisticated analysis could help detect ownership or other relationships between entities that have not been made public, or could find companies that have violated labour as well as environmental regulations. This kind of analysis will require major advances in web and economic sciences, but may serve the public interest in important ways.

An overriding question – and one with major implications for regulatory policy – is how effective transparency can be in comparison with more directive forms of regulation. While there has already been research in this area, including the wide-ranging analysis done by Harvard's Transparency Policy Project (see Fung et al., 2007), more work will be needed as open data makes new levels of corporate transparency possible. As important as transparency is, it should not be seen as a panacea or a substitute for stricter regulations where those are necessary.

Two examples of environmental regulation in the US show the potential impact of combining mandates for transparency with more traditionally directive regulations. The Clean Air and Clean Water Acts have been the basis of national pollution control measures. But at the same time, the Toxics Release Inventory, launched by the Environmental Protection Agency (EPA) in the 1980s, has publicised annual pollution levels from individual industrial plants, using transparency to shame the worst offenders into improving. Regarding fuel efficiency, government-mandated labels have given new-car buyers information on estimated miles-per-gallon for years, and were recently redesigned to make this information even more transparent and useful to consumers. But the government is not relying on transparency alone to improve fuel efficiency: in August 2012, the US Department of Transportation and Environmental Protection Agency announced ambitious new fuel efficiency standards that all vehicle manufacturers will have to meet (White House, 2012).

With new technology available to collect, analyse, and distribute large amounts of data, corporate transparency can become a market-changing tool. For perhaps the first time, our ability to analyse data is catching up with the complexity of modern corporations and their global activities. Government agencies and data-savvy journalists are both key players in the emerging data ecosystem, and will play critical and complementary roles in defining the future of corporate transparency. We should never expect transparency and disclosure to take the place of more directive government regulation. But the current efforts to improve corporate transparency, and thus corporate accountability, are beginning to show their potential to help individual consumers and the public interest.

Notes

1   Personal communication by Joel Gurin with Schwark Satyavolu, CEO of BillShrink, June 2010.
2   http://collegecost.ed.gov/catc/Default.aspx.
3   http://nces.ed.gov/collegenavigator.
4   http://nces.ed.gov/ipeds/resource/net_price_calculator.asp.
5   See the description of this initiative at http://webarchive.nationalarchives.gov.uk.
6   Personal communication by Joel Gurin with Georgina Nelson of *Which?*, 2012.
7   Meetings of Joel Gurin with *Consumer Reports* staff, Jan. 2012.
8   See www.openinggovernment.org.

References

Barstow, D., and Bergman, L. (2003) 'Dangerous Business: Deaths on the Job, Slaps on the Wrist', *New York Times*, 10 Jan.
Basel Committee on Banking Supervision (2010) *Report and Recommendations of the Cross-border Bank Resolution Group* (Bank for International Settlements).
CFPB (Consumer Financial Protection Bureau) (2013) 'About Us', updated 31 May: www.consumerfinance.gov/the-bureau.

Chopra, A. (2011) 'Modeling a Green Energy Challenge after a Blue Button', White House Office of Science and Technology Policy Blog, 15 Sept.: www. whitehouse.gov/blog/2011/09/15/modeling-green-energy-challenge-after-blue-button.

Chopra, A., Park, T., and Levin, P. L. (2010) '"Blue Button" Provides Access to Downloadable Personal Health Data', White House Office of Science and Technology Policy Blog, 7 Oct.: www.whitehouse.gov/blog/2010/10/07/blue-button-provides-access-downloadable-personal-health-data.

Dyson, E. (2012) 'The Quantified Community': www.project-syndicate.org/commentary/the-quantified-community.

Eccles, R. G. and Krzus, M. P. (2010) *One Report: Integrated Reporting for a Sustainable Strategy* (John Wiley & Sons, Inc.).

Executive Office of the President, National Science and Technology Council, *Smart Disclosure and Consumer Decision making: Report of the Task Force on Smart Disclosure*, May 2013: www.whitehouse.gov/sites/default/files/microsites/ostp/report_of_the_task_force_on_smart_disclosure.pdf

Fung, A., Graham, M., and Weil, D. (2007) *Full Disclosure: The Perils and Promise of Transparency* (Cambridge University Press).

Noveck, B. S. (2012) 'Open Data – The Democratic Imperative', 5 July: http://crookedtimber.org/2012/07/05/open-data-the-democratic-imperative.

Noveck, B. S., and Goroff, D. (2013) *Liberating Data for Impact: 990 Data and the Nonprofit Sector* (Aspen Institute).

Office of Management and Budget (2011) *Informing Consumers through Smart Disclosure*, Memorandum for the Heads of Executive Departments and Agencies, 8 September: www.whitehouse.gov.

Overbye, D. (2012) 'Big Data's Parallel Universe Brings Fears and a Thrill', *New York Times,* 4 June: www.nytimes.com/2012/06/05/science/big-datas-parallel-universe-brings-fears-and-a-thrill.html.

Slee, T. (2012) 'Do Civil Liberties and Privatization Belong Together?', in *Open Data Movement Redux: Tribes and Contradictions*, Whimsley Blog, 8 May: http://whimsley.typepad.com/whimsley/2012/05/open-data-movement-redux-tribes-and-contradictions.html#sec-4.

Strom, S. (2012) 'Uneasy Allies in the Grocery Aisle', *New York Times*, 13 Sept.

Thaler, Richard H., and Tucker, W. (2013) 'Smarter Information, Smarter Consumers', *Harvard Business Review* (Jan.–Feb.).

US Department of Transportation (2011) *Enhancing Airline Passenger Protections,* final rule 25 Apr., docket DOT-OST-2010-0140.

US Securities and Exchange Commission (2012) 'What is Interactive Data and Who's Using it?': www.sec.gov/spotlight/xbrl/what-is-idata.shtml.

Waldman, S., and the Working Group on Information Needs of Communities (2011) *The Information Needs of Communities* (Federal Communications Commission): www.fcc.gov/infoneedsreport.

White House (2011) *The Open Government Partnership: National Action Plan for the United States of America*, 20 Sept.: www.whitehouse.gov.

White House (2012) 'Obama Administration Finalizes Historic 54.5 MPG Fuel Efficiency Standards', 28 Aug.: www.whitehouse.gov/the-press-office/2012/08/28/obama-administration-finalizes-historic-545-mpg-fuel-efficiency-standard.

12

The Rise of NGOs and Nonprofit Media

Charles Lewis

William Shakespeare's oft-cited line written not far from Oxford four centuries ago that 'what's past is prologue' might help us properly consider the current state of transparency and accountability in government and media, including the specific subject of the rise of non-government organisations (NGOs) and nonprofit media in the United States. In regard to the specific issues before us, reflecting upon the past certainly provides useful insight into the present and the future. Indeed, the fuller, lesser known version of that famous aphorism actually alludes to the future but also reminds us that the actions taken *today* are quite relevant to what happens tomorrow: 'Whereof what's past is prologue, what to come in yours and my discharge' (*The Tempest*, 2. 1. 397).

In the past half century in the United States, we have lived through the confluence of several historically significant, information-related developments in the evolution of our representational democracy, the potential synergies of which are exponential and incalculable. For the purposes of providing context and perspective for the discussion that follows, consider that during this momentous period of time, we have *simultaneously* seen:

- The emergence of a broad consensus and expectation that the public has a right to know information and that our most powerful institutions *must* be transparent and *must* be held accountable. This popular presumption, by itself, is hardly new, dating back more than two centuries in the Age of Enlightenment. As a Founding Father of the United States and its remarkable Constitution, James Madison, once said, 'A popular Government, without popular information, or the means of acquiring it, is but a Prologue to a

Farce or a Tragedy; or perhaps both. Knowledge will forever govern ignorance: And a people who mean to be their own Governors, must arm themselves with the power which knowledge gives' (1999: 790). In 1948, the United Nations adopted the Universal Declaration of Human Rights, including Article 19, which formally asserted the right 'to seek, receive and impart information and ideas through any media and regardless of frontiers' (Glendon, 2001: 312). And in 1966, President Lyndon Johnson signed into law the Freedom of Information Act, which has been subsequently amended many times. Today over 90 countries have FOIA laws and administrative procedures, a potentially invaluable, investigative tool for 5.5 billion (out of 7 billion) people in the world attempting to hold those in power accountable (FreedomInfo.org, 2012; McIntosh, 2011; see also Roberts, 2006: 14–15; Sweden and Finland had the first laws, adopted in 1766, see Bjorkstrand and Mustonen, 2006: 4).

- The evolution of a dynamic, highly technological Information Age, in which, according to author James Gleick, information itself 'has become the modern era's defining quality – the blood, the fuel, the vital principle of our world … We are all patrons of the Library of Babel now, and we are the librarians, too' (2011: 426). In just a few decades, we have gone from the invention of the mainframe computer to the laptop computer and ever smaller multimedia computer devices to the internet, the World Wide Web, global search engines, and 2 billion wired users globally, from telephones to wireless cell phones and now 'smart phones', from typewriters to personal computers to stunning, high-definition tablets, from books to multimedia e-books, in personal communication from handwritten or typewritten letters to emails to 140-character tweets, etc. (Gabler, 1998[1]). This astonishing ability to obtain and process seemingly boundless bytes of computerised information has increased the public expectation of transparency and accountability, and dramatically bolstered the ability of journalists and other research-minded citizens to sort, process, and analyse massive amounts of data.

- As additional sources of online news, entertainment and other information have proliferated, consumer 'use of newspapers, news magazines, and television news is at a 50-year low' in the United States, according to Robert Picard, the director of research at Oxford University's Reuters Institute for the Study of Journalism (Picard, 2009). The resultant loss in annual advertising revenue has resulted in *one-third fewer* newspaper reporters and editors now covering those in power than there were 20 years ago while the number of public relations specialists attempting to 'manufacture consent' have *doubled* during the same period of time (Downie and Schudson, 2009). Given that kind of disturbing disruption, the extent of in-depth, accountability journalism has seriously diminished. Pulitzer Prize applications in the public service, explanatory journalism and investigative reporting categories have decreased by roughly 35% the past quarter-century (Walton, 2010, based on calculating the simple average of the cited 'decreased' percentages in applications for the three following categories, 1985–2010: applications for the public service 'Gold Medal' fell 43% from 122 to 70, for investigative reporting, 21%, from 103 to 81, and for explanatory journalism, 43%, from 181 to 104).

- And of the at least 20,000 people who have been downsized from their newspaper newsroom jobs as reporters and editors since 1992, *fewer than 5%* of them appear to have moved into the 'new journalism ecosystem' of nonprofit news organisations. Since 2004, more than 60 new nonprofit news organisations have been created throughout the US, 17 of them at colleges and universities (Lewis et al., 2011; Walton, 2010).[2]

- Today, there are also approximately 1.5 million nonprofit NGOs operating in the United States alone; they exist, in the words of the US Department of State (2012), 'to represent virtually every cause imaginable'. NGOs undertake a wide array of activities, including political, social, economic and other advocacy. And in recent years, there has been a notable increase in the growth in one particular type of NGO, public policy research organisations, better known as think-tanks, and that growth has been nothing less than explosive. 'Not only have these organisations increased in number, but the scope and impact of their work has also expanded dramatically,' according to James McGann at the University of Pennsylvania, who annually tracks their evolution. There are now 6,480 think-tanks operating in 169 countries, 57% of them in North America and Western Europe. In the first decade of the new millennium, think-tanks have 'witnessed a new phenomenon of global networks and partnerships', which have 'become an effective mechanism for transferring knowledge and information internationally' (McGann, 2011: 5–16). Their high-quality content is released via assorted publishing venues, from multiple websites, daily blogs, books, monographs, magazines, newspapers and newsletters, radio and television and web documentaries, and even their *own* television and radio programmes.

Indeed, not only are these organisations operating as in-depth journalists function – taking months or even years to gather information before publishing and then, upon publication, issuing short releases, single multimedia stories, full pdf online or otherwise as books, op-eds published elsewhere, etc. – to a greater extent than before, several have been hiring respected print reporters and authors full-time and on a contract basis. It is, I would suggest, a natural and perhaps even inevitable evolution. As the need to do more in-depth and global-aperture journalism has increased, and the extent of traditional newsgathering capacity and resultant coverage has instead actually decreased, retrenching for financial reasons, these often very well-funded rising NGOs have shrewdly and nimbly moved into very important, specialised niches of neglected subject matter and helped to fill glaring public information needs. Thus, this phenomenon must be recognised as a robust and dynamic part of the emerging new journalism ecosystem.

This evolution also signifies an important, emerging new hybrid form combining high-quality, in-depth journalism and topical social science research, written with varying degrees, depending on each individual case, of little or even no discernible advocacy to 'soft advocacy' to full-throated advocacy. These various professional and heavy public research affinity groups have been quietly proliferating in plain sight in recent years, barely noticed as a potentially significant new development in the respective recent histories of both journalism and political science and other social science disciplines.

Human Rights Watch

For example, it is no secret that the most granular, on-the-ground research and reporting on human rights issues around the world, extending to innovative uses of new technologies such as satellite imagery photography and bomb-data analysis, is being done by Human Rights Watch, published in nine languages and online translatable into scores more – not the *New York Times* (in English- and Chinese-language editions plus the *International Herald Tribune*) or any other single daily newspaper. Human Rights Watch functionally began operating in the form of regional organisations such as Helsinki Watch in 1978, ultimately combining energies to become Human Rights Watch in 1988; in 1997 it shared in the Nobel Peace Prize as a founding member organisation in the International Campaign to Ban Landmines. Its 'accurate fact-finding [and] impartial reporting' and documentation are certainly evident in over 100 reports and briefing information published *annually* about human rights conditions in about 90 countries. Led by former federal prosecutor Kenneth Roth, who oversees 280 full-time human rights experts and advocates, lawyers, journalists, and academics operating from offices now in 14 cities on four continents, Human Rights Watch is funded by major foundations and individual donations, and it does not seek or accept contributions 'from any government or government-funded agency'. In 2011 its far-flung research and advocacy activities cost $50.6 million; that year the organisation also received the first instalment of a 10-year, $100 million commitment of support from billionaire George Soros, whose son Jonathan Soros serves on the Board of Directors.[3]

Of course, anyone investigating and reporting about such a contentious and politically sensitive subject as human rights abuses will inevitably encounter controversy and denials and counter-charges. In 2009, Robert Bernstein, the founder and former board chairman of Human Rights Watch for 20 years, who also happened to be the former president and CEO of Random House, publicly excoriated his old organisation in a stunning editorial in the *New York Times*, writing that Human Rights Watch, through its reports, was 'helping those who wish to turn Israel into a pariah state'. Of particular frustration to him and some other long-serving board members was that there now appeared to be a different, shifting standard about how to assess human rights abuses. The Middle East, Bernstein wrote, 'is populated by authoritarian regimes with appalling human rights records. Yet in recent years Human Rights Watch has written far more condemnations of Israel for violations of international law than of any other country in the region' (Bernstein, 2009). And months later, a *Wall Street Journal* editorial revealed that the organisation 'had solicited donations in Saudi Arabia by trumpeting the criticism it faces from "pro-Israel pressure groups"' (Birnbaum, 2010).

Veteran Human Rights Watch board member and attorney Kathleen Peratis responded to Bernstein's overarching frustration about the organisation's disproportionately critical reporting about Israel vis-à-vis other Middle Eastern human rights-abusing countries:

There is broad consensus on the board of Human Rights Watch in support of its Middle East work in general and its Israel-Palestine work in particular ... I am a Jew, a Zionist and a full-throated supporter of the work of Human Right Watch ... There is no bias against Israel at Human Rights Watch except in the minds of those who erroneously believe Israel is harmed by honest criticism. Far from harming it, I believe this work strengthens Israel.

And she referred readers to 'our extensive research on most of the other countries and entities in the region such as Hamas, Hezbollah, Iran, Syria, Libya, Saudi Arabia' (Peratis, 2010).

Ultimately, as the *New Republic's* Ben Birnbaum – who interviewed Bernstein following his startling op-ed and wrote an in-depth review of precisely what had led to such an unusual act of a founder publicly rebuking his own organisation – acknowledged, '[Human Rights Watch] is widely considered the gold standard in human rights reporting – an organization whose conclusions nobody can ignore'. Despite this controversy and others that are simply inevitable in this kind of work, I agree, and that is, indeed, the general consensus view.

Global Integrity

Currently the most thorough country-by-country field research and diagnostic analysis, peer-reviewed and collectively chronicled by ground-view social science experts, other knowledgeable citizens, AND journalists, tracking the precise state of corruption in countries throughout the world – using a global 'network of more than 1,500 on-the-ground analysts and our unique scoring system ... data and qualitative analysis drawn from more than 300 indicators' – is being done by Global Integrity, as opposed to any single traditional daily news media source (Global Integrity, 2009, with subsequent updating email with Nathaniel Heller, Dec. 2012).

On this assessment and how a new international research organisation with offices in Washington and Cape Town, South Africa, was born, I am admittedly not objective. It was my idea. As the founder and executive director of the Center for Public Integrity in Washington in 1989, including its International Consortium of Investigative Journalists (the first global network of premier investigative reporters, initially 100 in 50 countries, now up to 160 in 60 countries on six continents, collaborating across borders and cultures to report about abuses of power around the world) in 1997, through its aggressive, award-winning journalism and published work over the years, the Center had eventually come to be seen as an international authority on both political corruption and investigative journalism. And from years of travelling and speaking abroad, I had become concerned that the extremely dangerous, heroic corruption reporting in the world is too micro and Sopranos-like in its bad guy crime focus, often lacking context and sometimes, besides the sensational, personal scandal titillation, lacking much broad, public relevance.

While in Tashkent, Uzbekistan, in 1997, as part of a fact-finding research team investigating horrific ethnic violence years earlier in the Fergana Valley, sponsored by the Council on Foreign Relations, I had an epiphany that inside and outside that repressive country, all citizens – from foreign investors and companies with offices there to tourists as well as truly endangered indigenous human rights activists and journalists who had seen their colleagues killed – seemed to lack current, credible online information about the quality of governance, rule of law, civility, press freedom, and accountability. There was no satisfactory, comprehensive, 'one-stop-shopping' organisation or website generating such vital insight or regional context, enabling residents and visitors to easily compare these things country-by-country. From the Center's national survey investigations into US conflicts of interest in the state legislatures and in Washington, I believed we had discovered a more sweeping, analytical way of examining cronyism and corruption and the conditions that had helped to enable such abuses of power. What if our often macro investigative methodological approach in the US could be adapted to the entire world?

In July 1999, I asked Nathaniel Heller, a newly arrived, recent University of Delaware grad and Center Soles Fellow to help me explore a new way of monitoring and reporting on corruption, government accountability, and openness around the world. It culminated years later in an unprecedented, 750,000-word Center report – by far the largest ever – published online in 2004, titled *Global Integrity*, prepared by 200 paid social scientists, journalists, and peer-review editors in 25 countries on six continents. This massive project, directed by Marianne Camerer, an internationally respected anti-corruption social scientist from South Africa, spawned a new nonprofit organisation with a more academic, social science orientation and quantitative methodological component and with greater and more diverse funding and capacity needs than the Center for Public Integrity.

The Center has never accepted project or general funding from any government source, but there also appeared to be insufficient foundation or individual donor interest in this issue to financially sustain such ambitious, labour-intensive work globally about corruption, especially if it was done annually. If I didn't spin it out from the funding-restrictive Center, the exciting project would die, along with its unique approach and innovative, multifaceted reporting and research methodology. One of my last official acts as Center executive director in December 2004 was to recommend to the Board of Directors that this exciting new enterprise be spun off as a new global independent nonprofit organisation (Lewis, 2013[4]). The Board approved my recommendation unanimously and months later, Global Integrity became a 501(c)(3) tax-exempt organisation in 2005, co-founded by Nathaniel, Marianne, and yours truly.

Since then, Nathaniel has built it up to a full-time staff of 13 people, including co-founder and international director Marianne Camerer in South Africa, and a 'growing network of more than 1,300 local experts in more 120 countries', paid in 2010 with $1.96 million in revenue raised from disclosed, donated funding from foundations, corporations, and national and multilateral government entities including the World Bank, the Inter-American Development Bank, the United Nations Development Programme (UNDP-Oslo) Governance Centre (interested in 'democratic governance ... and as a means to achieve the [anti-corruption] Millennium Development Goals'), etc. The organisation publishes a sophisticated, very extensive, annual *Global Integrity Report*, utilising reporters and social scientists in each country profiled and generating substantial worldwide news media coverage upon its release. Global Integrity organisationally describes itself as 'an innovation lab that produces high-quality research and creates cutting-edge technology to advance the work of a global network of civic, public, and private reformers pursuing increased transparency and accountability in governments'.[5]

Nathaniel (and other social entrepreneurs across the country with their own separate projects) has also been exploring the possible development of a new type of company described by the *New York Times* as 'intended to put social goals ahead of making profits', called a 'flexible-purpose corporation ... part social benefit and part low-profit entities', known as a limited liability company or L3C (Strom, 2011). It is called Foglamp, now a project and 'service of Global Integrity' that generated 'maybe $150,000' in earned as opposed to donated income in 2011. 'Foglamp revenue isn't at a point where it's crucial to spin it off', Nathaniel told me.[6] But eventually Foglamp could very possibly become an incorporated, revenue-generating entity 100%-owned by the nonprofit Global Integrity. With its own separate website, Foglamp is utilising the Global Integrity on-the-ground international network of contract-hired researchers and journalists in 120 countries. For Foglamp is a 'customizable in-country research service helping investors and professionals better understand opportunities in overseas markets'. Researchers and journalists may be asked to write 'client-designed memos', 'follow-up calls and field updates, email, instant message and phone exchanges with on-the-ground subject matter experts', and other 'custom services', which could include 'in-country meetings, custom trips and bespoke expert surveys all tailored to client needs'.[7]

This is, of course, decidedly unjournalistic, and such 'client' interactions are and will be very uncomfortable and frankly unimaginable for some reporters and researchers to participate in, awkward and embarrassing activities for an old dog veteran journalist like myself with traditional, twentieth-century professional reporting sensibilities. At least it is not a *required* activity, it is an option – it is entirely up to each individual reporter or editor available to Global Integrity as a contractor to be hired whether or not to participate. According to Nathaniel Heller:

> *Despite the conventional wisdom that grizzled, veteran investigative reporters would shy away from conducting private paid projects for Foglamp clients, in only one case during the past three years, spanning more than 50 projects for a range of hedge funds and consulting firms, has a Global Integrity contributor declined a Foglamp project opportunity for 'yuck factor' reasons.*[8]

But also, no one ever suggested that Global Integrity is exactly a news organisation, though its reports and books are prepared in part by retained journalists, reporters and editors and enthusiastically received and covered by them.

Finally, beyond Global Integrity, there is another, larger point to be made, which further illustrates the new blurring of lines between professions and previous journalistic sensibilities. Two of the *largest* news staffs in the English-speaking world today are Bloomberg and Thomson Reuters; the former is a private corporation, the latter is public. But news is a 'relatively small factor in the bottom line of both Bloomberg and Reuters'. As *Adweek* reported, their respective, high-end subscription-based businesses and financial intelligence for clients contribute a huge part of their annual revenue – 82% for Bloomberg, 90% for Reuters. And the 'core news content produced by the two companies is not exactly what one would call public-interest journalism. Rather, it is made up of stories geared to making, as one critic puts it, "a handful of people even richer"' (Freeland, 2010; Moses, 2012).

It all seems sadly emblematic of these difficult times for gathering and publishing serious, important research and reporting, the various, valiant efforts to find an unfickle, genuinely interested, online reading and paying audience, anywhere, and the ongoing search for a financially sustainable business plan for publishing such work. Welcome to our increasingly mercenary milieu.

New America Foundation

And of course, the nature of Google and other global search engine queries now is that 'who' published it is less noteworthy than which words are 'tagged' and other online traffic algorithm factors; which is why Wikipedia for years has been one of the most viewed sites in the world and the *New York Times* and *Washington Post* and other individual daily 'here's today's news' newspaper and other media outlets are not. (Wikipedia's self-described definition is 'a multilingual, web-based, free-content encyclopedia project based on an openly editable model'.[9]) It means that purveyors of serious, original content can conceivably publish something extremely topical, and that story or report can rocket to the upper echelons of web traffic.

This melding of heavy in-depth research, analysis, and writing with very topical subjects, presented with all of the latest digital age sensibilities and content written in many instances by displaced career journalists now adeptly operating from another (or sometimes simultaneous) venue and 'platform', is a very important, indeed extraordinary development. And it frankly has hardly been addressed in most 'future of journalism' observations to date.

For example, consider for a moment the New America Foundation, based in Washington, DC. It was created in 1999 by founding president Ted Halstead and founding chairman of the board James Fallows, a highly respected journalist and author, formerly the editor of *U.S. News & World Report*, NPR commentator, and currently a national correspondent for the *Atlantic Monthly* magazine. New America's self-description is as a 'nonprofit, nonpartisan public policy institute that invests in new thinkers and new ideas to address the next generation of challenges facing the United States'. Today, it employs 142 people and has an annual budget for FY 2012 projected to be $19.1 million.[10] The director of the Foundation's National Security Studies programme is CNN's national security analyst, veteran journalist Peter Bergen, who among other things interviewed Osama bin Laden prior to 9/11 and is the author of four books, three of them *New York Times* bestsellers.

The Foundation has no fewer than 31 fellows, some of the most highly regarded journalists in the US, such as Joel Garreau, former long-time *Washington Post* reporter and editor and author of numerous books; Tim Wu, a professor at Columbia Law School and author of the acclaimed book, *The Master Switch: The Rise and Fall of Information Empires*; Pulitzer Prize-winning writer for ProPublica and the *New York Times* magazine Dr Sheri Fink; Jason DeParle, a long-time *New York Times* reporter, etc.

The second president of the New America Foundation was Steve Coll, stepping down from that leadership role in 2013 and a former *Washington Post* managing editor, a two-time winner of the Pulitzer Prize for his books and currently also a staff writer for the *New Yorker*. It is extremely unusual for the head of a public policy institute to also be an active, current staff writer for any national magazine, but one interesting recent trend in the US is just that, wearing two (or more) professional hats, simultaneously. Another 'two-fer' has been former Columbia University Graduate School of Journalism Dean Nicholas Lemann, who was and also remains a current *New Yorker* staff writer. Coll, the new Columbia Journalism dean, will also continue as a staff writer for the magazine.

Donors to the New America Foundation are identified alphabetically on the website, bracketed by the amount they have given. There are, of course, numerous donors annually on the way to a $19 million annual budget. It receives government funding from the US Department of State and the Swiss government, numerous well-known foundations from the Carnegie Corporation, the Knight Foundation, the Peter G. Peterson Foundation, the Wyncote Foundation, the Irvine Foundation, the MacArthur Foundation, the Open Society Institute, and many others.

There is also no shortage of corporate funding, from Merck & Co., Aetna, Microsoft, Nike Foundation, and many others. The three most generous donors, each giving at least $1 million or more, in 2011 were The Ford Foundation, the Bill & Melinda Gates Foundation, and Eric and Wendy Schmidt.

Schmidt is also the chairman of the New America Foundation Board, and from 2001 to 2011 he was the CEO of Google, and he is now the executive chairman. Not only is he responsible at Google for 'the external matters of Google: building partnerships and broader business relationships, government outreach and technology thought leadership, as well as advising the CEO and senior leadership on business and policy issues'. Schmidt is also a member of the President's Council of Advisors on Science and Technology, and the Prime Minister's Advisory Council in the UK.

The reason that is quite interesting is that the New America Foundation has a robust research programme around its Open Technology Institute, dealing with 'policy and regulatory reforms to support open architectures and open source innovations and facilitates the development and implementation of open technologies and communications networks'.[11] From an objective journalistic standpoint, what may be most notable sometimes are not the policy-related subjects an organisation chooses to examine, but the extent to which certain publicly relevant topics are *not* addressed or critically analysed. So much of what the Open Technology Institute is doing in terms of policy-related research has direct relevance to Google, right now, and none of it appears to be remotely critical of the gigantic company's policies or practices. For example, in terms of policy, the Foundation has not substantively addressed certain difficult policy issues for Google such as consumer privacy or online consumer protection vis-à-vis children, health, finance, etc.

The main point from the brief discussions of Human Rights Watch, Global Integrity, and the New America Foundation is that these organisations and so many others like them, by dint of their sheer public presence, enlarge the public space for sometimes significant truth-telling in our society by employing a substantial number of exceptional journalists.

Add to that the numerous nonprofit journalism centers operating throughout the US today, 17 of which are operating from university campuses and thereby attempting to inculcate core journalistic values and technical know-how in new generations of reporters, editors, and others in order for them to be able to continue and extend this essential work. In late 2011, when my Investigative Reporting Workshop researchers and I examined the IRS 990 tax documents and other materials, we found that the cumulative total of annual funding and number of employees for the 75 journalistic organisations profiled in our database was $135 million and 1,300 full-time employees, respectively. And as the Investigative News Network (INN), created in 2009, becomes larger, adding new member organisations and forging creative new ways to combine energies, skill sets, and content into effective content management and syndication systems, and the Global Investigative Journalism Conference movement moves into its second decade, the nonprofit public space for investigative journalism these days is a very exciting place to be.[12]

Finally, what is substantively possible when it comes to these scrappy nonprofit reporting organisations and their potential national or even international impact in terms of transparency and accountability? At the Center for Public Integrity alone, for the first time in journalism history, we posted every available financial disclosure form for state legislators in the nation, more than 7,400 elected officials, and collaborated with 45 newspapers in 45 states to identify literally hundreds of inherent conflicts of interest. We obtained and published a list of all overnight White House guests in President Bill Clinton's first year in office, and published a report, *Fat Cat Hotel*, about how major Democratic Party donors were rewarded with overnight stays in the Lincoln Bedroom.

The Center helped to pioneer the early use of online searchable databases and documents, posting everything from independent political organisation '527' data to tobacco company documents obtained in Britain and analysed by journalists on five continents, which revealed that British American Tobacco was illegally smuggling cigarettes across borders in order to avoid millions of dollars in customs duties.

We went through hundreds of thousands of state and federal records in 1996, 2000, and 2004 and posted 'Top Ten Career Patron' lists for every major White House aspirant, which we closely analysed and published in *The Buying of the President* books.

In 2003, weeks before the US invasion of Iraq, the Center posted secret draft 'Patriot II' legislation, and in October, for the first time in any American armed conflict, the Center posted all of the known US war contracts in Iraq and Afghanistan. *Windfalls of War* first identified that Halliburton and its then-subsidiary Kellogg Brown & Root had received by far the most money from those contracts, and it won the first George Polk Award for Internet Reporting. In this instance, 20 researchers, reporters, and editors worked for six intense months, filed 73 Freedom of

Information Act requests and we also successfully sued the Army and State Department in US District Court, in order to publish this information and update it in 2004.

The Investigative Reporting Workshop at American University in Washington, DC, began publishing major investigative stories in partnership with national media outlets in March 2009 and since then has published more than 50 national investigative news stories, not counting periodic updates and partnering with the PBS programme FRONTLINE, www.nbcnews.com, BBC News, the *Financial Times*, ABC *World News Tonight*, the *New York Times*, the *Washington Post*, Politico, McClatchy newspapers, and others. Workshop reporting was read by more than 1 million unique visitors on our website in the first two years of operation. Already the Workshop is the largest university-based investigative reporting center in the United States, and the only one in the nation's capital.

For three years, amid the Great Recession, Workshop senior editor Wendell Cochran's unprecedented and very popular BankTracker project, in partnership with msnbc.com (now nbcnews.com), has taken and analysed Federal Deposit Insurance Corporation (FDIC) data for all 8,000 banks in the US and posted this quarterly on the Workshop site, and expanded it to include some 8,000 credit unions from separate data. On the eve of publishing the first story, the American Bankers Association urged us not to do it, for fear there might be a 'run' on banks. The *New York Times* had had similar misgivings and had decided not to proceed. We did, there was not a run on any bank, and the project has since received a national journalism award. Now the *Wall Street Journal* has also started periodically presenting the data.

Veteran award-winning reporter John Dunbar of the Workshop in early 2012 posted public and private data showing broadband service prices and speed for the Washington, DC, metropolitan region, revealing major 'digital divide' disparities between urban, suburban, and rural neighbourhoods. Following that, using three datasets, we posted a national interactive map, revealing the precise extent of broadband adoption rates, zip code by zip code.

At the Workshop, our FRONTLINE documentary production staff had close encounters of the worst kind, which producer Catherine Rentz recently chronicled, with the Federal Aviation Administration (FAA) in the research gathered for a recent, national award-winning documentary called *Flying Cheaper* about how major airlines outsource maintenance overseas.

We have many other investigative projects in the pipeline, all of which involve federal or state government documents which we are attempting to obtain and glean the essential information from, before posting it all on the web for the American people to see. This work is time-consuming, expensive purely in terms of the cost of labour, and requires great analytical skill in discerning the important from the mundane. We could not attempt to do this work without the philanthropic support of foundations and individuals. More broadly, of course, the entire freedom of information community and culture of collaboration are invaluable to us, and vitally necessary in this imperfect representational democracy of ours.

It is increasingly apparent that holding those in power – public power or private power – accountable is and must be a global, and thus increasingly collaborative undertaking, given how fundamental reliable information is to democracies and to the entire concept of self-governance everywhere. Public interest, academic, NGO, journalistic, and other investigative-minded organisations and individuals increasingly must share their information, knowledge, and expertise. And journalists must redefine the possible, and, for example, become more welcoming of substantive input from knowledgeable citizens and the common, shared interest and value in public accountability. At American University, within the School of Communication and with the other Schools, I have formally proposed that we create a new interdisciplinary, academic field known as 'Accountability Studies', combining the perspectives and know-how of such fields as forensic accounting, political science (e.g. corruption-related research), investigative history, public anthropology, human rights law, and many others. We are all now at the dawn of a new, twenty-first-century age of shared accountability, across disciplines, borders, languages, and cultures.

Centuries ago the great Italian astronomer Galileo Galilei wrote, 'All truths are easy to understand once they are discovered; the point is to discover them.' For peoples throughout the world, this has always been a formidable challenge with potentially huge consequences, and it certainly remains so today. It also happens to be a very exciting time.

Notes

Full disclosure: Charles Lewis is personally associated with several nonprofit journalism or research organisations mentioned in this chapter.

1   Two billion internet users is based on data compiled by the World Bank through 2010: http://search.worldbank.org/all?qterm=number+of+internet+users+in+the+world&Search=go.
2   Research about the number of US-based nonprofit news organizations varies widely depending on the precise methodology, the time period, etc.
3   See www.hrw.org./partners; and Statement of 2011 Functional Expenses, www.hrw.org/sites/default/files/related_material/financial-statements-2011.pdf
4   See also www.globalintegrity.org/about/story.
5   www.globalintegrity.org.
6   Via email, 28 September 2012.
7   www.foglamp.org/about.
8   Via email exchange, 12 December 2012.
9   Wikipedia contributors, 'Wikipedia:About', *Wikipedia, The Free Encyclopedia*: http://en.wikipedia.org/w/index.php?title=Wikipedia:About&oldid=568463685.
10 Via email from Clara Hogan, New America Foundation, 28 September 2012.
11 http://oti.newamerica.net.
12 For INN see www.investigativenewsnetwork.org. It was created in July 2009 and now has 82 nonprofit news organisations as members, with others expected to be joining by the end of 2013. Globally, training and educational conferences among journalists formally began in 2001, and in late 2013, the eighth Global Investigative Journalism conference will be held in Rio de Janeiro, Brazil. Over 3,300 reporters and editors have attended these events, from nearly 100 countries, to date. See www.GIJN.org.

References

Bernstein, R. L. (2009) 'Rights Watchdog, Lost in the Mideast', *New York Times*, 20 Oct.: www.nytimes.com/2009/10/20/opinion/20bernstein.html.
Birnbaum, B. (2010) 'Minority Report: Human Rights Watch Fights a Civil War over Israel', *New Republic*, 27 Apr.: www.tnr.com/article/minority-report-2.
Bjorkstrand, G., and Mustonen, J. (2006) 'Introduction: Anders Chydenius' Legacy Today', in J. Mustonen (ed.), *The World's First Freedom of Information Act*

(Anders Chydenius Foundation): www.access-info.org/documents/Access_ Docs/Thinking/Get_Connected/worlds_first_foia.pdf.

Downie Jr., L., and Schudson, M. (2009) *The Reconstruction of American Journalism*, Columbia University Graduate School of Journalism, 20 Oct.: www.cjr.org/reconstruction/the_reconstruction_of_american.php.

FreedomInfo.org (2012) '93 Countries Have FOI Regimes, Most Tallies Agree', 19 Oct.: www.freedominfo.org/2012/10/93-countries-have-foi-regimes-most-tallies-agree.

Freeland, C. (2010) 'The Rise of Private News', *Columbia Journalism Review*, 22 July: www.cjr.org/feature/the_rise_of_private_news.php?page=all.

Gabler, N. (1998) *Life the Movie* (Knopf).

Gleick, J. (2011) *The Information* (Pantheon/Random House).

Glendon, M. A. (2001) *A World Made New: Eleanor Roosevelt and the Universal Declaration of Human Rights* (Random House)

Global Integrity (2009) *The Global Integrity Report: 2009 Methodology White Paper*: http://report.globalintegrity.org/methodology/whitepaper.cfm.

Lewis, C. (forthcoming, 2014) Note: This is an unpublished and as yet untitled book manuscript (Public Affairs).

Lewis, C., Butts, B., and Musselwhite, K. (2011) 'A Second Look: The New Journalism Ecosystem', 30 Nov.: http://investigativereportingworkshop.org/ilab/story/second-look.

Madison, J. (1999) 'Letter to William T. Barry, August 4, 1822', *Writings* (Library of America).

McChesney, R. W., and Nichols, J. (2010) *The Death and Life of American Journalism* (Nation Books).

McGann, J. G. (2011) *The Global Go-To Think Tanks, 2010* (University of Pennsylvania): www.fpri.org/research/thinktanks/GlobalGoToThinkTanks2010. pdf.

McIntosh, T. (2011) 'FOI Laws: Vary Depending on Definitions': www.freedominfo. org/2011/10/foi-laws-counts-vary-slightly-depending-on-definitions.

Moses, L. (2012) 'Bloomberg and Reuters: The Future of News', 2 Apr.: www. adweek.com/print/139320.

Peratis, K. (2010) 'Correspondence: We're Actually Good for Israel', *New Republic*. 26 Apr.: www.tnr.com/article/politics/correspondence-were-actually-good-israel.

Picard, R. G. (2009) 'Tremors, Structural Damage and Some Casualties, but no Cataclysm: The News about News Provision', background paper to the presentation by the author at the US Federal Trade Commission Workshop,

'From Town Crier to Bloggers: How Will Journalism Survive the Internet Age', 1–2 Dec. 2009: www.robertpicard.net/files/PicardFTCbackgroundpaper.pdf.

Roberts, A. (2006), *Blacked Out: Government Secrecy in the Information Age* (Cambridge University Press).

Strom, S. (2011) 'A Quest for Hybrid Companies that Profit, but Can Tap Charity', *New York Times*, 11 Oct.: www.nytimes.com/2011/10/13/business/a-quest-for-hybrid-companies-part-money-maker-part-nonprofit.html.

US Department of State (2012) *Fact Sheet: Non-Governmental Organizations (NGOs) in the United States*, Washington, DC (Bureau of Democracy, Human Rights and Labor): www.humanrights.gov/2012/01/12/fact-sheet-non-governmental-organizations-ngos-in-the-united-states.

Walton, M. (2010) 'Investigative Shortfall', *American Journalism Review* (Sept.).

13

Keeping American Accountability Journalism Alive

Leonard Downie Jr.

Voting rights became a prominent issue in the 2012 US election campaign after a number of Republican-controlled state legislatures enacted new requirements for voting, including certain kinds of state-issued photo identification. Democrats and voting rights advocates argued that this could make it more difficult to vote for many Americans – particularly the poor, minorities, the elderly, and college students. Republicans said the laws are necessary to prevent voter fraud. American news media covered the controversy, but few had the resources to dig beneath the surface of the political bickering.

A significant exception was the annual university student-staffed News21 national investigative reporting project, based at Arizona State University's Walter Cronkite School of Journalism and Mass Communication (Downie, 2012b). The project is funded by the John S. and James L. Knight Foundation, the Carnegie Corporation, other foundations, and participating universities. In 2012, 24 selected student journalists from 11 American universities – Arizona State, Syracuse, Harvard, Maryland, North Carolina, Elon, Florida, Nebraska, Oklahoma, Texas, and Oregon – spent eight months investigating US voting rights in a video-conferenced spring semester national seminar and a summer newsroom at the Cronkite School in Phoenix. They reported in 40 cities, 21 states, and Puerto Rico, conducted more than 1,000 interviews of state and local officials and prospective voters, and reviewed more than 5,000 documents.

The student reporters made public records requests in all 50 states to create the first comprehensive database anywhere of reported cases of election fraud in the US. Their analysis of the 2,068 cases of alleged voter fraud in the US since 2000 showed that, while some fraud has occurred, the rate was infinitesimal, and in-person voter impersonation was virtually non-existent, contrary to the argument for strict photo identification requirements. It also showed that a significant amount of alleged election fraud consisted of mistakes made by both voters and volunteer election workers in the nation's thousands of state, county, and city electoral districts, which do not have uniform rules or procedures.

The student reporters documented a coordinated effort among conservative Republican legislators to introduce laws tightening voting requirements in 37 states. They exposed active partisanship by senior government officials supervising voting in some states. They interviewed black and Hispanic Americans and university students who expressed fears they might not be able to vote in states with new election laws. They reported the potential for clashes between aggressive poll watchers for both sides on election day. And they showed how most states forbid millions of convicted felons from regaining the right to vote after serving their prison sentences and returning to civilian life.

Altogether, the News21 student reporters, working under the direction of professional journalists on the Cronkite School faculty, produced 20 stories and an abundance of photos, videos, and interactive graphics and databases for the project's multimedia website – votingrights. news21.com – and, free of charge, for partnering news media across the country. Stories from the project were published and posted in print and on the websites of the *Washington Post, Philadelphia Inquirer, Arizona Republic, NBC News*, Center for Public Integrity, and a number of other newspapers and nonprofit news sites. Through these partners, the voting rights stories reached hundreds of thousands of newspaper readers and millions more online – including more than 7 million page views alone for the stories posted on nbcnews.com. The News21 election fraud database findings have been cited countless times in other news media reporting and commentary.

News21 is a notable example of an increasing number of new models for producing and sharing investigative reporting about government and other centres of power at a time when the future of such accountability journalism is at risk in the chaotic reconstruction of American news media. As commercial news media shrink their staffs while struggling to reinvent themselves and survive, emerging nonprofit news organisations are working on their own and with commercial news media to fill gaps in accountability journalism.

Many of these national, regional and local nonprofits were started within just the last few years, often by journalists who left commercial news media. They have been funded by charitable foundations, philanthropists, and other donors, and by universities at which some of the nonprofits are based. Most of their staffs and the readership of their own websites are still relatively small. Yet a number of them reach much wider audiences, as News21 has, by successfully offering their journalism to newspapers, television networks and stations, public radio stations, and other nonprofit news websites.

However, many of these nonprofit news organisations are still financially quite fragile, scrambling for grants and donations from year to year, as their founders focus as much on fundraising as on journalism. Some startups have already failed. Others have had to reduce staff and expenses. Most are still seeking widespread recognition as a necessary public good, which they hope would attract sustaining philanthropy and supportive government policies.

Accountability journalism in the United States

American investigative reporting began with revolutionary-era pamphleteers who harassed British colonial rulers and then the Founding Fathers. In the early twentieth century, investigative reporters and authors, christened 'muckrakers' by President Theodore Roosevelt, exposed exploitive business monopolies, urban slum conditions, and government corruption, prompting enactment of anti-trust and food safety laws and the popular election of the US Senate. After a hiatus during the two world wars and the Great Depression, accountability journalism gradually revived, beginning in the 1960s, amid the upheaval of the civil rights, counterculture, and anti-Vietnam War movements.

Columbia University's Pulitzer Prize board created its annual award for investigative reporting in 1964. The three television networks of that era began broadcasting investigative reports around the same time. The 1964 US Supreme Court decision in *New York Times v Sullivan* made it much more difficult for American public officials being scrutinised in the media to sue successfully for libel. The Freedom of Information Act, passed by Congress in the mid-1960s, made more government information available to journalists and citizens. The 1971 Supreme Court decision, *New York Times v United States*, which allowed the *New York Times* and the *Washington Post* to resume publication of the Pentagon Papers during the Vietnam War, made prior restraint of the press virtually impossible under the First Amendment to the US Constitution.

Investigative reporting became entrenched in American journalism after media and government investigations of the Watergate scandal culminated in the resignation of President Richard Nixon in 1974. Generations of journalists, inspired by the *Washington Post*'s Bob Woodward and Carl Bernstein, became investigative reporters, and their work was given top priority by many newspapers, magazines, television networks and stations, and book publishers. The Investigative Reporters and Editors group was founded in 1975 to train and share techniques among investigative journalists. The nonprofit Center for Public Integrity was started in Washington in 1989 to systematically mine government records for investigative reports and books. Accountability journalism about almost every aspect of American society – government and politics, business and finance, education and culture – won the lion's share of each year's journalism prizes. Computers and the internet eventually helped make accountability journalism more sophisticated and precise – and its audience and impact greater.

But, at the same time, dramatic changes in audience and advertising in the digital age started rapidly undermining the economic model that had subsidised much of the investigative reporting that flourished during the resource-rich golden age of American newspapers and commercial broadcasting in the last third of the twentieth century. Most of their newsrooms – along with their journalistic ambitions – have been steadily downsizing. Even in newsrooms in which investigative reporting remains a priority, there are now significantly fewer journalists and resources devoted to it (Downie, 2012a).

In something of an understatement, the 2011 report of the US Federal Communications Commission's Working Group on Information Needs of Communities concluded:

> *Although there is tremendous innovation in the commercial (news media) sector, and it is difficult to predict what will come next, it is not inevitable that commercial media markets will solve all the problems we face, especially the provision of relatively unprofitable, labor-intensive accountability journalism. (Waldman and Working Group, 2011)*

The potential of nonprofit accountability journalism

The most promising alternative so far is the expanding but still unstable ecosystem of new and varied nonprofit, internet-based news organisations – many of which are focused on accountability journalism. Taking into consideration America's size, federal system of government and numerous population centres, these startups, although still essentially experiments, are vital contributors to government and public affairs accountability and transparency at the national, state, and local levels (Downie and Phillips, 2012).

Four-year-old ProPublica, a New York-based nonprofit initially financed by large grants from the Sandler family foundation in California, has already made a significant impact nationally. Its 34 journalists, many of them prize-winning investigative reporters hired away from commercial news media, work out of a Wall Street newsroom under the direction of the former managing editors of the *Wall Street Journal*, Paul Steiger, and *Portland Oregonian*, Stephen Engelberg. They have produced influential accountability journalism about many challenging subjects, including the underlying causes of the American financial crisis, how the federal bailout and stimulus money has been spent, the financial ties between physicians and the medical industry, the environmental dangers of off-shore oil production and on-land natural gas drilling, the under-diagnosed and untreated traumatic brain injuries of American soldiers, the unmet health claims of foreign employees of American military contractors injured in Iraq and Afghanistan, and the legal status and treatment of terrorism detainees at Guantanamo Bay.

In 2011, ProPublica distributed 110 of these kinds of stories to more than 25 different print, broadcast and digital media partners across the US, including the *New York Times,* the *Washington Post,* and *Los Angeles Times*, commercial and public television networks, and National Public Radio. ProPublica has collaborated with journalists at other news organisations on accountability projects, as it did with the *Washington Post* on an investigation of presidential pardons of convicted criminals. ProPublica also has patiently stayed with investigations over long periods of time – producing hundreds of stories about the federal bailout and stimulus spending, for example, and more than 50 each about money in politics and the status of Guantanamo detainees – a persistence unmatched by most American news organisations.

Much of this work has involved obtaining and analysing government information, or using other reporting methods, including soliciting information from citizens, to find what the government or other institutions won't make available. In addition to using this information for its investigative stories, ProPublica, with a grant from the Knight Foundation, has packaged it into subject-specific interactive database 'news applications' on its website, where it is available to the public and other journalists and news organisations (Downie and Phillips, 2012).

These kinds of collaboration among nonprofit startups, commercial news media, and public broadcasting are steadily increasing across the country. They are beneficial for the nonprofit accountability journalism sites, whose journalism gains much greater impact; for commercial news media and their audiences, who gain journalism they would not otherwise have; and for American citizens, who gain an increased measure of governmental and institutional accountability. In another understated but important conclusion, the FCC working group report stated that 'collaboration among media – including for-profit and nonprofit media – will and should be an important ingredient in the new system' (Waldman and Working Group, 2011).

Dozens of models similar to ProPublica have been created on the state and local level from coast to coast in the United States. Three years ago, for example, editor Evan Smith and Texas investor and philanthropist John Thornton launched the nonprofit *Texas Tribune* in the state capital of Austin after they had 'watched the decline' of the state's commercial media and their accountability and public affairs coverage, as Smith recounted at a conference on nonprofit accountability journalism held at the Cronkite School in 2012. 'If the for-profit media could no longer produce the kind of serious journalism that raises the level of civic journalism in our communities – a fundamental element of our democracy,' Smith said, 'then we have to create a new model to do it.'

With a staff of 35, including 17 reporters, and a 2012 budget of $4 million, mostly from Texas donors, the *Tribune* produces accountability journalism about the state's government and politics for its website and, free of charge, for news media partners that include several dozen Texas newspapers and television and public radio stations. It also mines government data to produce interactive databases about government services and performance. 'We are lifting the lid on the inner workings of government,' Smith said, 'so the average person is better informed and can make better choices.'

The Center for Investigative Reporting (CIR) in Berkeley, California, has become even more ambitious. For three decades, it was a nonprofit outpost for award-winning independent investigative reporting about national issues, which it shared with newspapers, magazines, and commercial and public television networks throughout the country.

Three years ago, CIR started California Watch, which produces high-impact accountability journalism about that state's government and public affairs for a large network of newspapers and broadcast stations throughout California, in addition to its own website. In 2011, for example, it told millions of Californians, in stories and an interactive state-wide database, how the government was failing to enforce its own earthquake safety requirements for thousands of public schools. California Watch editor Mark Katches said at a meeting of journalists in late 2012 that the startup had already evolved into 'a wire service for investigative reporting' for the state's many news outlets.

In 2012, CIR took over the Bay Citizen, a startup nonprofit local news website in San Francisco. CIR's executive director, former Philadelphia and San Francisco newspaper editor Robert Rosenthal, said, in an interview, that the three combined nonprofits will be able to produce national, state, and local accountability journalism with a total staff of 70 and a budget of more than $10 million, raised primarily from large foundations and philanthropists. Unlike ProPublica and *Texas Tribune*, CIR is also paid modest fees for some stories and video packages it provides to newspaper and broadcast partners.

'We have five ABC (television) affiliates, nine or ten newspapers, and they all pay us a fee for a certain amount of stories each day,' Rosenthal said. 'I don't think syndication is a sustainable model necessarily. But it's generating … the first year, 2011, $75,000 … this year, $500,000. Video is where the money is.'

Similarly, the *Voice of San Diego*, an award-winning local accountability journalism site supported primarily by foundations and donors in that southern California city, is paid for investigative and public affairs reporting that it shares with the local NBC-owned television station and the local city magazine. It and some of the other nonprofits also sell small amounts of advertising on their sites. And many solicit business sponsorships and voluntary audience memberships, which have long been major sources of revenue for American public radio and television stations.

The financial vulnerability of nonprofit accountability journalism

Too many of the startup nonprofit accountability journalism sites scattered around the country are still quite fragile financially. Most of them still depend primarily on startup grants from philanthropic foundations. To date, only a small minority of the foundations of various sizes in the US have made such grants, and most of them have been for only a few years each. The foundations expect the nonprofits to find other ways to sustain themselves over time. 'Sustainability, to foundations, means we don't fund you anymore,' said Grant Oliphant of the Pittsburgh Foundation, which financed the launch of a local accountability news site to collaborate with other news media in that city. The Knight Foundation, whose money comes from a former newspaper-owning family, has been encouraging more American foundations, big and small, to join it in making grants to news nonprofits and actively help them to become sustainable.

As a result, fundraising is a preoccupation for fledgling American nonprofit news organisations. 'We will break even this year for the first time,' *Texas Tribune* editor Smith said at the Cronkite School conference. 'I have said more than once that I feel like Indiana Jones outrunning the boulder. I cannot look away from the ground in front of me for a second or I will get killed. I am constantly out friend-raising, fund-raising, brand-raising. All of those things feed into the sustainability of the operation.'

To do this effectively, a news nonprofit must be designated as a tax-exempt charitable organisation by the Internal Revenue Service under section 501c(3) of the US tax code. That designation allows philanthropic foundations to keep their own tax-exempt status while giving money to the nonprofits, and it enables citizen and business donors to take tax deductions for their contributions to them. ProPublica, the Center for Investigative Reporting, *Texas Tribune*, and many other news nonprofits have 501c(3) designations. But each of them received it after applying individually to the IRS, rather than automatically, because nonprofit journalism is not specified as a charitable endeavour in the tax code.

As nonprofit news startups proliferated, IRS approvals of 501c(3) designations for them slowed to a crawl, with delays stretching many months into years. The IRS has not said why. But it appears, from what the agency has asked applicants, that it is questioning how much they resemble or differ from commercial news organisations – this is, whether they should be considered charitable organisations. Some startups have been able to pay existing 501c(3) charitable organisations to serve temporarily as their 'fiscal agents' for grants from foundations and other donors. But several startups have failed while waiting for IRS approval, and advocates of nonprofit journalism fear that the delays may have a chilling effect on others who want to start one.

'It will be a travesty if we lose this fight over whether organizations such as we're talking about are legitimate nonprofits or not,' the Pittsburgh Foundation's Oliphant said at the Cronkite School conference. 'These organizations are performing a social good.'

The FCC working group report concluded that 'policymakers should recognise that cleaning up ambiguities in the tax code for nonprofit media is potentially a crucial step toward enabling nonprofit entities to develop sustainable business models' (Waldman and Working Group, 2011). At its suggestion, a small group of news nonprofit and tax law experts is considering recommendations to make to the IRS.

The role of public broadcasting

America's numerous public radio and television stations are already long-established, IRS-recognised nonprofits. But they have lagged in producing accountability journalism. With a number of notable exceptions, most public radio stations across the country devote little resources of their own to news coverage, although many of them broadcast hours of National Public Radio (NPR) news programs each day. Most public television stations broadcast only an hour-long weeknight national newscast and occasional national investigative documentaries that a few public stations and independent producers distribute through the Public Broadcasting System.

Public broadcasting in the United States is a loose collection of hundreds of local radio and television stations spawned by an act of Congress in 1967. The federal government gives only about $400 million a year to them in grants through the quasi-independent Corporation for Public Broadcasting (CPB). Public radio and television stations, largely owned by colleges and universities, nonprofit groups and state and local governments, must supplement their relatively small CPB grants with their own fundraising from individual donors, philanthropic foundations, and corporations. Most of that money pays for the costs of that fundraising and the stations' overheads and programming, rather than for news reporting.

The exceptions are stations that have been successfully and economically merged or joined in collaboration by their nonprofit owners in places like New England, New York, Minnesota, Oregon, and California.

There are now several efforts under way to increase national and local accountability reporting by public radio, for which overheads and programming costs are significantly less than for public television. NPR, a cooperative financed by member stations, has created a national investigative reporting team and is working with some of its member stations on joint investigative projects. It is also encouraging partnerships between local public radio stations and newspapers in their cities. The CPB has made grants to groups of public radio stations in regions around the country for experiments in collaborative accountability reporting on subjects including the environment, demographic change, agriculture, and economic development. Other public radio stations are collaborating with nonprofit website startups in their communities on local investigative reporting, some with grants from Knight and other foundations. These efforts are somewhat belated, considering the nearly half century existence of American public broadcasting. But they are a needed and potentially significant part of the evolving ecosystem of nonprofit accountability journalism.

The role of universities

One of the most promising additions to that ecosystem is the accountability journalism being produced by a still modest but steadily growing number of university journalism schools. Student journalists, working under the supervision of professional journalists hired onto the schools' faculties, comprise the staffs of local news sites, state news services, and regional and national investigative reporting projects based at these universities. Their journalism is increasingly being published and broadcast by commercial news media that can no longer produce some of it themselves (Downie, 2011–12).

At Arizona State University's Cronkite School, students staff Cronkite News Service bureaus in Phoenix, the state capital, and Washington, DC, which serve about 30 newspaper, broadcast, and news website clients throughout Arizona. Their in-depth accountability journalism has examined state government, politics and campaign finance, state–federal relations, environment and land use, healthcare, and immigration and demographic change. The Cronkite School also is the headquarters for the annual foundation-funded News21 national investigative reporting project, which has produced accountability journalism about transportation safety, food safety, and voting rights that reached millions of newspaper and online readers during the last three years. News21 students also developed, from federal and state government records, comprehensive digital databases of election fraud cases and responses to food-borne disease outbreaks in all 50 states, which are accessible to everyone.

Maryland, Northwestern, Columbia, Wisconsin, Minnesota, Northeastern, Boston, American, and Southern California are among other major universities with student-staffed news services, news websites, or investigative reporting projects that collaborate with commercial and other nonprofit news media. They are supervised and sometimes partnered by professional journalists, including prize-winning investigative reporters, who have left commercial news organisations to join the faculties of these universities. With $5.6 million in grants from the Knight and Peyton Anderson foundations, Mercer College in Macon, Georgia, has brought the newsrooms of the struggling local newspaper, the *Telegraph*, and a Georgia Public Radio station onto campus in its Center for Collaborative Journalism, so that professional journalists, students, and faculty can all work together.

Advocates of university journalism schools producing professional-level journalism and collaborating with commercial and nonprofit news media make comparisons to the teaching hospitals of university medical schools and the legal clinics of university law schools. Knight and five other national philanthropic foundations funding journalism education and nonprofit journalism have formally urged all journalism schools to adopt the 'teaching hospital' model. 'Some leading schools are doing this, but most are not,' the foundations stated in an August 2012 open letter to the nation's university presidents. They warned that journalism schools that do not change 'will find it difficult to raise money from foundations interested in the future of news'.

Other roles for philanthropy and nonprofit entities

There are also other ways in which philanthropic foundations and nonprofits are trying to protect and advance accountability journalism in the rapidly changing American news media environment. The Ford

Foundation, which has made grants to such news nonprofits as ProPublica and the Center for Public Integrity, has given money for the first time to commercial newspapers for public interest reporting. In May 2012, Ford gave $1 million to the *Los Angeles Times*' innovative coverage of immigrant communities, the US–Mexican border region, and the California prison system. In August 2012, Ford gave $500,000 to the *Washington Post* for national and local investigative reporting about politics, money, and government. The grants enable the newspapers to hire new journalists devoted only to new reporting on these subjects, which must be publicly available without copyright, as nonprofit news organisations do. In the case of the *Washington Post*, this would be in addition to its existing accountability journalism, such as its ongoing investigation of potential conflicts of interest of members of Congress, based on their reported financial holdings.

Questions have been raised about whether entire existing newspapers should become tax-exempt nonprofits if they are no longer commercially viable. A few American newspapers are already owned by foundations created by previous owners, as is the *Tampa Bay Times* in Florida, or by religious institutions. But it would take an endowment of billions of dollars to produce enough income to buy and run a sizeable newspaper.

For now, the most promising possibility for American accountability journalism to survive and prosper, in addition to the priority still given to it by some downsizing commercial news media, is increased collaboration between them and the various new nonprofit news organisations dedicated to it. The Investigative News Network (INN) was founded by a number of those nonprofits in 2009 as a clearinghouse for back office support, business development, publishing and distribution practices, content sharing, and joint reporting projects. For example, INN member nonprofits in several states published stories on their websites from the News21 national voting rights project.

Investigative Reporters and Editors (IRE) and its subsidiary National Institute for Computer-Assisted Reporting (NICAR), nonprofits founded and operated by investigative journalists, provide training, information databases, networking and other resources for thousands of investigative journalists and their news organisations, both commercial and nonprofit. IRE's DocumentCloud enables them to digitally upload, store, manipulate, analyse and share government and other documents in their reporting. With a $50,000 grant from Google Idea, IRE also offers small amounts of seed money for journalists and news organisations working on promising data analysis for investigative reporting.

Other nonprofits, some of them issue-advocacy groups, maintain searchable databases of federal court records, legislation in Congress and state legislatures, federal and state election campaign contributions, the activities of lobbyists and foreign agents, and other government data. The Reporters Committee for Freedom of the Press, a nonprofit financed by foundation, corporate, and individual donors, helps journalists, news media, and government transparency organisations exercise their First Amendment and Freedom of Information rights. It provides free legal information, training, advice, and, when necessary, legal action, plus online guides to federal and state open government laws, databases, and court records. Similarly, the non-partisan, Knight Foundation-funded National Freedom of Information Coalition and its state chapters lobby for greater open government and improved FOI laws, and its Knight FOI Fund offers financial support for FOI and open government litigation.

The role of government

The First Amendment to the US Constitution guarantees American journalists and news media more freedom from government interference – and financial support – than any other nation, including Great Britain. But the relationship is not as simple as that. The federal and state governments decide what information and databases to make available on proliferating government websites. They can fight requests made under federal and state Freedom of Information laws or require exorbitant fees to fulfil them, forcing expensive legal battles or delaying the release of information well beyond when it would have most useful for timely accountability journalism. The federal government also can threaten with prosecution officials who disclose classified information without authorisation and threaten with subpoenas, for the identities of those sources, the journalists obtaining and publishing the information. Despite promising more openness and transparency in government operations, for example, the Obama administration has been particularly aggressive in investigating disclosures of classified information.

Writing in the *IRE Journal*, an expert on Freedom of Information laws and government transparency, University of Missouri Journal School associate professor Charles N. Davis (2012), argued that decades-old federal and state FOI laws and practices need to be substantially reformed in the digital age to make more records accessible and usable in electronic forms and to reduce or eliminate access charges left from the era of paper files in manila folders. 'FOI is at a crossroads,' Professor Davis wrote. 'Digital technology offers the promise of democratized governmental information as never before, but the gap between what is possible and what is required by the law grows wider every year.'

From the beginning of the nation, as Columbia University Journalism School professor Michael Schudson and I noted in our 2009 report, 'The Reconstruction of American Journalism', the US government has provided varying kinds of limited support for the news media. The Post Office Act of 1792 authorised a subsidy for newspapers sent through the mail, a primary form of news distribution at the time. As noted above, Congress acted in 1967 to partially subsidise public broadcasting with federal money administered by the Corporation for Public Broadcasting. The Newspaper Preservation Act of 1970 allowed newspapers in the same city to form joint operating agreements to share revenue and costs in a futile attempt to prevent single-newspaper monopolies in most cities. More recently, federal agencies have allowed to wither regulations requiring equal time for political discourse on the federally regulated broadcast spectrum and forbidding joint ownership of newspapers and broadcast stations in the same urban markets, both of which became archaic in the digital age. And the Internal Revenue Service has had a role in the creation of nonprofit news organisations by deciding which of them qualify for tax-exempt status.

What can be done

In our 2009 report, Professor Schudson and I argued that it would be a logical extension of this history of a limited role for government to create a national Fund for Local News with money the Federal Communications Commission could collect from communications licensees. Grants from the fund could be made in open competition through independent state Local News Fund Councils for innovative local news coverage by nonprofit and commercial news organisations. This could also be a model for indirect government support for other forms of accountability journalism. But, given the country's current political polarisation and budget and debt crises, nothing like this can be expected to appeal to Congress any time soon.

More practical, timely, and urgent is our recommendation that the Internal Revenue Service should be more open to authorise any independent news organisation substantially devoted to reporting on public affairs to become a tax-exempt nonprofit entity, regardless of its mix of financial support, including commercial sponsorship and advertising. This could be done by IRS recognition that all news nonprofits qualify as 501c(3) organisations, so long as they do not engage in political activity or lobbying, or even the creation of a new charitable organisation category for public service journalism.

The IRS should also be more expansive in allowing existing 501c(3) s and philanthropic foundations to support news nonprofits and even accountability journalism within commercial news media, such as the Ford Foundation grants for in-depth and investigative reporting by the *Los Angeles Times* and the *Washington Post*. More national, regional, and community foundations – and their national councils – could push for such changes and significantly expand their own financial support for nonprofit and other forms of accountability journalism as a public good similar to other recipients of their philanthropy.

The Corporation for Public Broadcasting (CPB) should be more aggressive in pushing public radio and television to reorient their mission to provide significantly more national and local news coverage, especially accountability reporting. The CPB could expand its current experimental grants for collaborative reporting by regional groups of stations. It could require a specified commitment to news coverage for all grantees, including public television stations. It could move more aggressively to encourage needed overhead-saving combinations of the nation's numerous, often overlapping public stations to free up money for news and for the stations' support of National Public Radio's national news and accountability reporting. Among the leading regional consolidations of public stations providing aggressive news coverage are Minnesota Public Radio, with more than 40 stations in six states in the upper Midwest; Oregon Public Broadcasting, with 20 radio and five television stations in Oregon and Washington in the Pacific Northwest, and New York Public Radio, with seven stations in the New York City metropolitan area and neighbouring New Jersey.

Congress and state legislatures – and federal and state agencies – should update and expand FOI laws and procedures to take advantage of new technologies to make available more government information more easily and inexpensively. Working with the National Freedom of Information Coalition and its state chapters, government agencies could reduce burdensome FOI bureaucracy and FOI exemptions and document redactions. Foundations and philanthropists concerned about government transparency could finance more aggressive action, including litigation when necessary, to expand FOI more rapidly.

Public universities, the largest in the US, should convert more of their journalism schools into 'teaching hospital' models of producing journalism while studying it. This could enable them to both attract more foundation support and better fulfil their responsibilities to their states' citizens. They could join Arizona State's Cronkite and other pioneering journalism schools in becoming centres for professional journalism, digital media innovation, the development of new news media business models, and the convening of and sharing information for struggling accountability journalism nonprofits.

As they realise how much change is occurring in the news media ecosystem, American citizens also should play a role in public policy decisions and consumer choices that could determine the future of accountability journalism.

Steven Waldman, senior media policy scholar at the Columbia Journalism School and author of the FCC working group report, wrote in the *Columbia Journalism Review* (2012) that news consumers should sort out sources of original and accountability reporting from the news summaries, aggregation, gossip and opinion that now fill so much of the digital media. They could make purposeful consumer decisions to support that reporting, Waldman argued, by regularly patronising it and the news organisations providing it – increasing their audience and their appeal to advertisers – and by finding and donating to news nonprofits specialising in accountability journalism.

'Our job, collectively, is we need to sell this,' Cronkite School Dean Christopher Callahan said to the news nonprofit and foundation leaders at the conference on accountability journalism in 2012. 'We need to go out to other communities, to other journalism leaders, to other philanthropists who are not involved in this space and get them excited about it. We need to make sure that word is spread.'

Leadership for keeping American accountability journalism alive is emerging from leading commercial news media, nonprofit startups, universities, and foundations and other philanthropists. Much more will be needed to sufficiently inform citizens, persuade policy-makers, increase funding, and preserve accountability journalism as a priority at surviving news organisations.

References

Davis, C. N., 'Journalists Should Seek FOI Reforms', *IRE Journal*, 35/2 (2012).

Downie Jr., L. (2011–12) 'Big Journalism on Campus' *American Journalism Review* (Dec.–Jan.).

Downie Jr., L. (2012a) 'Forty Years After Watergate, Investigative Journalism is at Risk', Outlook, *Washington Post*, 10 June.

Downie Jr., L. (2012b) 'Behind the Story: Who Can Vote?', Investigative Reporters and Editors, 14 Aug.: ire.org.

Downie Jr., L., and Phillips, W. (2012) 'Making a Difference: Philanthropy and the Future of Local Accountability Journalism', white paper based on the Feb. 2012 Cronkite School conference on 'The Role of Philanthropy in Local Accountability Journalism', presented at the Carnegie–Knight Deans conference at Harvard University, June.

Downie Jr., L., and Schudson, M. (2009) 'The Reconstruction of American Journalism', *Columbia Journalism Review* (Nov.–Dec.).

Waldman, S. (2012) 'What You Can Do', Support Reporting blog, *Columbia Journalism Review*, 14 Aug.: www.cjr.org/support_reporting/what_you_can_do.php.

Waldman, S., and the Working Group on Information Needs of Communities (2011) *The Information Needs of Communities* (Federal Communications Commission): www.fcc.gov/infoneedsreport.

Index

RISJ/I.B.TAURIS PUBLICATIONS

CHALLENGES

Transformations in Egyptian Journalism
Naomi Sakr
ISBN: 978 1 78076 589 1

Climate Change in the Media: Reporting Risk and Uncertainty
James Painter
ISBN: 978 1 78076 588 4

Women and Journalism
Suzanne Franks
ISBN: 978 1 78076 585 3

EDITED VOLUMES

Media and Public Shaming: The Boundaries of Disclosure
Julian Petley (ed.)
ISBN: 978 1 78076 586 0 (HB); 978 1 78076 587 7 (PB)

*Political Journalism in Transition: Western Europe in a
Comparative Perspective*
Raymond Kuhn and Rasmus Kleis Nielsen (eds)
ISBN: 978 1 78076 677 5 (HB); 978 1 78076 678 2 (PB)

Transparency in Politics and the Media: Accountability and Open Government
Nigel Bowles, James T. Hamilton and David A. L. Levy (eds)
ISBN: 978 1 78076 675 1 (HB); 978 1 78076 676 8 (PB)

The Ethics of Journalism: Individual, Institutional and Cultural Influences
Wendy N. Wyatt (ed.)
ISBN: 978 1 78076 673 7 (HB); 978 1 78076 674 4 (PB)